femmes of **POWER**

ULRIKA DAHL is a femme-inist writer and a regular contributor to Scandinavian queer and feminist debate. With a PhD in cultural anthropology and Women's Studies from University of California at Santa Cruz, she teaches Gender Studies at Södertörn University College in Stockholm, Sweden and is currently working on a monograph tentatively entitled *Femme as Figuration: Rethinking (queer) Femininities*. Her Swedish book *Skamgrepp*, a series of critical essays on feminist (sexual) politics, normativity and queer kinship is forthcoming from Atlas Förlag in 2009.

DEL LAGRACE VOLCANO is a gender variant visual artist and cultural producer working with the body and gender/sexual identity notions for social, political and pleasurable purposes for the past twenty-five years. Del has produced four monographs, *Love Bites*, Gay Men's Press 1991, *The Drag King Book* (with Judith Halberstam), Serpent's Tail 1999, *Sublime Mutations* 2001, and *Sex Works*, Konkursbuchverlag 2005. Volcano's work has been cited and reproduced in numerous publications, journals and books on visual art and queer and feminist theory and has exhibited in galleries and museums worldwide.

femmes of POWER
Exploding Queer Femininities
**DEL LAGRACE VOLCANO
& ULRIKA DAHL**

A complete catalogue record for this book can be obtained from the British Library on request.

The right of Del LaGrace Volcano and Ulrika Dahl to be identified as the authors of this work has been asserted by them in accordance with the Copyright, Designs and Patents Act 1988

PHOTOGRAPHY | © 2008 Del LaGrace Volcano
MAIN TEXT | © 2008 Ulrika Dahl
Copyright © in each essay is held by the author

All rights reserved. No part of this book may be reproduced, stored in a retrieval system or transmitted in any form or by any means, electronic, mechanical, photocopying, recording or otherwise, without the prior permission of the publisher.

First published in the UK in 2008 by Serpent's Tail,
an imprint of Profile Books Ltd
3A Exmouth House
Pine Street
London EC1R 0JH
WEBSITE | www.serpentstail.com

ISBN 978 1 84668 664 1

DESIGN | Elina Grandin
PRINT | Graphicom, Vicenza, Italy
COVER IMAGES | FRONT: The Bird Club: Dyke Marilyn and Bird laBird, London 2006 | BACK: Atlanta Femme Mafia, Atlanta 2007

10 9 8 7 6 5 4 3 2 1

Mixed Sources
Product group from well-managed forests, and other controlled sources
www.fsc.org Cert no. CQ-COC-000015
© 1996 Forest Stewardship Council

Dedicated to Jeannine Della-Grace, 1939–2007
– my first femme icon

DEL LAGRACE VOLCANO

photo by Della Grace, San Francisco, 1982

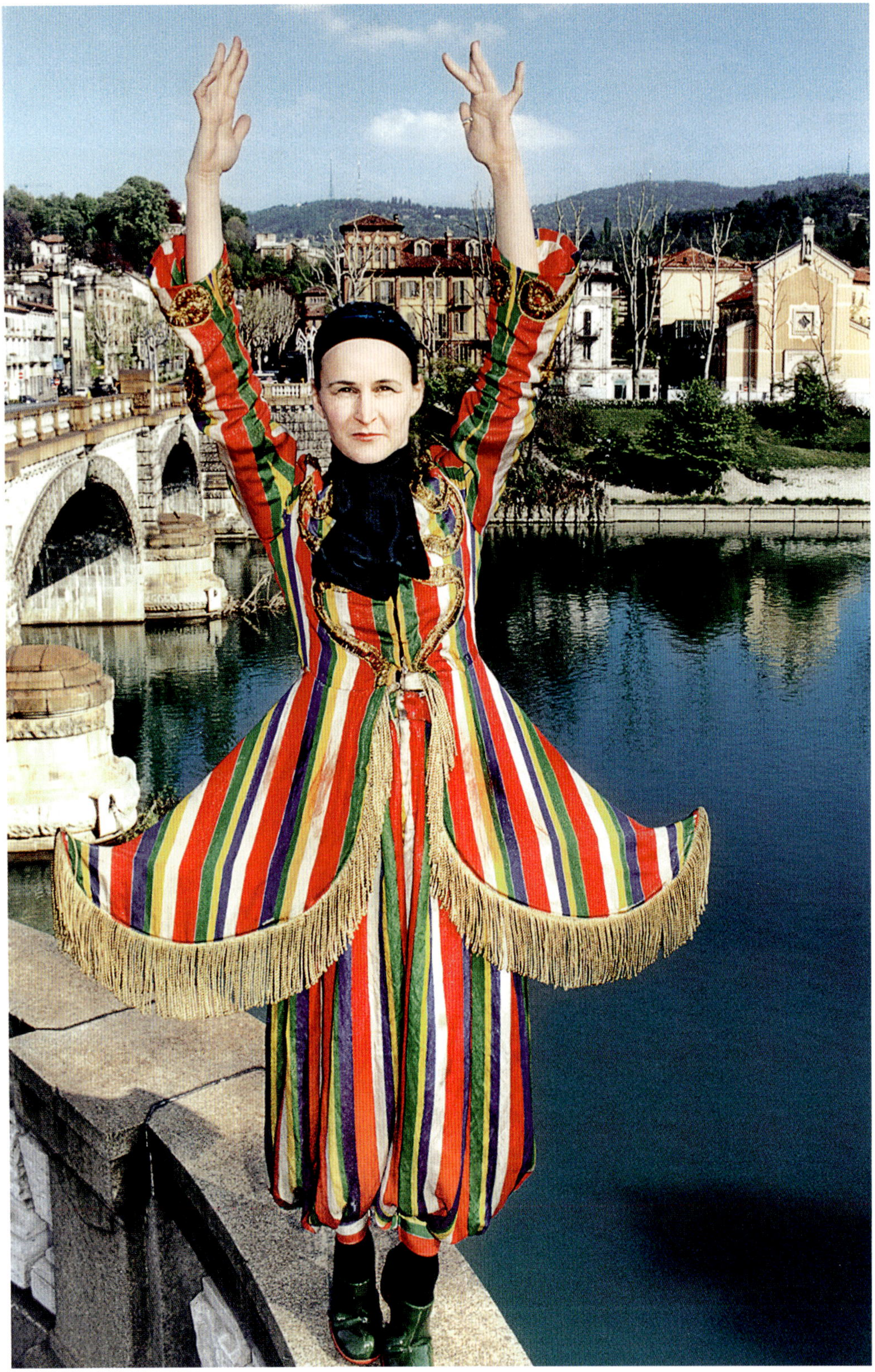

TABLE OF CONTENTS

DEL LAGRACE VOLCANO | **Introducing Images** 9 |
ULRIKA DAHL | **Introduction: A Letter to Femmes of Power** 18 |
INGE 'CAMPBELL' BLACKMAN | **Fem** 29 |

THE FEMME FREQUENCY 30 | *The Third Eye of a Latina Power Femme* 37 | *Beard-Adorned Lady* 38 | *TransFemme Theory with Miss File* 40 | *The Black Roots of Dyke Marilyn* 47 |

COPIES WITHOUT ORIGINALS: ON FEMME DRAG 50 | *Portland's Diesel Femme* 56 | *Las Damas* 59 | *East Atlanta's Showgirl Divas* 62 | *Fierce Maven Femme* 67 | *Bird La Bird: A Tweet with a Coverchick* 68 | **ITZIAR ZIGA** | **Playing with our Latin Female** 73 |

EPISTEMOLOGY OF THE FEMME CLOSET 78 | *The Face of Swedish Transfeminism* 86 | **PRATIBHA PARMAR** | **Pocket-sized Venus** 91 | *Femme Anti-War Activism* 97 | *Bandit Queen of Manchester* 98 | *To Be Young, Pretty and Queer* 103 | *Quatrième Génération Fem* 106 |

THE BAD GIRLS' GENEALOGY 112 | *Berlin's Feminist Sexpert* 118 | *Danish Pillow Queen Femme* 122 | *Interview with the Vampire Queen* 126 | *Mommy Far from Heaven* 129 | *Earn Your Reputation* 133 | *Defying the Laws of Ageism* 138 | **LOIS WEAVER** | **Still Counting** 141 |

SHOWGIRLS QUEERING THE STAGE 147 | *Femme Hag Pussy Power* 155 | *Parliamentarian Pin-up* 159 | *Rock Stars and Riot Grrls* 160 | *Femininity without a Country* 169 | *Creative Navigator of Heightism* 172 | **KRISTA SMITH** | **Fat... Femme... Fierce... Kentucky Fried** 175 |

FEMME FUTURES 180 |
AMBER HOLLIBAUGH | **Afterword: Femmes of Power** 185 |

Contributors Index 189 | **Bibliography** 190 |

Brixton Brady, Turin, Italy 2002

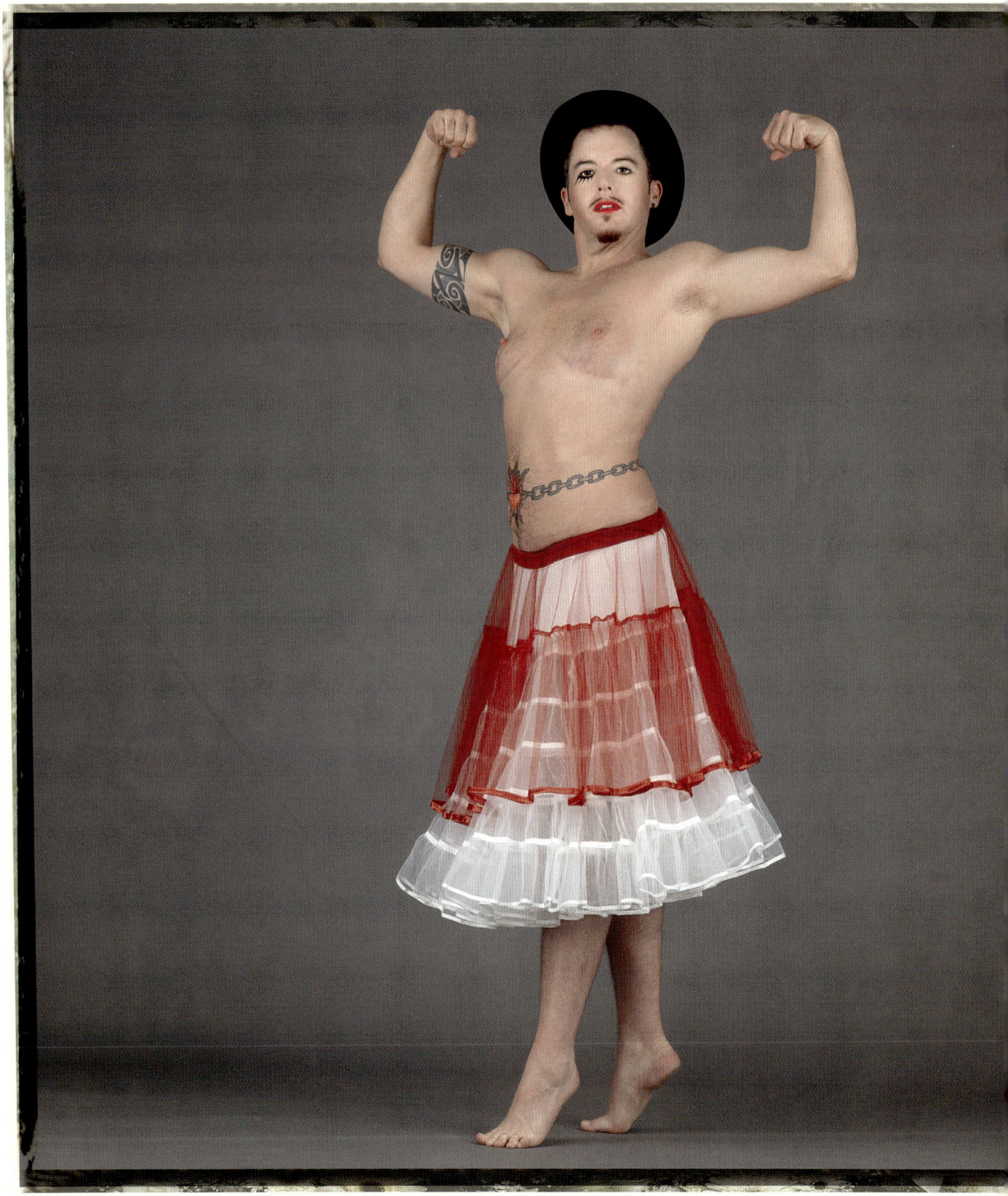

DEL LAGRACE VOLCANO
Introducing images

GROWING UP I wasn't sure I was female. As I grew further I wanted to be a lesbian but wasn't sure I would meet even the most basic membership criteria (though eventually I created a 'femme dyke' persona that worked well for over fifteen years). It wasn't until my early twenties that I was sure of at least one thing – I was an artist. Quite an accomplishment for anyone assigned female at birth in a culture that only calls male artists 'great'.

So far my strategy (of subversion) has been to focus on basic questions like, who am I and where do I belong? Where is that place called home? From the outset I have been one of my own subjects and often use my (multiple) selves as primary source material. I've also worked with thousands of subjects: people who have something to show and tell about the nature of power and who gets to represent the 'having' of it. I began by photographing and making films about my biological family and when I moved north to San Francisco I became part of a radical sex positive lesbian community and continued making 'family photographs'. By the mid-nineties my family had expanded to include trans-gendered, non-gendered, hyper-gendered, asexual, bisexual, tri-sexual, intersex and even a few ordinary heterosexuals. Ulrika Dahl calls me a

Del LaGrace Volcano, Gerard Rancinan, Paris 2004

'queer community photographer', a label I initially resisted because I was an *artist* and to be seen as archivist of any sort is not something the art world values. Then I remembered where I lived and decided I could be both!

The Drag King Book was my first time collaborating with an academic. Jack Halberstam was already writing about female masculinity and brought an intellectual rigour to the project that would have otherwise been lacking. In 1995 when we began our collaboration we were near the sharp edge of the new millennium. The drag king star was on the ascendant rising fast and the media was absolutely mad about the boy! I was thrilled to see female and trans-masculinities taking up space in print, on stage and on screen. At long last there were challengers to a throne that had been occupied for decades almost exclusively by drag queens, who, while entertaining, were too apolitical for my taste. Drag Kings on the other hand seemed much more invested in challenging social injustice on multiple fronts; the kind of action that makes my queer heart beat.

Documentary films like *Gendernaughts* and *Venus Boyz* were screened at queer film festivals worldwide and in art house cinemas throughout Europe. Drag King contests, conferences, and communities began to spring up all over the western world and occasionally beyond. *The Drag*

10

King Book went to a second print, a rare achievement for a queer photo book and an exhibition of photographs from the book even featured in an episode of *Sex and the City*. Drag Kings became like a non-toxic washable crayon on the cultural landscape. Progress? Well, that's debatable... Back in the UK television programmes like *Self-Made Men* were screened on Channel Four. 'Is it a boy or a girl?!' was tabloid television's favourite fodder for a short while. For about five minutes even transsexual men were hot property and there were benefits – political, social, and for a few professional queers such as myself, even temporary financial gain.

But you didn't have to scratch far below the surface to see that once again queer femininity, as well as femaleness in general, was being left out of the equation, or reduced to little more than a supporting role. Why is it that masculinity of all types is so astonishingly over-valorised in LGBTQ and even feminist circles? Has my own ph/autography (as Jay Prosser calls it in his introduction to *Sublime Mutations*), with its focus on female and transmasculinities for over twenty years, been part of the problem? If so then it's time I became part of the solution!

My work and my life are inextricably entwined and so when I became lovers for the first time with a femme-(y) woman, Miss Wild Windh, with whom I also collaborated politically, photographically and intellectually for almost four years, a new universe opened up. At the same time I fell for Dr Dahl and was inspired by her leonine verbosity and passion for making queer femme-inism a priority. These two queer women rocked me to the core and challenged me to rethink my entire relationship to femininity and femmes, in terms of desire, absolutely, but also in terms of my own photographic practice.

OVER THE YEARS I took a fair amount of criticism for not photographing feminine women, as much as some people thought I *should*. Although I am inclined to rebel against any *should*, it would be closer to the truth to admit that I actually didn't know *how* to queer femininity, photographically speaking, without providing more fuel for heterosexist fantasies of feminine lesbians waiting for a real man. I also asked myself if the world actually *needed* any more images of 'pretty women', since proud, powerful images or portrayals of masculine women are still so rare on screen or in print.

It was a slow burning fire that caused my femme epiphany. For seven wonderful years I collaborated with the late Brixton Brady, an utterly befuddling gender queer creature, who identified as an effeminate man, albeit with extraordinary street style. At the dawn of the new millennium I was in Santa Barbara, California and met Krista Smith and Jessica Eve Humphreys, femme members of the local drag king troupe, The Disposable Boy

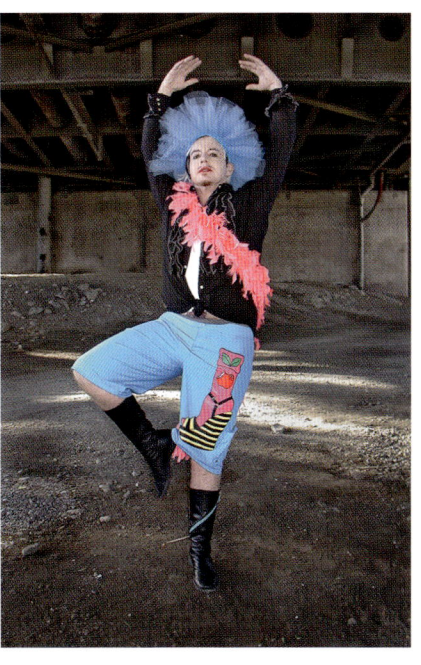

Wendy Delorme & Louis(e) deVille, Paris 2006 | Del LaGrace, created in collaboration with Indra Windh, Stockholm 2004

12

Toys. I was introduced to fat femme activism by two big girls who knew just how sexy they really were and weren't afraid to show it. A few years later in London a dream came true and I finally met the extraordinary Amber Hollibaugh, who I had semi-stalked as a baby dyke when she worked at Modern Times Bookstore on Valencia Street in San Francisco. When she gave her standing ovation keynote address at the Femme Conference in 2006 it was like coming home to something inside myself. I cried and clapped along with all the others, feeling happy blessed to be part of such an emotionally intelligent and sincerely intersectional movement. A movement that has learned from both herstory and history, that puts political theory into lived practice and queers as femme-ininity in a manner that is light years away from mere titillation.

So where am I, an off-white, self-proclaimed hermaphro*dyke* located in relation to this project? For a long time I worried that my masculine outer layer would have a negative impact on my photographic relationships, especially with femmes. When I was making photographs for *The Drag King Book* I was an 'insider', a drag king – or at least a kissing cousin. Fast-forward almost ten years and my femme (pretender) history would not be known or apparent to the (mostly) women whom I was working with on this project. Would they see me as a man? Or worse, a 'wanna-be white man' aiming his phallic lens at their already over-objectified bodies?

In *The Queer Theory Reader*, Indra Windh wrote that 'gender happens between bodies,

Indra Windh & Dalia Schweitzer,
Club Wotever 2004

not [just] within them' and I would expand this notion to include how race also happens between bodies. The way in which I experience myself as white has been altered by my ostensible maleness. Even though I call myself off-white (for a number of reasons, including ancestry which includes non-white great grandmothers and in resistance to all notions of racial purity), I am read as a white, usually gay man. Therefore I must simultaneously take responsibility for the perception others may have of me (regardless of my hermaphroditic codicils) and perform an alchemical homeopathic act, transforming the shit of white male imperialist history into the precious substance of human connection, which is just one ingredient in my photographic recipe book.

IN MY MASTERS thesis in 1991 I wrote that I wanted to 'examine those seldom seen and rarely talked about photographic moments that exist before the image is created and after the image is "consumed" by the spectator. Traditionally the relationship between the photographer and the model is gendered, with the male being the photographer and the female being the photographer's object. What might an image look like if both the photographer and the photographed inhabited the subject position, or even if the subject-object dynamics oscillated between them in a way that caused the spectator to question his or her own positioning? It is the "play of looks" that I want to explore, within the framework of desire and its visual representations. By unearthing some of the processes involved in representations of desire we can begin to examine the dynamics of desire present in the relationship between the photographer, the photographed and you.'

More than fifteen years later I am working towards what I call a queer feminist methodology; a working ethos committed to making images *with* (speaking) subjects rather than taking images *from* passive or silenced objects. Ever since I began making pictures the photographic model release has been an albatross around my neck (and this is one bird I have no interest in saving from extinction). As you might be aware, the model release gives the photographer (alone) the power 'to use, reuse, intact or in part, composite or distorted... for any purpose whatsoever, in perpetuity'. And yet many of us sign on the dotted line without fully understanding what this means. The history of photography is also the history of the violent and ubiquitous exploitation of those who are considered marginal and disposable with the camera as the weapon of choice. There are good reasons why some cultures are camera shy.

What I want and need is for the people I work with to feel empowered by both the process and the final product. For me this means that the *way* the image is created is as fundamental as the image itself. The agreements I make with the people I photograph has been inspired by the 'copyleft'

movement, a copyright licensing scheme in which the photographer surrenders some rights under copyright law and which also allows the photographer to impose some copyright restrictions provided certain agreements are adhered to, such as crediting the photographer. Putting these principles into practice has not been a walk in the park on a sunny day, especially when there are so many individuals to check in with and get approval from. It's a tricky business to figure out but I am committed to making queer femme-inist interventions into 'traditional' (patriarchal and racist) photographic practice however, wherever and whenever I can.

Femmes of Power is the product of multiple collaborations and years of shifting sands. These collaborations, between me and the people with whom I make photographs; between Dr Dahl and myself; between the good doctor and each of our 'subjects'; between text, image and design; and finally, between you and these pages; are pregnant with possibilities. This might be the closest I ever get to giving birth and this baby is long overdue! Please welcome her and watch her grow into the femme of power she was born to be!

ACKNOWLEDGEMENTS

Ulrika Dahl, for her remarkable tenacity, her femme wit and wisdom and for always believing that this project was important. Matt/ilda Wurm, for always being there for me in heart, body and mind. Simo Maronati for giving me a comfy bed to sleep on when mine was far away. Billy Goodfellow for being bestmate butch eye candy when called upon. Campbell for the FEM text and queer consultancy work above and beyond. Shanti Freed for stunning art direction and finesse. Anna-Maria Sörberg for emotional project management, support and friend-ship. Elina Grandin for design genius and totally twisted yet absolutely lucid logic. Jeanette Andersson for making my images look so good! Iain Moreland for last minute textual fine tuning. Dagmar Fink for a tough and insightful femme-insist critique. Mary Mizelle for some Deep South sunshine and sea just when I needed it most.

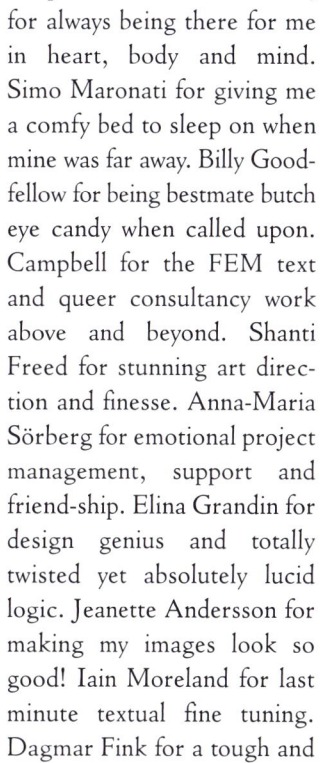

Finally I want to acknowledge the queerly feminine and all of us who, through absolute resilience and tenacity, are landscaping a brave new femme world unbound by the regulation and the rule of patriarchal law.

Disposible Boy Toys, Santa Barbara, California 2002 |
Blue Vulva & Luigi, Stockholm 2003
next spread: Indra Feminist Pants, Halmstad 2003 |
Flying Femme, Ulrika Dahl, Halmstad 2003

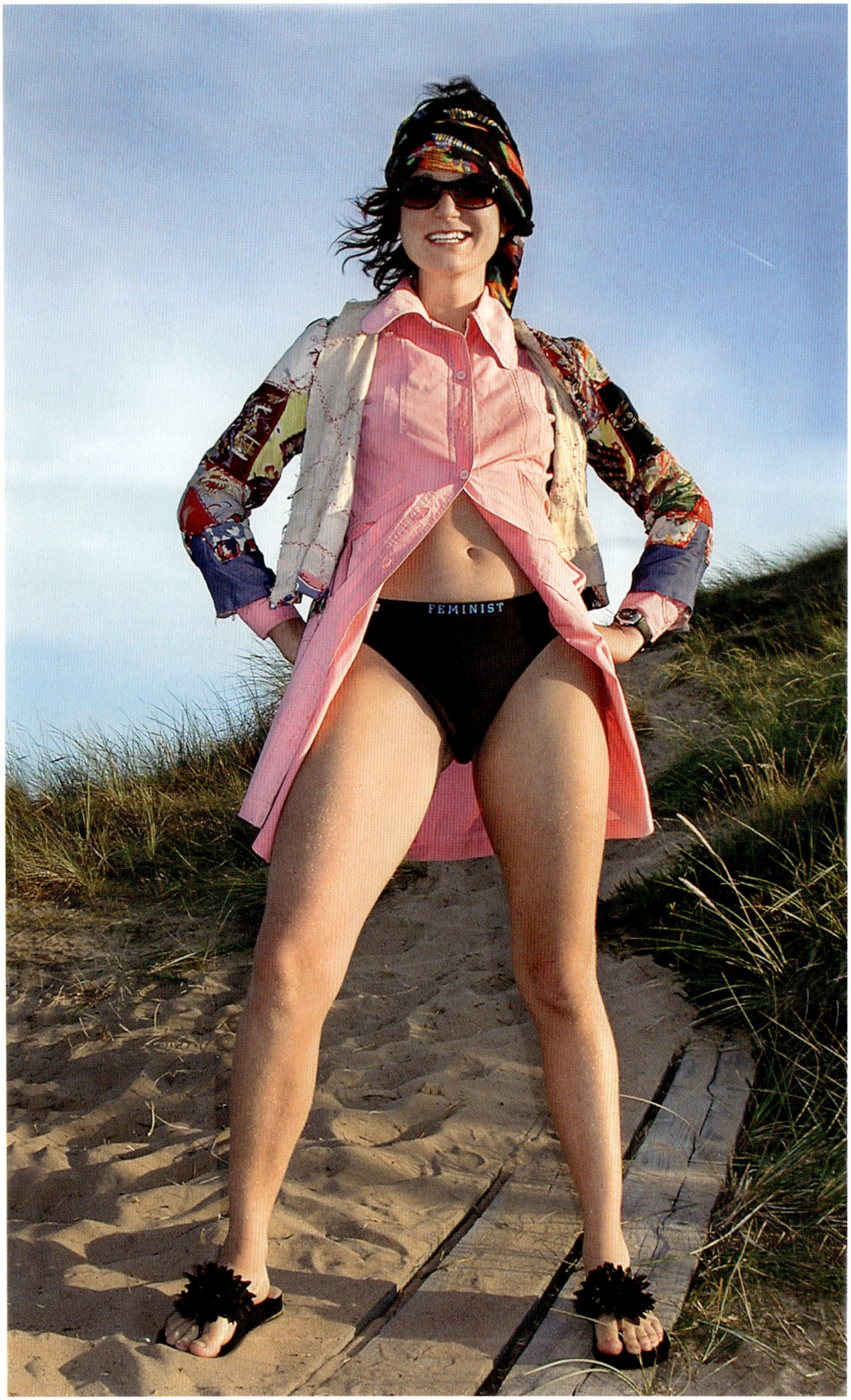
FEMINIST

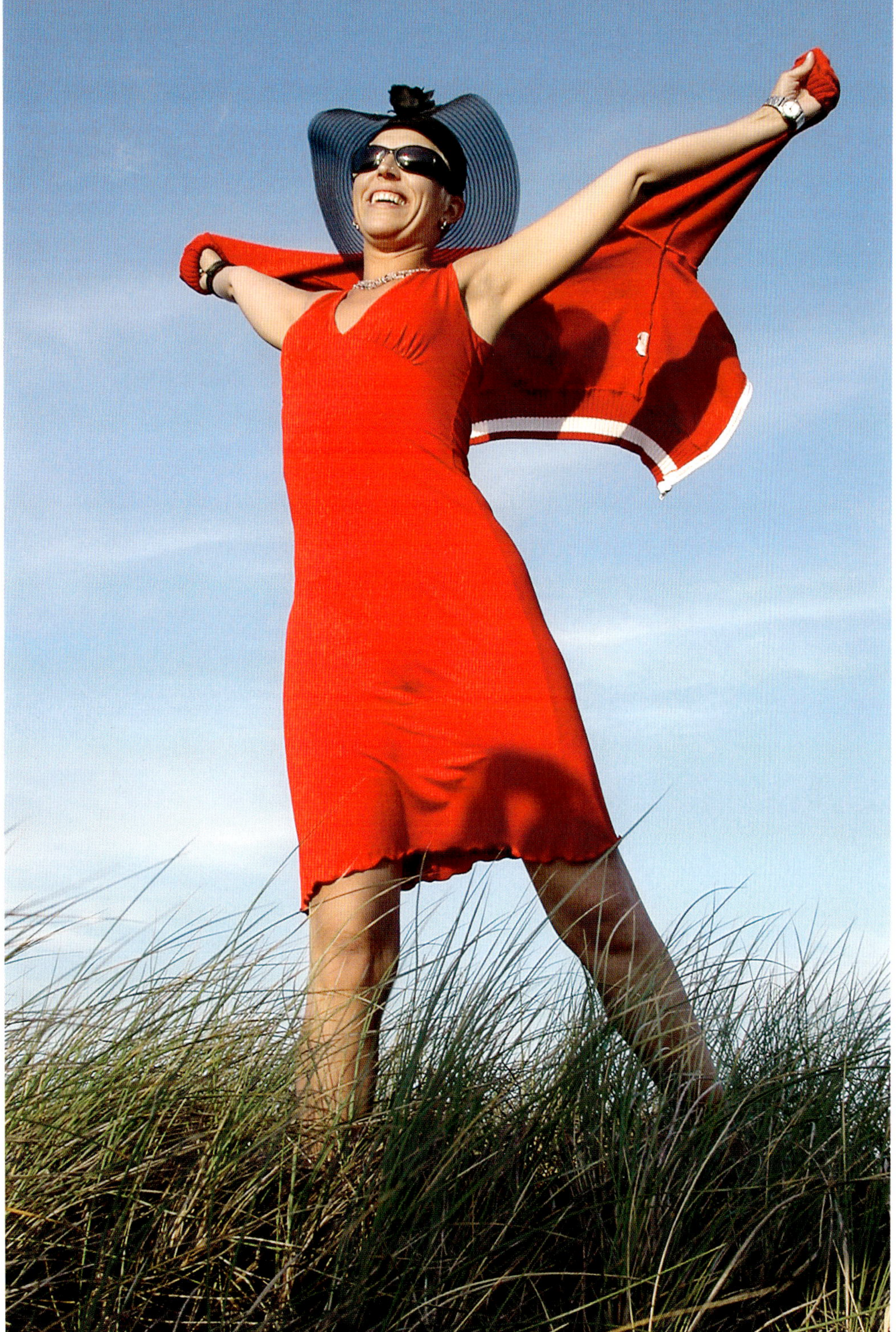

ULRIKA DAHL

Introduction

I want to liberate femininity from its history – in my mind, in my body and in my communities. I want to liberate it from the hands of the privileged who withhold access to it, and use it as an excuse to oppress others. I want to demolish its reputation as cause for violation. And I want to take it from under the pestle of the dyke community and celebrate it as a radical expression of queerness. TARA HARDY 2000:181

Dear Femmes of Power,

As I write this, I think about how many of you have described your first femme moments, your first passions and performances, or when you first deliberately indulged your queer femininities. It's exhilarating and a little terrifying. In a heterosexist world that continues to tell us that femininity is the ultimate available object for universal consumption and contempt, taking a stand on and through (queer) femininity, as we all do and know, is both intense pleasure and clear and present danger. Who will understand and who will misread? Neither femme nor femme-inist theory, you have all reminded me, is easy or natural. To us, femininity is neither phallic fantasy nor default, it's beyond surface and it certainly does not passively wait to come alive through a (male) gaze. Fiercely intentional, neither objects nor objective, we have stuff to get off our chests. But speaking bittersweet truths to power takes both busty bravery and some serious padding.

Some may say I am a bad scientist. I am indeed

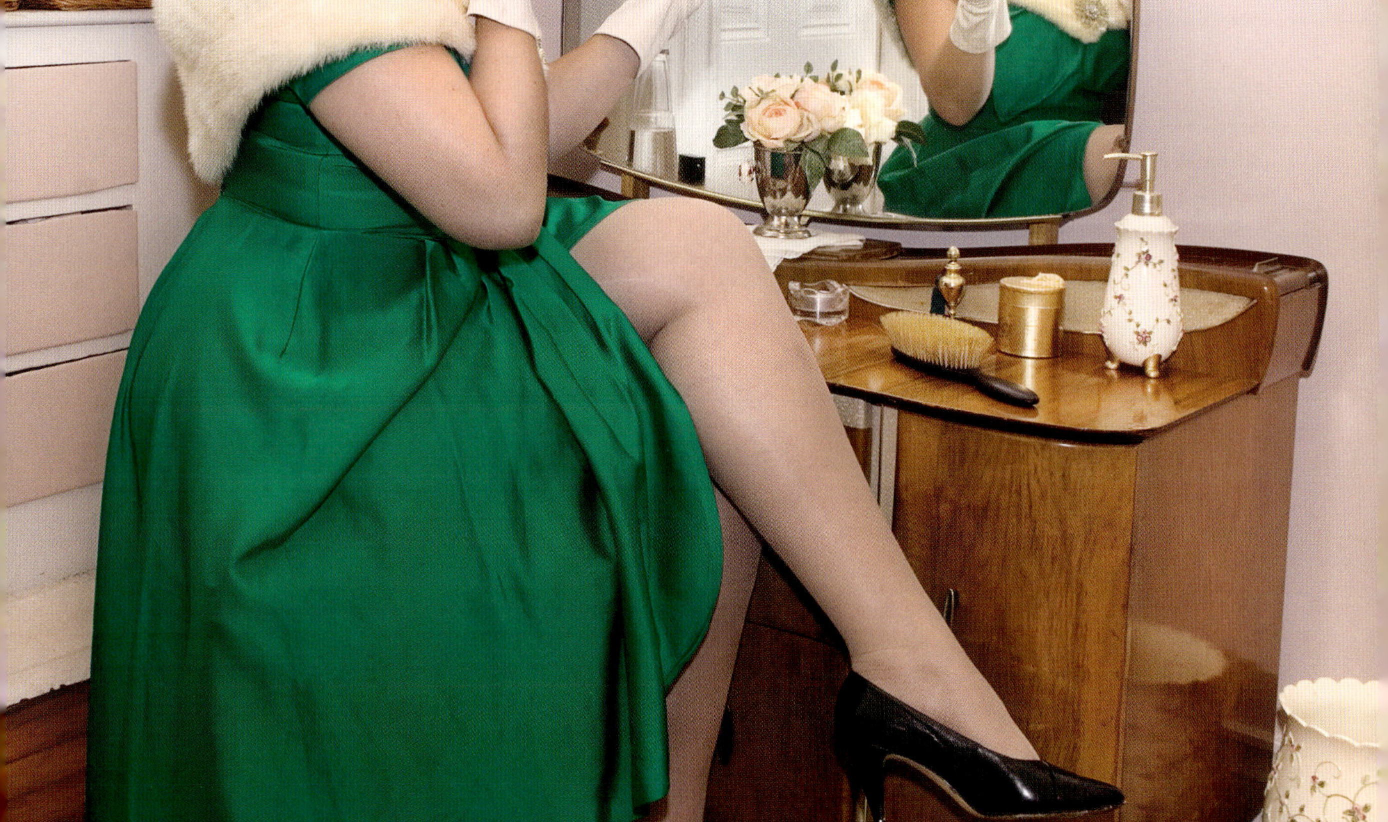

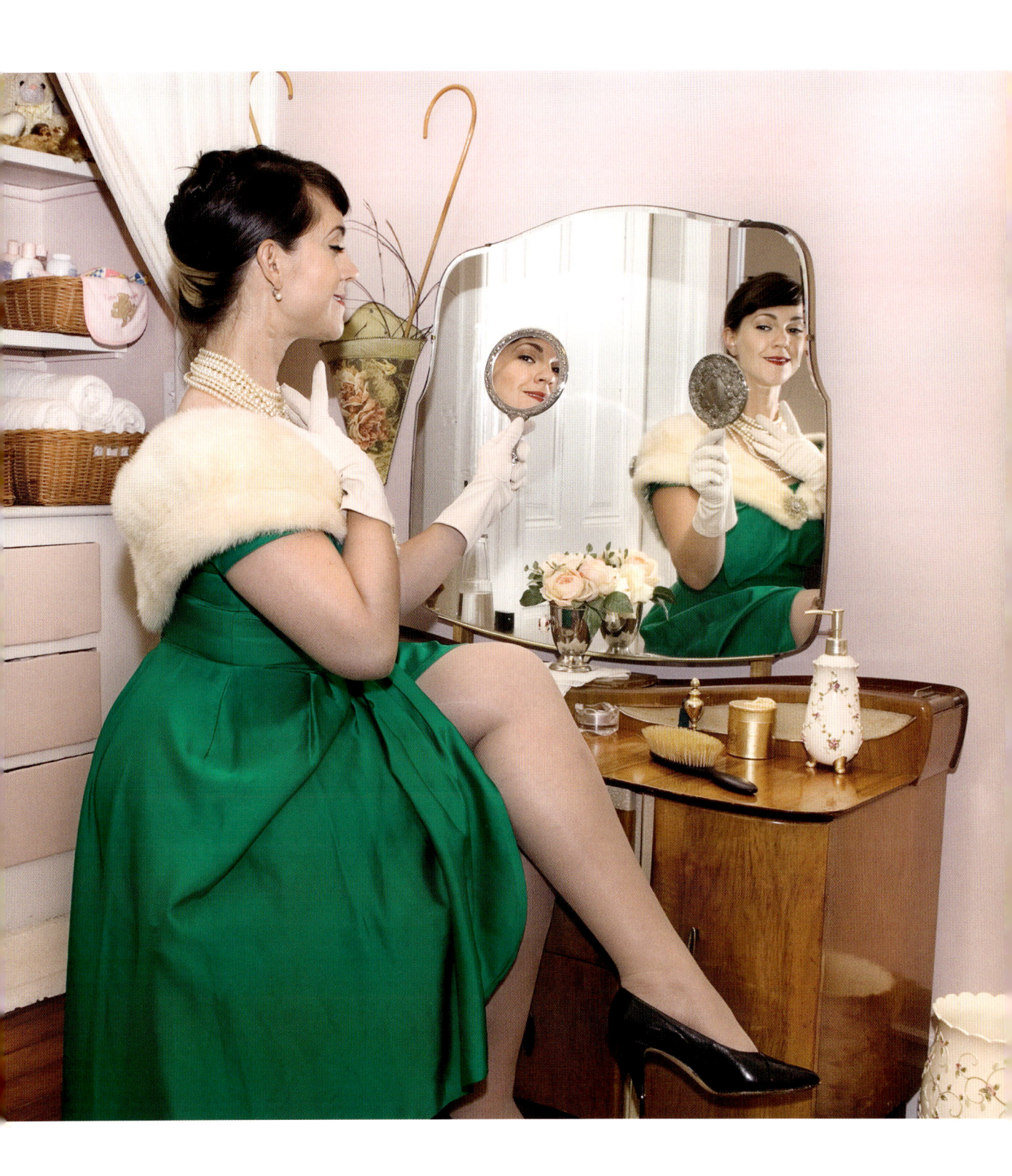

both object and subject of my own research. My bleached blonde Northern Swedish ambition lacks the requisite scientific objectifying distance and to me, the personal is still political.

Like Tara Hardy in the opening quote, I join a long legacy of femme writers who want to liberate femininity from its heterosexist history, in ourselves as well as within our communities. This is – thank you, Joan Nestle and Amber Hollibaugh – our persistent and dangerous desires. However, just because my gaze in the mirror is not distant does not mean it's narcissistic. You, my queer sisters, are spectacular and you have taught me that there are many ways to walk in the world as a femme-inine subject. Every conversation we've had and photo we've made with you – and there are over sixty of you, from twelve different cities and seven countries – contains amazing life stories and speaks of situated stakes. You are all larger than life in your love, your bodies, your desires and your activisms. This book is not a single, linear narrative or literal translation of the multiple and exploding meanings of femininity modelled and made by you. These are love letters and celebrations.

As a femme I have found and formed my own femme-inine identity/theory through connection, vintage and trade. I reject the imperialist fantasy of scientific 'discovery' and question a capitalist consumption logic that feeds on always inventing something new. I was raised by feminist anthropologists, and yes, I write with ethnographic attitude, but above all, as this book shows, the power and pleasure of femme lies in generous and generative mirroring and copying, imitating and citing. So let's call ourselves contributors to what Lisa Duggan and Kathleen McHugh [2002] have called *Femme Science*. The femme scientist, they declare in their legendary *Fem(me) Manifesto*, is in the third phase of research. She is past objectivity and explanation, she has an explicit goal, even as she uses the force of the oxymoronic and the paradoxical. Importantly, the femme scientist solicits collaboration, which is what I have done with you. To me you are all articulate and brilliant theorists of the pleasures and pains of femininity. Together we give a cheeky red painted middle finger to Big Science and its urge to discover, reduce, label and patent. Why? Because the femme-inine principle reminds us that world needs political fictions as much as it needs theoretical systems and because you are all visionaries.

GRRLS, I HAVE TO SAY, I've lost count of the number of times I've been asked to define what femme is. Like you, I might be able to if I was to speak only for myself, but femme never sits still and she is always in relation. It's true, many of us will say we can recognise each other, not only adjusting outfits in the ladies room or on the arms of the people we desire, but also on the streets and in bars, even when we are not read as queer.

Few of you have wanted to nail down what enables us to do so, but one thing is clear: it's not as simple as a question of polish or length of nails. You may transition into femme-ness, earn your reputation, tune into the frequency, be born a (drag) queen, be seen only in the eyes of your lover or, as Reina Lewis put it, be 'raised to cleanse, tone and moisturize', but you all are proud, fierce and intentional. The Atlanta Femme Mafia declares: 'femme is an umbrella under which we find solace, not an ex-clusionary or re-strictive predetermined formula', and like our cover girls from London's Bird Club say: 'anybody can be a Bird'. Refusing to create one master theory of queer femininity is thus an act of resistance and solidarity.

A lot of mascara and ink has been spent conceiving passionate poetic theory about what the world looks like through a femme figure and most of it, like femininely coded labour, is that of love: underpaid and undervalued. That is, femme has not been central to neither feminist nor queer theory. As a 'professor' entangled in fishnets and networks and committed to femme-inist citational practice, I here point to some femme tales in the form of a bibliography rather than through academic aerobics. In this book I want the show to be yours. Your lived theories emerge at the intersection of movements of queer activism and feminism, anti-racism and fat activism, transactions and sexual politics. You went back into the closet and come out of do-it-yourself traditions, you play dress-up, ooze from biomythographical poetry and explode off stages in queer subcultural Meccas. You celebrate and channel great heroines and icons of femininity – not because you are duped by advertising but because who tells us more about

The Femme-inist Ethnographer @ Work, San Francisco 2006 | previous spread: The 3 Faces of Morgana Maye, San Francisco 2006

the changing value and meaning of femininity than the mass-produced and reproduced pin-up? Who is better equipped to give the world a theory of sexual politics than those who make a living from it? You show that most blondes have dark roots, that making an income on sex can mean many things and that when the pin-up is allowed to speak, she straddles stacks of feminist theory. I am doing femme theory, not only for my own pleasure but because produced and performed, sincerely ironic and deadly serious, femme pulsates in my dreams, in my bulimic wounds, my dirty tricks, my dress-up box, my feminist politics, my perverse desires and, most of all, in my longing for queer sisterhood.

Liberating femininity from its history in our bodies and communities is easier said than done and we are used to being misread and unseen. Each time I've questioned myself and this project, it's the bravery of what you have shared and taught me, the privilege of working with all of you, the endless conversations we've made together, and how each meeting has been so incredibly important, that has kept me going. Your willingness to get in front of Del's camera and be poster girls for this particular daily (r)evolution makes the world of difference to all who never dare or want to. In Del's images and in our encounters, femme is more than a visible declaration of identity. As a gesture, a posture, a gaze and a spirit, I've seen femme reflected in your eyes and in the eyes of lovers and kin (my own and yours, and sometimes, yes, we've shared them). You have been fatally sharp reflections in dressing room mirrors, at times in the corner of my eye, and as Canadian femmes Anna Camilleri and Chloe Brushwood Rose [2002] note, sometimes it's in a femme's look away that she appears. As Turner, femme-identified FTM in Atlanta knows, there have been moments when I have not recognised you. I will keep looking and I hope you will find me too.

Visible and invisible, tangible yet intangible, brand new and age old, there is no universal recipe for making a femme or queering femininity. Rather, as you all show, femme is at once a private matter of space, a local business and a transnational community project. Your stories point to the need for both queer reading skills and cultural literacies in the particular histories which you live in, cite, disrupt and explode from.

Itziar Ziga, Barcelona 2007 | Stockholm Pride Femme Workshop 2006

Biological clocks or not, femmes honour our mothers and commit blasphemous loving twists on our pasts and what was passed on. Refusing to pick sides, you have commitments to multiple communities and legacies, be you Bengali, Chicana, White Scandinavian, Desi, Black, Jewish, Irish, Lankan, Guyanese, Basque or German. Our experiences of exile and passing, migration and diaspora across borders and in/between both majoritarian and queer communities, differ greatly and remain the femme movement's most important sites of continued interrogation.

Together you show that femme is in between both sheets and streets, in the borderlands, and this offers hopes of possible partial connections – even as we remain painfully aware of the heightened border policing in the world and of our communities. Femmes in times of (sex) war can all choose to be on the side of struggle and to show up to be counted.

THIS BOOK IS a testimony of a particular queer kinship route. In an era of increasing airplane pollution and virtual community-making and self-promotion, activists and dissidents have many ways to find and keep up with fellow travellers with similar tastes and tales. Most of you I've met because Del and I are particular kinds of nomadic subjects who have had the privilege of making home, love and community in many places over the past decade. As the writer of these love letters, it matters that I was raised speaking Swedish and ethnographically trained in English. These stories, like most things that I am and do, have emerged in/between two languages that feel equally native and alien and they, like our meetings, have often required multiple translations – and at times, translators. The portraits here are in many ways fragments of the chosen family album of two Euro queers in collaboration and occasional conflict. Del and I have followed threads and crumbs, hooked and hustled, we have listened to the wise words of community elders and outspoken critics.

While we are both deeply marked by our status in relation to the US and by our partial belongings to (albeit) different generations of queer America, this dying empire is neither the sole origin or the ultimate measuring tape for femme. If anything, our 'T' time with the Queens and Kings of England and the Serpent's Tail that whipped us into shape have made us decide not to put the US and American queer politics at the centre of this book. Amidst a great range of queer urban Meccas in the so-called land of the free, we could only make pilgrimages to three: San Francisco, Atlanta and New York. Among both American sisters and Eurobabes alike it's very clear that 'femme' is neither simply French for 'woman' nor is it only or simply code for feminine lesbians. But the Paris Fem Menace uses a different (American) spelling than I do and we all know that the term femme and the meaning of queer femininity have different and diasporic histories in Germany and Spain, than it does among the descendants of those who once left and went west or whose ancestors were forced to. As a new generation of Swedish and Danish queers both embrace and reject the identity politics that seemingly arrived with the queer 'American' theory that was supposed to deconstruct it, queer femininity carries different meanings to Andy and Signe, Sofie and Jun, including those who pronounce it 'famme', or use it as an adjective rather than a noun. Some of you do not use the term femme at all to describe yourselves.

My writing in this book – an array of letter styled portraits, interviews and clustered themes, rather than a linear ('scientific') narrative – is a strategic choice. It's inspired by the tradition that Femme 2006: Conversations and Explorations proposed. Attending this San Francisco conference of workshops and performances, created by a coalition of North American femme activists with very limited resources, was for me an important part of this journey. Femme 2006 aimed 'to create a Femme-positive environment and to honour differences'. The goal of this gathering of over 400 femmes and our allies was 'to create a space to explore the complexities of Femme identity, including (but not limited to) questions of privilege, invisibility, intersecting identities, class mobility, aging, and the differences between femininity and Femme identity', which is what I've tried to do as well. As you all note, ours is not a unity through sameness (classic identity politics), but rather strategic solidarity through points of connection and collaboration. We share activist legacies of empowerment, attend to relations of power and dare to have a vision for a future of femme-inism.

In addition to my dialogic and thematic accounts, Inge 'Campbell' Blackman, Pratibha Parmar, Lois Weaver, Itziar Ziga, Krista Smith and Amber Hollibaugh, all of whom have also been important dialogue partners in this project, offer 'key-notes' on particular themes. We are, in short, honoured and inspired.

Anna Camilleri and Chloe Brushwood Rose declare that 'what cannot be seen, what cannot be held or pinned down, is where femme is – she can not be domesticated' [2002:11]. Indeed. Here femme is not 'represented' as stable or coherent. Rather yours are exploding and unruly queer femininities. To that end, I present femme as a queer and feminist *figuration*. As my teacher, hopeful feminist theorist Donna Haraway, has argued, a figuration can be 'a mode of theory when the more "normal" rhetorics for critical analysis seem only to repeat and sustain our entrapment in the stories of established disorders' [2004:47]. A genre rather than a gender (as Dandy theorist Jami Weinstein puts it), femme is in a state of becoming, emerging from the stories we tell, the artifacts and technologies we employ, the desiring bodies we live, from our citational practices and the representations we make. Collecting both hopes and fears, showing possibilities and dangers, here femme is rooted in your stories because as Haraway reminds us, 'stories are always more generous and capacious than ideologies' [2004:3]. Together we show that the femme figuration is a non-linear political fiction, at once literary and imagined, material and embodied.

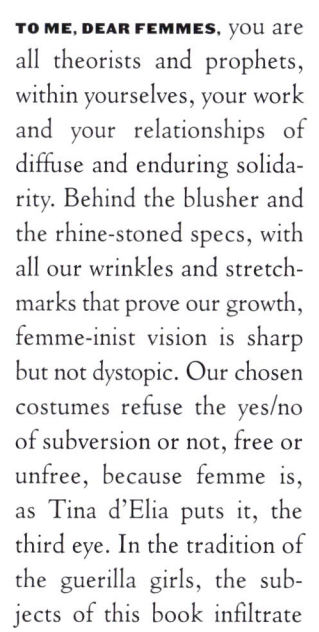

TO ME, DEAR FEMMES, you are all theorists and prophets, within yourselves, your work and your relationships of diffuse and enduring solidarity. Behind the blusher and the rhine-stoned specs, with all our wrinkles and stretchmarks that prove our growth, femme-inist vision is sharp but not dystopic. Our chosen costumes refuse the yes/no of subversion or not, free or unfree, because femme is, as Tina d'Elia puts it, the third eye. In the tradition of the guerilla girls, the subjects of this book infiltrate the over-saturated world of feminine advertising and sissy bashing. Yes, we wear lipstick because it makes us feel better and we are willing to share. Like eternal tricksters straddling impossible dichotomies, we continue to take up space with our desires, sincere ironies and refusals to be either/or.

In queering femininities you all go beyond the radical individualism of identity politics. Playing with, rather than fully rejecting the 'dominant ideology' of femininity, means engaging in what queer scholar Jose Esteban Munoz [1999] calls a

Signe Flyvsk, København 2007 | Reina Lewis, London 2007

strategic act of disidentification. By neither assimilating in its structure nor strictly opposing it, femmes try to 'transform a cultural logic from within, always laboring to enact permanent structural change while at the same time valuing the importance of local or everyday struggles of resistance' [1999:11–12]. In bodies marked, adorned and adored, as a figuration, exploding femininities are always in relation, situated, but accountable for and speaking from more than our self-appointed positions; we each have our own location in worlds and histories, including those of feminisms and queer communities.

Like all size queens, I like it big. No matter how huge our dreams for this book, these are partial perspectives and there are obvious absences. You, dear femmes, do not 'represent' all corners of the world, not even of the western world, let alone the metropoles we so often celebrate – nor have you been asked to. This book comes out of conversation and exploration and it highlights some of the subjects, stories and stakes we've encountered on this journey, but far from all. Like a figurative cat's cradle game, we've made some patterns that can be passed on and reconfigured. Remember, there is no manual, no entrance exam or dress code, but that because we have each other far beyond this book, we are able to live in this world. *Femmes of Power* is about us and for everyone, but makes no claims to be the ultimate representation of femmes or what it means to queer femininity.

Femme science, Lisa Duggan and Kathleen McHugh argue, 'is addressed to the future, a future where femininity as we know it ("normal", ego-less, tolerant of, and therefore complicit with, deception) will have been completely superceded' [2002:168]. This is our contribution. Now, dear Femmes of Power, allow me to introduce you to each other, and all of you to our readers. I hope that all gendered beings (regardless of queer credentials) everywhere can find points of connection, dare to see yourselves in these fragments of femme and continue to explode the meaning of femininity.

Femme Luv and respect always,

Ulrika

ACKNOWLEDGEMENTS

My enduring gratitude to Del LaGrace Volcano, for friendship, wisdom and collaboration and to the *Femmes of Power* for doing this with us. I am blessed and full of love for my family, friends, lovers, allies, colleagues and students whose faith, support and critical engagement has sustained me for many years. Special Thanks to Jami Weinstein for queer partnership and dandy brilliance; to Lena Sawyer, Josephine Wilson, Krista Smith, Rosie Lugosi, Amber Hollibaugh, Devrim Mavi, Indra Windh, and Campbell Ex for ideas and feedback on writing; to Elina Grandin and Anna-Maria Sörberg for outstanding form and loving management, the queerest eye and all your time; to Cherry Smyth for excellent editing and Serpent's Tail for amazing patience; to Tiina Rosenberg, Nina Lykke and especially Judith Halberstam for early encouragement and continued support; to the organisers and participants of the Femme 2006 conference for femme vision. Lastly and most of all: To all femmes, past and present, for your inspiration, courage and work in this world, every day. I honour you.

Mafia Femme Aly, 'Have Love Will Travel',
San Francisco 2006

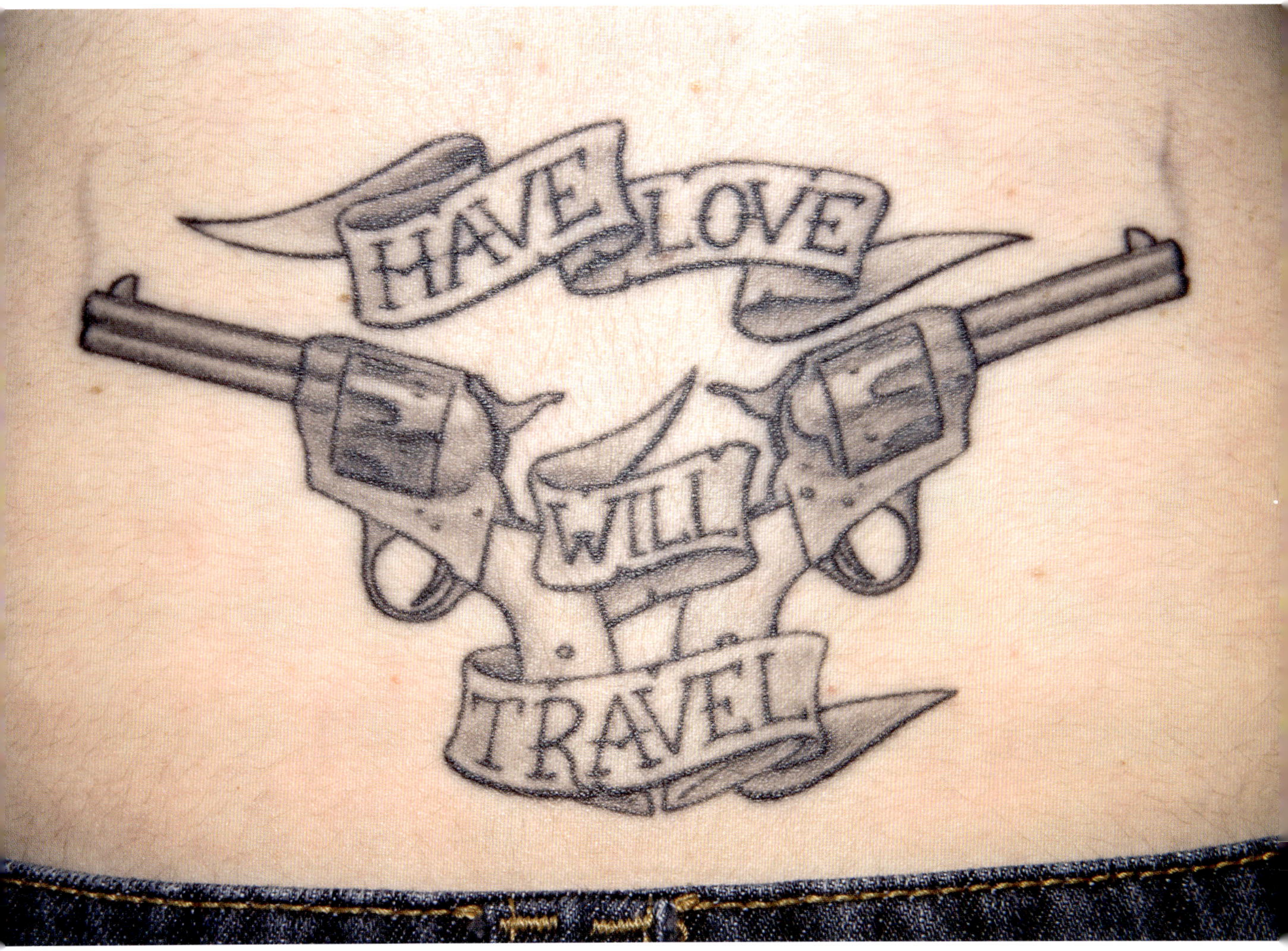
HAVE LOVE
WILL
TRAVEL

28

FEM

INGE 'CAMPBELL' BLACKMAN

Dear Femme,
Ever wondered what it would be like
   if Eve had *not* been
chased from the Garden of Eden?
Had not tasted that forbidden fruit?
Seductive woman!
Is your femme-ness stained by original sin?
You dress to please me, your butch lover,
   your man-royal,
and others accuse you of passing.
We both know your desire for me is the
   revolutionary act.
And yes, sometimes, I break my promises.
Although
I love you
You hate me
I hate you
You love me
You love
the woman inside the man that I am
even though beside me
the closet swings open and
there is nowhere to hide.
And when you are invisible.
You become my gender spy, my queer
   Mata Hari.
And those heels, painted lips and swinging hips,
Send out a code that only I can read
We created this love
We take the straight and bend it into shape.
Yes you *are* the girl but that does *not* make you weak.

Remember!
The bloodlines from powerful goddesses
   run through you.
You hold the power to create and destroy.
Your womanly magic
So terrifying
they burn you at the stake.
But you, refuse to die.
I pack and my hardness pleases you
Pandora opened her Box,
And unleashed demons.
But between your thighs
I find divine sweetness and sacred power.

Let us unlearn the patri-lies.
Sweet femme, you choose to surrender to me
and I enter deep inside you,
I am stone.
And yes
I would switch for you,
your yin becoming my yang.
We play in our own enchanted garden
   inventing new rules
from old games. You be my mistress,
   my wife, my virgin, my
whore, my bird, my lover, my friend.
We stand naked,
You content in your woman-body
Me awkward in mine.
You can
Cut me down to size.
Am I eunuch or stud?
You will decide
Dearest femme,
Do you need me as much
as I want you?
I am forever your daddy, boi, stud, your geezer,
husband, your gentleman friend.
Desire over biology.
Always.

Deni Francis, London 2007

The femme frequency

THE FIRST TIME I locked eyes with a butch my stomach dropped. I didn't understand what I was feeling, I had no name for what Amber Hollibaugh years later called 'knowing you're toast'. When I was first seduced by a butch, I couldn't speak for two days. Even my compulsory writing halted and my feminist fuse short-circuited. Stunned I sat in my room in the communal household and listened to the Pacific waves, trying to calm those inside me. I couldn't explain the need it had unlocked in me. So one last time I did resort to toast. That is, to bingeing – something I'd secretly done for as long as I'd been sexual. Luckily, I've now accepted that I'm toast and a complete butchaholic. It is butches who've seen me, who've taught me to be in my body and to like it. Perhaps the uncontrollable hunger I've been struggling with all my life is simply the awkward girl I've always been yearning to own both the queer desire to be desired and the desire to desire.

'Femme is at its essence a frequency you tune into,' mused London-based Caroline, a 'Zenbyker-Femme', music producer, pleasure activist and practitioner of the healing arts. 'Butch–femme is a dance of equal opposites, a kind of energy frisson. It was like a magnet, I was drawn to it and I had to open to it, it was primal,' she continued. I can only agree. I can't explain why I get weak in the knees for a butch with power tools, a tie around a strong neck or a firm grip on my hand. Following in the persistent and dangerously desiring footsteps of, among others, Joan Nestle and Amber Hollibaugh, many of us live and defend the historical lesbian legacy of femme and butch. Femmes have a well documented history of supporting and desiring queer masculinities fiercely and powerfully, even when it's unintelligible to the (straight) world or when butches have gotten all the queer credentials. What this frequency actually means in the streets and between sheets varies a great deal, but one thing is clear: femme desire is neither a bad copy of a heterosexual original, nor is it simply tied to butch and ultimately, queer desires are never completely free of racialised and heterosexist ideas of gender.

Dr Valerie Mason-John, London-based award-winning author, performer and foundational theorist of black lesbian sexuality in Britain, declared: 'I'm most definitely femme, I only ever sexually polarise around butches or boys. I know I'm not butch because I've never had the fear of being outed as a dyke in public nor have the fear or discomfort of being mistaken as a man. However as a femme I do fear being sexually harassed by men on the streets to

Deni Francis (& Crin Claxton), London 2007

31

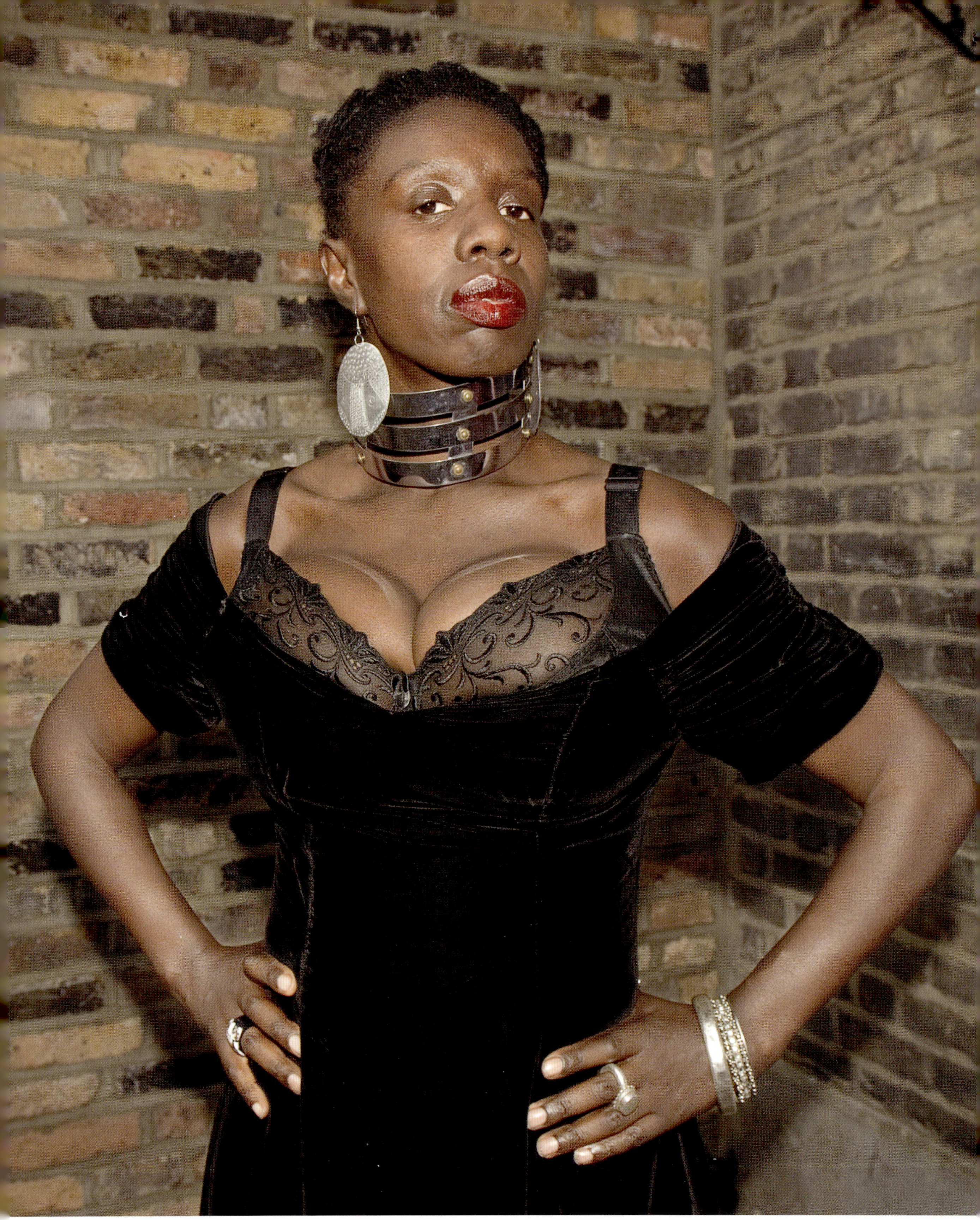

the extent that I can't always wear what I want to. During my twenties I felt an unspoken pressure to be butch in bed from white women, as if we, black women, had to be sexually dominant. Queer culture had a huge impact on me when I realised I could be femme one day and something else the next. Above all I realised I didn't have to be butch in bed and that there is power in being a femme lesbian. Femme is a revolution of female identity. It's not about how one dresses, it's about one's attitude, and values.'

Carving out space for queer feminine pleasure in a heterosexist and racist world is an accomplishment. The femme tradition is both charged by and filled with tales that challenge ideas of femininity as always and only tied to (sexual) passivity. Writer, therapist and life-long Bay Area femme Dossie Easton glowingly announced that 'at sixty-two I'm training a young butch to top and it keeps getting better!' Dossie spoke of the power of receptivity and recited her 'Do me queen' poem. At Femme 2006 Dossie read it accompanied by dancer Veronica Comb and it was a frequency that left many spellbound:

I have always been completely hopeless at playing hard to get / I get desperately confused when I am supposed to pretend / I don't want to, when I do, I do / Sleaze comes easy to this greedy queen. Story of my life: Pants-on butch meets easy-off skirt.

Valerie Mason-John, London 2007 | Solange Garjan, Atlanta 2007

Greed, you know, is just the other side of generosity, solid gold when you / Grasp the whole coin. / Do me queen. Do me do me do me do / do me slow / do me soft / do me sweet / do me now!

SOLANGE GARJAN from Tennessee chronicled how her 'plumage' has affected her lesbian relationships. 'In a world where violence against women is a constant reality and where our sexuality is simultaneously exploited and resented, my lover was scared that I would attract the wrong attention and she was afraid of my sexual aesthetic and power. But actually, the more confident I was and the more I projected that in the street, the less I was harassed.' At a gathering at Mafia femme Andi's house in Atlanta, Solange spoke of the powerful pleasures of bottoming to her stud. 'It's important to who I am. Topping/bottoming is circular and exponential in nature, it feeds on itself, spiraling up and out and deeper and deeper. Surrendering I feel quite free and my passion fuels the passion of my lover, which in turn further fuels mine.' Rachael, proud Donna of the Atlanta Femme Mafia, talked of being a fierce femme top who likes to strap it on for her bois. And in her professional and personal life, Mistress Morgana figures the feminine power of leading both women and men into the pleasure of submission and surrender.

Many will insist that neither being lesbian nor a butch desire are necessary femme ingredients, although for Ylva Maria, Maya, Jun, Maria Dixen and Virginie, it is desiring men, past and present, that has made them question calling themselves femme. Tina Batya is proudly bi and to her the Atlanta Femme Mafia is a space where she feels included. 'I can't tell you how much I appreciate that, because it's more than disheartening when people try and tell you that your sexuality doesn't exist or make you feel there's no place for you. You're too queer for the straight people and too straight for the gays.' The many femmes who partner with transmen speak of the complexities of invisibility in both queer and straight worlds. 'Being with my FTM partner, we pass as a straight couple, but when I'm with my feminine play partners, we come across very queer,' said Signe, who like Wendy and Barbara also enjoys femme-on-femme play. Atlanta-based Turner, a femme-identified FTM spoke of another mis/recognition: being read as butch or male in relation to his bio femme girlfriend Carey. Josephine and Kate, as femme-on-transfemme dykes, are at once distinctly homo and utterly queer. And for Sofie in Stockholm, the power of the *flicka* (girl) femme doesn't need to be tied to desire at all; she advocates asexuality, distinct from what she sees as 'the sexual excess of femme bad girls'.

Femme theorist Kathryn Payne [2002] defines femme as 'deliberate feminine sexual agency' and ultimately femme desire is both intentional and indeterminate. Regardless of gender/sex, of our individual objects of desire, or of the positions taken in sexual practice, one thing is loud and clear: femmes' desiring practices place their pleasure centre stage, powerfully rearticulating what femme queen Shar Rednour [2000] has called coming in a cornucopia of sexualities and getting off on being the object of desire. Tuning into any femme frequency is a transformation of presumed feminine objectification into subjective choice and proudly declared agency. It is a femme-inist reconfiguration of Big Daddy Freud's pleasure principles.

Caroline, London 2006

35

DRAFT BEER
CARLSBERG
STELLA ARTOIS
SIERRA NEVADA
AMSTEL LIGHT
Munchies 75¢
Popcorn
dart for a GUINNESS

The Third Eye of a Latina Power Femme

Dear Tina,

Entering your San Francisco studio where we met to talk before the photoshoot, I recalled the first time I visited you in 2000. Shar Rednour and Jackie Strano's film *Hard Love/How to Fuck in High Heels*, in which you were one of the local stars, was premiering. I admired your bravery, talent and beauty – there was something glamorous and silver screen diva-like about you, like you were channelling your heroines Bette Davis and Rita Hayworth. Your husky voice and loud laughter also has a hint of your other hero Groucho Marx and the tomboy you were as a kid showing through. 'I cannot hide my femininity,' you said now, putting on strappy heels and a gorgeous evening gown. Yours is not a high femme position and it involves neither motherhood nor housework you said, adding that, 'I've tremendous admiration for high femmes because it is a lot of work to even walk down the street in such shoes.'

Your Boston childhood dreams were less Joan of Arc – 'the obvious heroine for a Catholic girl' – and more Wonder Woman. 'I've always been a feminist and femme in my queer life. It's like having a third eye that makes you see injustice and through misogyny,' you said. 'I've not always had language for it but I've always had the lipstick and the attitude of a power femme.'

When we first met, Shar and Jackie's queer porn – made in San Francisco butch–femme aesthetic, was part of a new wave of making femme desire and sexuality visible. What I found so powerful about you and many others in that scene was the combination of activism, sex and art, and you also worked at CUAV, Community United Against Violence, as director of the hate-violence survivor programme. Among other things, you worked on the campaign to raise awareness around the case of GwenAraujo, a Latina transgender youth who was murdered in 2002, and California's hate crime statute. 'As a Latina femme,' you said, 'I'll always first and foremost identify with communities of colour and as an ally to transcommunities of colour.'

You're a proud mixed race Latina, power femme bottom, and an actress and a lover of the stage. 'As a child I wanted to tap dance at the altar in the Catholic church that my Italian father and Mexican-German-raised-in-Colombia mother shared.' You've been the MC of San Francisco's dyke march stage, conducted your own one-woman show, and in 2006, you had a part in Will Smith's film *The Pursuit of Happyness*.

You wanted a bar shot, feeling like Lady Luck and channelling Cristina Maria Carmencita Rivera – the first two names yours by birth, the third your mother's and the last your grandmother's. A power femme, you explained, 'shows up alone to the bar, that is part of the joys of cat and mouse chasing. Lady Luck awaits the arrival of her Transgender Latino blackjack king. When she finds him, she turns his luck around, never becoming his property, but happy to be on his arm.'

Tina D'elia, San Francisco 2006

Beard-Adorned Lady

Dear Lady Charlotte,

In 2003 you hosted the monthly Trans Cafe at RFSL, Sweden's national LGBT organisation and were among the first to be interested in discussing queer femininities with me. An 'ordinary middle-aged Swede with Central European background', you're a linguist by training, currently working in customer relations. 'Some people don't seem to understand that I identify with a feminine, not masculine, gender,' you said. 'People rarely have a problem with my name but struggle with using female pronouns. To a linguist it's very interesting that pronominal and nominal gender are distinguished.' In a hand-written letter you carefully delineated your theories:

'For me femininity is both a feeling and an expression. The feeling is a certain kind of sensitivity that I think is different from the masculine. The expression is like a form of language. Its form happens on several levels, including clothing, decorating style, movements, use of language and voice. Clothes are most feminine when they enhance feminine body forms. I value femininity highly, in myself and in others. I have a strong positive identification both with femininity (as expression and feeling) and with femaleness over all.' Always the lady you wrote: 'With this image I want to show everyone that I – a woman, a transwoman and a beard-adorned woman – exist and that I'm part of this society. I do so next to our country's most public and political place, The Swedish Parliament, because the laws made there by my elected representatives should give me support and protection. Del really understood what this meant.'

When we met over vegan food and a beautiful view of Old Town, we bonded over our love of lacy fabrics, leopard patterns, tight-fitting dresses and pretty shoes. You stood up and pointed to your tight jeans and pink sweater. 'I feel very feminine wearing this,' you said. 'I hardly ever wear jeans,' I replied, a little unsure about what you meant. 'They show my feminine form and my rather broad hips, leaving nothing to the imagination,' you continued. Finally I understood, it's what the jeans do *not* show of your pre-op body that matters. That day you were troubled: your 'sex change investigation' (as Swedish authorities call it) had been stalled. The 'experts' didn't understand your beard, even though you'd shown them images of well-known bearded ladies.

Like Jennifer Miller, Elese, and Amelia in this book, you wear your facial hair with pride. Indeed, yours is a bearded theory: 'A well shaped and kept beard is a beautiful ornament that shouldn't belong to men only. It can also beautify a woman's face, regardless of whether she is born or has become one. I've always found beards both aesthetic and alluring. My emotional associations with beards are linked to warmth, maturity and stability. To believe myself able to grow a good beard and feel myself worthy of it, is not something I've taken for granted. It's been a step-by-step process that feels a bit like a success. Aesthetically speaking I'm very pleased with it, I think it's improved the proportions of my face.'

Charlotte Karlsdotter, Stockholm 2007

39

TransFemme Theory with Miss File

Twas on 'The Night of Tall Women and Short Men' in London that Josephine and I first began to talk. Ms Wilson had already visited Stockholm with the Wotever cabaret and had affinities with my queer kin and I with hers. That night, whilst dirty dancing, we exchanged thoughts on queer academia and soon we'd begun an intense conversation about gender, femme, theorising and long distance love. In 2007 Josephine relocated to Stockholm to be with her honey Sofia while completing her dissertation. She continues to perform and dance under several names, including as the illustrious Miss File, a strict teacher whose comments on burlesque, sexuality and the straightjacket of femininity challenge and crack us up. Dr Doll asked her to share some of her transfemme theory.

Dear Miss Wilson, how did you become such a fabulous femme? As a transwoman and a feminist, what's the appeal in claiming a femme identity?

— When I first began transitioning, the commonly expressed understandings of 'trans' really didn't fit my sense of self. I went to support networks, read books, watched TV, trying to find out 'who' I was, and was frustrated at every turn. I didn't match what I thought these people, communities and organisations were describing. I despaired at the thought that I wouldn't find any common ground and felt quite isolated. I wasn't a woman in the traditional 'straight' sense, and now I wasn't a woman in the traditional 'trans' sense either. I then came across Shar Rednour's fabulous *The Femme's Guide to the Universe* and felt an immediate affinity. She presented the possibility of an un-restrictive, un-apologetic, intelligent, witty, funny, sexy and confident femme-inine identity that I felt was ideal, if only I could find the confidence to step into my femme self. I read as much about femme as I could and even if none of the authors I read were trans themselves, I felt like their 'femme subjectivity' (for want of a better term) fit my trans-self. Aside from that, the common femme/trans-femme(female) experience of having to critically engage with, re-appropriate and revalue femme-inities appealed to me.

It answered questions I'd been grappling with both politically and personally. I transitioned in a feminist and traditionally lesbian/gay political environment where I had to justify why I should want to be a woman, when clearly transitioning at all (and especially inhabiting a femme identity), fed into the dualistic, patriarchal, anti-queer and/or anti-feminist, model of gender. I knew, from personal experience, that this wasn't true and when I realised I was femme, I could argue back much more confidently and cohesively. It was a subject position to work from, make my own and thus give something back to.

Yeah. It seems that as queerly feminine subjects we often inspire, reference and feel affinity with one another. As a gender scholar, how does being femme inform the work that you do?

— Femme is important to me for two reasons. One, I am femme and as a researcher who feels the self has an impact on my work, I locate my self as femme within my research and argue that

Josephine & Sofia, Club LASH, Stockholm 2006

41

42

it matters. Two, in my research I find huge overlaps in how transpeople engage with their alternative gender subjectivity and how femmes do it, especially transpeople who are also femme. I like to draw together and clarify the common issues that face the myriad of queer communities that cross identity lines. The issues that femmes face with visibility are similar to what some transpeople face (not being seen as queer for example). The existential questions about the prescriptive nature of gender and how to deal with and ultimately fuck with it cross these identity lines and are common to both femme and trans (butch, genderqueer, etc). Femme's an excellent example of the critical engagement with prescriptive, problematic gender formations by an individual/community and their attempts to use it, twist it and make it their own in an empowered way. But femme, like any other (queer) identification comes in all shapes and sizes and it's not the identity that unites us but the issues that we face. We may not all have the same gender, but we all have to deal with the 'problem' of gender and our common issues include why the world at large sees femme-ininity as something inherently lesser and disempowering. It's these common issues that I want to theorise to question simplistic understandings of identity and allow us to come together through these issues rather than in-fighting over who is who, who fits where or who is better.

I agree. It's about the alliances we make. The Transfabulous Festival in London with its open definition of 'trans' has been a powerful model. So do you think there is a (need for) femme-inist movement?

– Femme is a set of common identifying principles that for some people form an identity that they can inhabit and claim. I wouldn't argue for an exclusive femme-inism. Rather, femme should

Miss File @ The Hootchy Kootchy Club, Stockholm 2007

be considered, valued and examined in its own right and given its own position within feminism/queer studies and politics as a whole. Such a femme-inism should seek to value femme and femme-inity within a wider context of examining gender variety and with a complex understanding of what it means to be or choose to be gendered in certain ways. More prescriptive philosophies seem to draw the lines between identities very rigidly. I want femme-inism as an approach or philosophy to blur those lines whilst also valuing and creating a space for people who identify strongly as femme to show that our political commonalities are greater than our differences. There are common themes between those of us who choose to identify as femme, but it is our variety that gives us our ultimate strength.

So how would this impact our understanding of desire and sexuality in relation to femme?

– I like that femme doesn't have a prescriptive sexuality. Though femme is often clearly linked to lesbians, there are bisexual femmes and femmes that identify their sexuality as poly, omni, or other. It is also possible to be a straight femme. Admittedly, labels like straight, lesbian and gay can feel restrictive too, if they are used to limit one's choices. I like being a dyke in that sense, but I also accept that I cannot predict who I will find attractive. That said, it seems I have a femme-on-femme, or more specifically in my darling Sofia's case, a very particular femme-on-'neo-questioning-femme' tendency. As long as dyke/lesbian are permeable concepts in my mind then I will happily use them. Plus it is fun to piss off the prescriptive types who insist that trannies can't be dykes. Another thing I like about femme's non-prescriptive nature, along with its emphasis on re-appropriating and twisting traditional understandings of gender norms, is that it alters our understandings of sexuality. If we can claim femme-inity as a valued queer identity, then we can also revalue other forms of sexual politics, such as s/m, polyamory, polysexuality, along with bisexuality and even queer heterosexualities.

– In femme, I found a way of expressing myself that made me comfortable and happy. It gave me the confidence to be different, and to find community and commonality with a variety of people. It's also given me a sense of fun, precociousness and mischievous politics.

Given that, how do you feel your femme expression has been captured here?

– Representation is key to femme/queer people and it's so tricky and so crucial to get right. I loved what Del said about making pictures together, instead of taking them of, or from, people. I'm usually uncomfortable being photographed but this made me feel we were working together – making images that were personal, but also public and would depict something genuinely 'us' to a readership we'd never met. No mean feat! I love Del's live performance photos because they reflect something of what I feel when I perform. The photos of me performing Miss File at Hootchy Kootchy show the audience's reaction, which I don't get to see when the bright lights are on. I got to see my 'expression' having an immediate impact. That's really special.

Miss File @ The Hootchy Kootchy Club, Stockholm 2007
The Hootchy Kootchy Hussies, Stockholm 2007

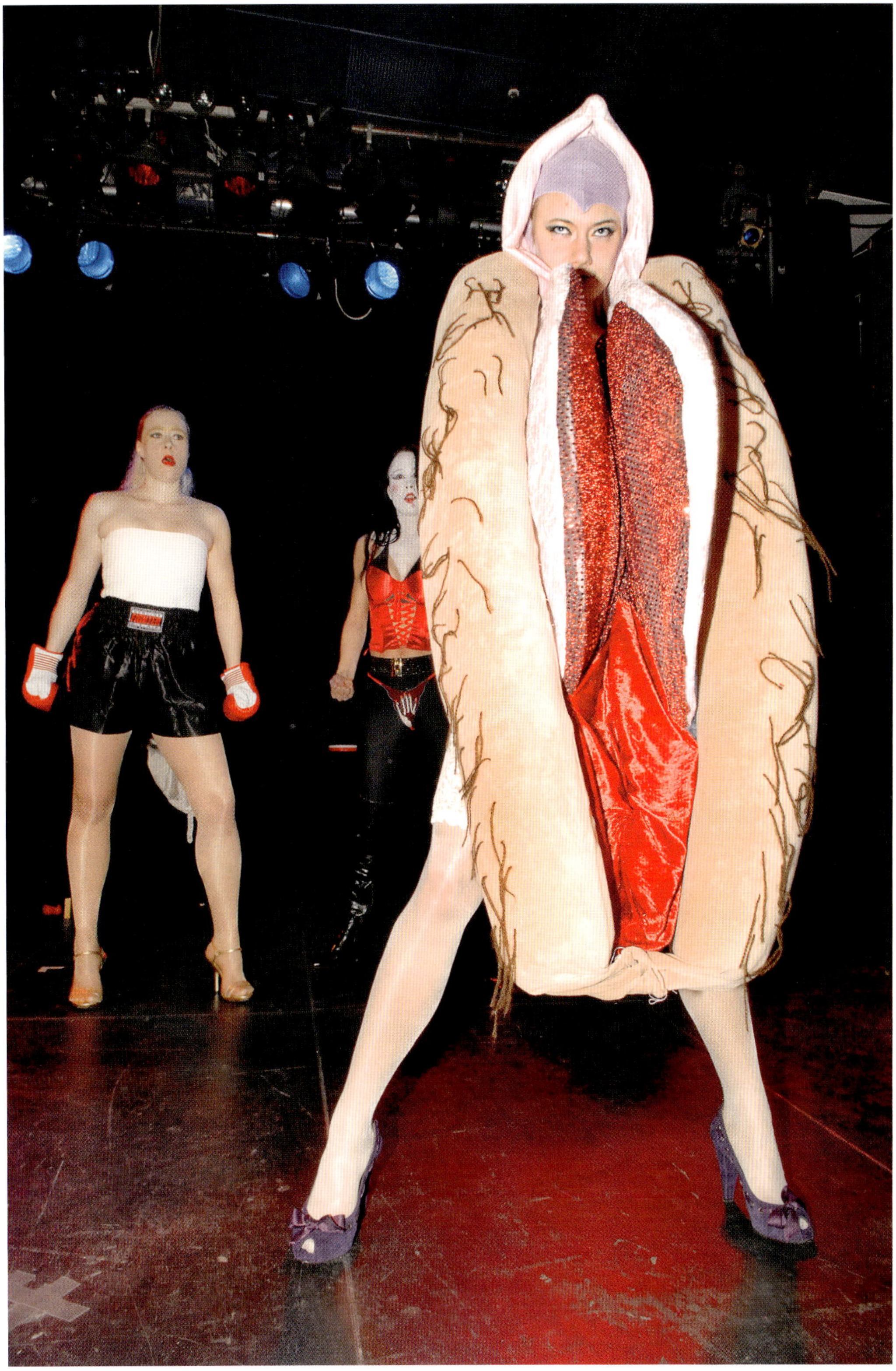

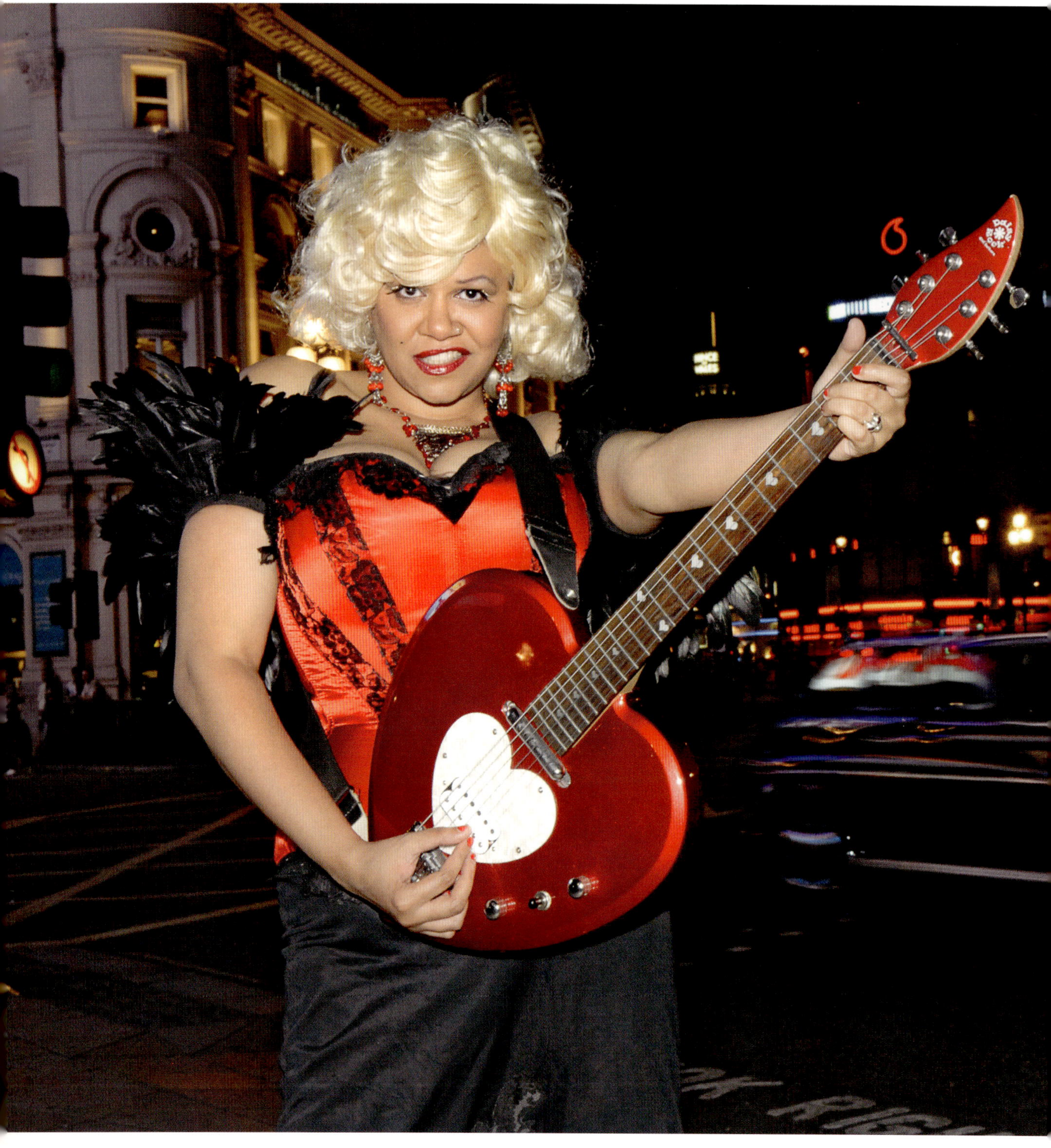

The Black Roots of Dyke Marilyn

Maria Rosa Mojo calls herself 'a queer wench with Spain, Barbados and Ireland in her veins'. As Dyke Marilyn she performed on London's queer scenes for many years and was a part of Club Wotever's Cabaret, with among others Josephine Wilson. A clever comedian, musician and writer, our cover girl has always explored darkness, as a rebel with a wish. With a BA with honours in Philosophy and Applied Psychology and an interest in identity and myth, she always finds cathartic elements to thread through her performances. With her 'big bosomy hugs', 'black hole theories', songs and heart-shaped guitar, Maria is a true femme star. I wanted to know more about Maria's cuntcentric theory of race, gender and desire.

When we first met during your performance at Stockholm Pride in 2004, it was instant femme sisterhood. What is femme to you?
– I came out in the mid-90s as a natural born femme, although I didn't use that label then. Femme continues to be about self-acceptance and empowering what I believe is an innate physical and mental sense of femininity. I view myself as both a woman and a femme, but it is my queerness that distinguishes the two. I identify

Dyke Marilyn, Piccadilly Circus, London 2006

as queer rather than lesbian because my lover is FTM. As a queer femme I've a heightened awareness of being a woman and the kind of fighting strength needed to stand up for femme recognition within often oppressive structures connected to internalised misogyny. Growing up with mixed parentage in Harlesden I'm only too aware of the prejudice labels can bring and, while being mixed race is a form of queer, I also see 'queer' as an anti-label which doesn't restrict my movement. My experience as a queer femme is psychological in that my thinking is feminine but with a queer bent, occasionally embracing masculine modes of thought. I can perform femme camp but also have a strong phenomonological experience as a woman in a curvaceous, bleeding body that expresses itself and reacts to its environment.

When Dyke Marilyn sings about how 'dildos are a girl's best friend' and challenges Daddy Freud by exposing her 'black roots' it's a powerful commentary on a feminine icon and phallocentric theories of identity. Can you tell me more about Dyke Marilyn?

– Through Dyke Marilyn I wanted to shatter the white idol of femininity. She is the bastard child of Marilyn Monroe and Jimi Hendrix who inherited Jimi's looks and Marilyn's guitar skills. She exposed her black roots by playing devil's advocate, showing that identities are disposable through the performance of them, that femininity and race don't have to be bound through stereotypes. Being a 'dark woman in blonde's clothing' never fails to be cathartic, nor to illuminate the ignorance that keeps you in your so-called place. The symbols within the name Dyke Marilyn seem to cancel each other out yet can co-exist at the same time. That's how I see queer, gender, and race: both fluid and contrary. Dyke Marilyn wasn't a natural drag queen, rather, the queen of dragging big, shiny, often phallic things, out of her closet. She loved to create an illusion and crash back to her roots through impersonation, singing, comedy and rock 'n' roll blues on the gee-tar!

Yeah, I'll never forget the confusion amidst the straights when you channeled Marilyn, Dolly and Jimi in one go at Stockholm's Hootchy Kootchy Club, nor how you were ready to personally throw out those who harassed Miss File! Now you're pursuing a different career, as Maria, a song writer and rock 'n' roll babe. How come?

– Dyke Marilyn was mostly a comedy act. Playing the blonde was a temporary illusion, but blondes have a way of taking over. When people start to box you in, it's important to get back to the roots of the matter, back to that raw creature clawing within us. When I was a kid, I had a recurring dream. I was offered a bit part in a movie. I was directed to wait in a dark forest, and on cue, pounce on my victim. I was the Big Bad Wolf, and my innocent prey? An angelic blonde girl, all sapphire eyes and naivety set in pure alabaster flesh. Flesh that my fake fangs hungered to devour. Flesh pronounced beautiful as the feminine ideal. Flesh that had got the part I'd auditioned for. I'd wake up growling... I would crawl to my bedroom mirror to face a brown girl with dark primal eyes. I'd want to embrace her, comfort her, but each time my nose would bump the solid surface as my breath, like a white fog, misted over the glass and obscured her image. Then my eyes would rise to the Marilyn Monroe poster on the wall... 'All Welcome...' her voice would beckon me in soft honey tones... 'C'mon Sugar...' and I would go to sleep willingly in a bittersweet fantasy that was never mine.

– Eventually... I got sick of dragging up and channelling the ghost of the white idol. What is at stake when you perpetuate the stereotypical myth of your physical binding, or strip naked on a white knuckled ride of an illusion? DM was important to my personal growth and confidence but not 'all' important. Now I feel truly in touch with the energy my music can create within myself and others. It isn't about being famous or being big in the industry, I'm no pop starlet obviously, it's about being that rebel with a wish, knowing that the universe is guiding you, battling on despite the demons.

If you were to imagine a femme-movement what would it look like?

– Lord! My brand of femme-inism would incorporate a recognition of strength and power that exists within the core of femme in the queer world. The ownership of the CUNT as a powerful symbol. Femme sexual expression for me is about owning my cunt. Our lesbian/gay/queer/bi/queer world is still prejudiced by the equation of feminity with weakness. Neither the cunt nor feminine expression are weak, both are vulnerable but strong in their tenacity. I delight in the magical and physical power of My Cunt and many others'. I delight in my beautiful brown flesh of black and white descent, and in my brazen femininity that remains in your face! There is a femme movement but the problem with groups is that they can also exclude. People who identify as femme shouldn't feel excluded due to stereotypical attributes considered to be un-femininine.

Dyke Marilyn, Soho, London 2006

Copies without originals:
On femme drag

DRESSED AS A school girl I was once kicked out of a public rest room by an infuriated lady who insisted that 'drag queens should still use the men's room'. I was puzzled. Usually it was my butch girlfriend who was policed at the doors of women's sacred spaces. At a dyke wedding that same summer, a child trying to get it right in a genderqueer world pointed at me in feathers and glitter and asked her mother: 'Is she real or is she a queen?' Where does femininity begin and where does it end?

Signe in København called herself 'a natural born drag queen' and spoke of learning to perform femininity with a twist from history's queens of femininity. Drag, like all clothing, is an everyday technique to engage, cite and disrupt gender traditions, always with the possibility of calling into question what is being conveyed through the technologies of dress-up. To some, femme-ininity is drag, others a transition, and to many of us, it is rooted in a simultaneous (both comical and painful) failure to approximate ideal womanhood and an explicit rejection of such an ideal.

Debra Kate, a US-born, Berlin-based *tunte* and a trans male femme, said: 'I want to take the ideas about how women are supposed to look, stretch them out like taffy and fold them back in on themselves. If a woman is supposed to wear make-up to look feminine, then shouldn't applying more make-up make her more feminine? If wearing lingerie makes you pretty for your man, then piling on extra layers of lingerie should be a sure fire way to achieve devastating beauty! At what point does the liberal application of femininity tip one over to the dark side of "Dude, that's not a chick. That's a guy!" That's the world I want to live in! My favourite look is a cross between a doll and a birthday cupcake, between a child's drawing of an animal and a clown.' Camping out in the periphery of respectable and normative femininity, drag is at once pleasure and possibility for dressing (up) sisterhood.

Drag, both as metaphor and materiality, has always appealed to Indra Windh, boxer, diva, criss-cross dressing gender theorist and pioneer of Sweden's drag king movement. 'I operate in and through the much-is-more principle which allows my fabulesse for masquerade, dress-up and theatricality get a lot of space and freedom to roam.' A changing wind refusing to stay in one costume, she added that, 'I've had the good fortune of finding play mates and likeminded people who take great pleasure and joy in the excesses and possibilities of the dress-up box. Together we have criss-crossed and mixed up gender

Debra Kate, Berlin 2007

51

52

expressions and codes in ways that were not even clear to us before we started, often with a twist and always with a wink. Humour, resistance, laughter and sex(iness) are the main ingredients. It's all about borrowing, stealing, trading and about the collective rituals of dressing up, doing make-up, making hair, trying on wigs, hats and shoes.' The girl's club costume Shanti and Indra wore for Wotever's sports night in London eventually traveled to Stockholm and became both a link in a queer kinship network and Parading Pussy Power for two fake blondes who were never fit to be cheerleaders.

'The more femme drag I indulged in the more defiant I felt touring around America,' said Leslie Mah, to whom femme is a transition from female. 'I was more than happy to shred the image of the dyke in lingerie. People were startled by the head-banging homo in glitter, eyeliner and boots because music fans are used to seeing straight boys perform this look. The truth is, tiny dresses are very comfy for jumping around and playing guitar, they offer full range of motion.'

Stav B, a Grecian-born, six-foot-tall, goddess performance artist who came to London because 'women like me don't have a way to express themselves where I come from', loves working with 'plates and boxes, spitting fire, satin ribbon and corset, dolls, microphones and thorny red roses, dramatic/theatrical make-up, humour and melancholy' and is constantly 'fucking gender up'. Posing as Frida Kahlo, she loved it when Del declared, 'there is simply no femme like you.' 'It's true,' Stav B replied. 'I am constantly masquerading, impersonating the other and enjoying every minute of it.'

Vagina Jenkins explained that 'because I'm so into costuming I find myself attracted to extremes in presentation, the thing that all those I desire have in common is their drag' and noting the pleasurable play of unpacking, she added that, 'it makes me want to deconstruct it all with tears, bites and buttons flying every which way.'

Indra, preferring the adjective *femmy* to the noun *femme* with regards to herself, praised femme drag as 'wonderful, expressive, incredibly hot, sexy, pleasurable, colourful and full of attitude when attributes that may appear traditional are used in a twisted pumped up way. Like in all other drag it is the cheeky, parodying excess that speaks to me.'

Asynja Gray has no interest in labels beyond being a dyke and pointed to the need to be practical in the frosty North. 'My femininity is in my pussy, not my clothes. I wear more feminine clothes in the summer when it is easier to wear less and be more naked. It keeps me cool when it's hot, it looks good and it's easy access for others!' Taking after her white Swedish artist mother and her African-American jazz musician father, Asynja works in theatre promotion and is a long-term organiser of Slick, Stockholm's most

Shanti & Indra, London 2004 | Pussy Power, Stockholm Pride 2004

popular queer club for label seekers and rejecters alike. A fan of looking smart, her drag is complex and in the case of images for this book, Scottish in origin. 'I've wanted a kilt for a long time but didn't know where to find an authentic one. One day I found a store that sold them and thought: it's time! The store clerk was very skeptical when he heard that I intended to wear it myself and said: "Yes, it's very masculine, for real men!" and turned his back on me! I went back twice and finally, when he wasn't there I got to buy it. I love weight of the fabric and what I can wear with it – heavy work boots, tall socks, shirt and tie and that it is very male but not, because I feel so hot in it. Actually, I feel more feminine when I wear the kilt, the same way that I do when I wear other male accessories, like a tie or a tweed jacket. I like that when people look at me they can't connect me with my style: I'm dressed like a sixty-year-old smartly styled man, but yet I am proud of being a hot middle aged black woman.'

Jun in Malmö, reflecting on her Japanese style roots and on 'bad taste' noted: 'Returning to Tokyo as a grown up, I found all the things I dream of in my head there. Platform shoes, clothes for small girls who are tough dolls. Style roots that I wasn't even conscious of, that are neither 'genetic' nor random. All is a mishmash of practicalities and physicalities – what can you get away with? I never felt that I could be a drag king – I'm too small and I didn't want to loose my high heels. And now I have my "natural" hair colour for the first time since age twelve and people tell me that it looks "so much better" than bleached blonde. They're missing the point! It was supposed to look fake.'

SO WHAT DOES it mean that a femme identified female born woman gets mistaken for a drag queen? That overdoing femininity makes you appear more masculine or wearing masculine clothing makes you appear more feminine? If a transwoman like Josephine finds a model for femininity in *A Femme's Guide to The Universe* and a femme learns femininity from drag queens who in turn are often seen as imitating 'real women'? Who is really imitating who? To many femmes of power, femininity does not originate in a femaleness, but is rather a kind of dissonance that goes far beyond conventions making us question where it came from and where it is going. While engaging with dominant ideologies of femininity, the femme figuration here employs what Jose Esteban Munoz [1999], scholar of queer (of colour) cultural production and radical drag, has called strategies of disidentification. That is, we are intentionally transforming the cultural logic of femininity by working both within and against it. And in the end, it seems to me, that as Judith Butler [1992] has taught us – herself citing drag queen performance – simply put, we are all unfaithful copies, copies without originals.

Stav B, London 2006 | Asynja, Stockholm 2008

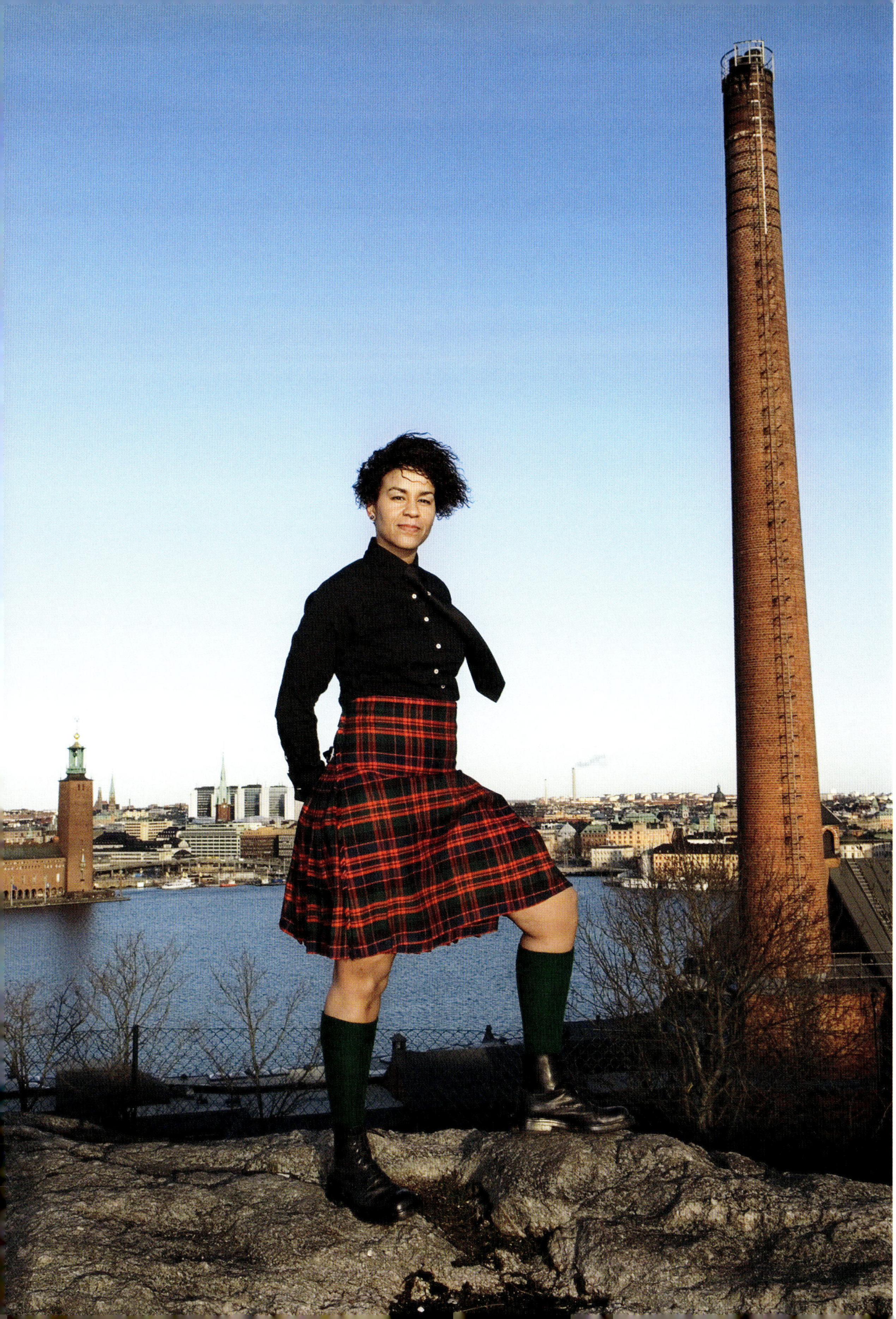

Portland's Diesel Femme

Dear Sossity,

At the Femme 2006 conference we kept checking each other out during key-note. Predictably, I loved your outfits – big boots and fish-nets, short leopard skirts, your 'Mama' tattoo and what you later called a 'No, I ain't your baby' attitude. Calling yourself a diesel femme, I, who barely passed my driving test, was impressed. Plus you sold your own reconstructed feminine gear made with a combo of costume and practicality. You spoke of being involved in Portland's very queer artist and activist scenes, saying, 'I'm a sacred temple whore, not a princess'.

Like for many others, coming out as femme in the early 90s was hard for you. Even as a member of Act Up! and Queer Nation, fishnets and long hair were not the ticket to acceptance in lesbian and feminist scenes. 'I'm a diesel dyke, in the working-class, take no shit, proud and loud tradition. My gender is femme. As much as I love butches, I got tired of my dyke strengths being minimised by them. Almost invariably, if I changed a tyre, used a power tool or picked someone up (sometimes literally), I was told I was "having a butch moment". It doesn't work like that. I'm a femme, and I do it, so it must be a femme, or even better, a non-gendered thing to do. Sometimes I still feel invisible out in the world, but more often I feel recognised and validated by other queers. It's not assumed that I'll be put off by mud, bugs, bikes or wrestling, or unable to hold my own.'

You described your femininity as the aesthetic result of dropping what doesn't suit you and adding dyke. 'What I do is rooted in who I am: a knife in my pocket and confidence in my stride; fighting invisibility for reasons political and personal; make-up that's like painting, and art that's like a protest march; giving out the Mama love, when I choose to, and letting my inner grrl play. It was a true honour and pleasure to do the photoshoot with my dear friend Jukie and the equally talented, fierce and beautiful Lady Monster and Celestina.'

Aside from making femme-inspired art and websites, you produce and MC the monthly x-rated open mic Dirty Queer at In Other Words, Portland's local feminist bookstore. You made us ache to visit what you described as 'a hugely diverse community that's very accepting of the wide range that "femme" can cover. In Portland it's widely known that when it comes to any gender, it's best not to assume at all.' I kneel to you and the Portland femmes still left to meet.

Jukie Sunshine, Lady Monster, Celestina Pearl & Sossity Chiricuzio, San Francisco 2006

57

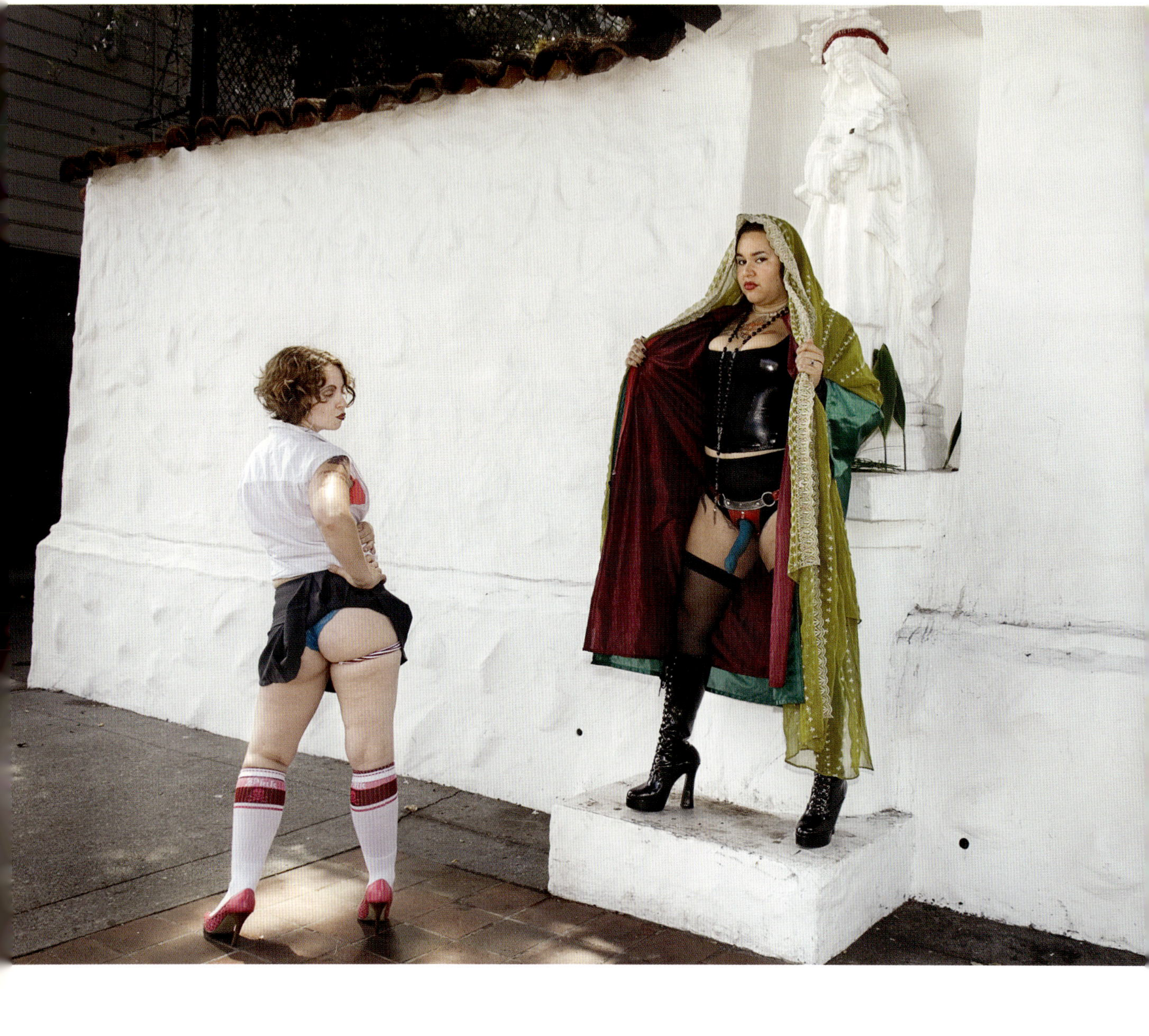

Las Damas

Dear Meliza & Celestina,

On the dark winter nights in Stockholm when I miss San Francisco and a certain kind of performance politics I can't find here, I often think of you, two of the most fierce Chicana femmes I know, and your articulate visions of queer girl politics, desire and political change. Making images and conversations with two experienced artists around Chula Street and Mission Dolores Church, our discussions went from pubic style to how the public always gets in the way of public sex, from trannie weddings in Vegas to racialised poverty in the US.

Meliza, the other day after I listened to your poem 'Do The Math', I found an old picture of you from the time when we first met, in Santa Cruz circa 1997. In it you've a shaved head and a big black Tribe 8 T-shirt and I remember you as one of the righteous babes hanging around the feminist bookstore Herland. When you speak about your transition from Female to Femme in Kami Chisholm's and Elizabeth Stark's film with the same name, it makes perfect sense. Your loud, assertive, slam poet voice was unforgettable from the moment you read the orgasm monologue in *The Vagina Monologues* at UCSC where you were

Meliza & Celestina, Mission Dolores, San Francisco 2006

the first in your family to go to college. Since then you've performed, written, organised and waited tables in the Bay Area and our paths have occasionally crossed.

'Femme is not always pretty or beautiful, to me it's dirty, ugly, funny and complex,' you said while getting changed for our photo session at the Women's Building in the Mission. You and Celestina had just performed at the Femme conference cabaret night, as well as your powerful poetry slam act as Las Damas with Julia Serrano. Now I watched you get ready, taking notes as you talked about yourself. 'As a mixed race Latina I'm like a secret agent. Not brown enough and not white enough,' you said. 'We wanted to play with and explode stereotypes of Latinas and to honour our pasts at the same time. Sleepy is inspired by the Cholas I went to high school with and desired while growing up in South Central LA.' Now your award-winning poetic theory of contemporary America and brazen 'kiss my ass' attitude is touring nationally with, among others, Michelle Tea's troupe Sister Spit.

Celestina, you too are a West coast girl. 'I'm a fierce, Chicana, femme, dyke, top, visual artist, bruja and a sex radical since I could hold my cock,' you said. As a performance artist always exploring erotic power for women and lesbians of colour, you've worked with the Liquid Fire project and been in two films celebrating *Voluptuous Vixens*. The day we made conversation and diner images with you and self-proclaimed size queens and big burlesque artists Jukie Sunshine, Lady Monster and Sossity, I learned about how you all celebrate your sexuality through your work and art. As Nuestra Señora de Las Putas you bring about pussy revolution and to me that includes a non-nostalgic dream of sisterhood. Your poem captures your priestess vision:

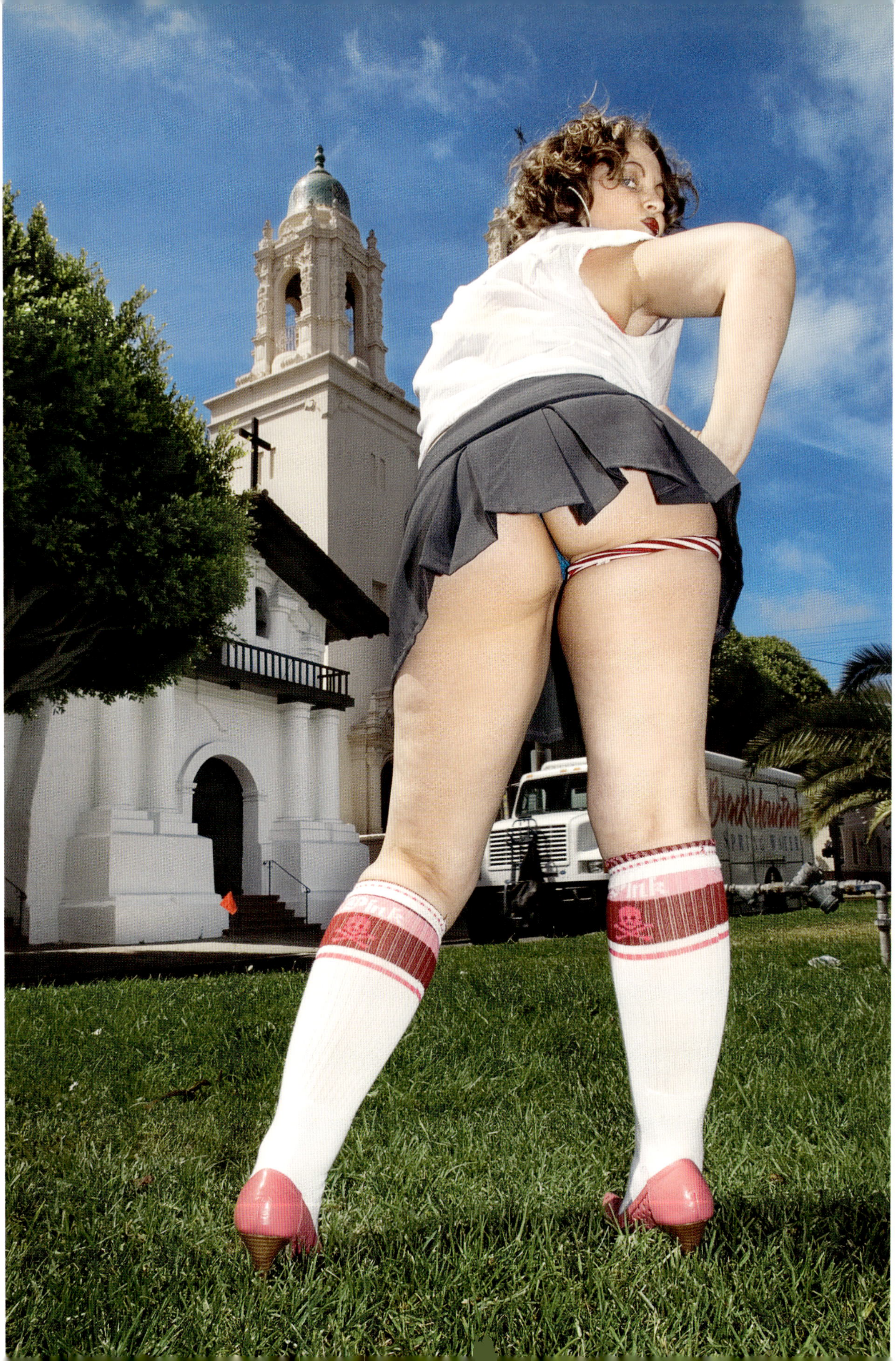

*I want to drip, drip ooze, come, give birth to the
Goddess and be penetrated by her divine cock.
I want to be split open like the holy cathedral doors.
Her heavy hands working her magic, decoding the
secrets inside my vessel. I want to writhe like a snake
through her blessed lava flow, shedding my skin.
Her molten eruption baptizing me naked, wet and
salty. I want to smear my blood like war paint all over
my body. Scream my name up to the heavens in a
sacred language untouchable except by the pure heart.*

*Kiss My Arse, Meliza Banales, San Francisco 2006 |
Soda Fountain Femmes, San Francisco, 2006*

*¡Yo soy La Reina de mi Corazon!
I want to listen to the powerful words of wisdom that
gush forth from my passionate pussy. ¡Sinvergüensa!
I want to see pussy revolution! Beautiful sisters,
hermanas chocolate, caramel, creamy, mixed, fat,
round, luscious, and proud, thin and elegant,
muscular and regal, every shape and color.
Learning from our selves, our desires, our sexuality,
and each other. No shame, No apologies.*

East Atlanta's Showgirl Divas

Dear Miss Jenkins,

Entering Paris, Decatur that chilly November night for the event organised by the Femme Mafia, it was impossible to miss you and miss Clover, two stunning best friends majestically seated at a slightly off-centre table, looking like you were cut out of a different time. Not members of the Femme Mafia, but certainly fiercely articulate about the racial and queer politics of Atlanta, about style and being femme in the South – the place you love and have never really left.

Veronica, you fancy yourself more a writer than a talker, but that night made clear that, as you said, you like being entertaining beyond being pretty and glamorous, you want to be memorable. 'I've my going-out-on-the-town drag which is usually thrifted vintage pieces or reproductions that remind me that I'm made like my mother and my grandmother. Thick and curvy in all the right ways. These are my favourites. I've always found myself on the outside, a cultural "other" and when I'm dressed to the nines in some sparkly, vintage get-up I feel like I'm reminding myself and others that the "other" is a glorious contrast to the mundane.'

Both in your personal life and as burlesque show girl Vagina Jenkins, your style is about drag and wearing a series of costumes that leave any viewer unsure of who you might be. 'I've my riding-to-work-on-my-motorcycle drag which says "she's tough." I've my slingin-coffee-for-seven-bucks-an-hour drag which is utilitarian and mysterious and hints at a private life I may/may not have. Dark red nail polish: is it an attempt at beauty or does it hide the coffee grinds in my nail beds? Short black work skirt: is it stylish and minimalist or just stain repellant?' Yes, these are the questions of queer femininity. As a performer you take your influences from 'strong, graceful African-American femmes of all genders', including Pam Grier and Harlem Shake Burlesque, Billy Holiday and Josephine Baker.

Like many others, you migrated to Atlanta. 'I read articles in *Essence*, *Jet* and *Ebony* about Atlanta being this new black Mecca, comparing Harlem Renaissance, the Black Arts Movement and present day Atlanta and I had to be part of it. There are a lot of queers in Atlanta even if they tend to run in different circles. I figured more black folks might equal more black queers to romance. Ironically, my current partner is actually the whitest person I've ever met – she's from *Vermont* for fuck's sake!'

That said, and even though you hate being teary about things, Heather is your heart, your other half, your partner in life. 'Because I'm so into costuming I find myself attracted to extremes in presentation. What they all have in common is their drag: Heather knows how to make a suit look comfortable and has the good sense to always have a matching tie clip and cufflinks; the thick-as-all-outdoors femme working the customer service desk at Sevenanda who's always displaying her amazing cleavage; the boy working at Kolo who has no visible body hair and looks like he might be a pierced extra from a Blade

Clover X & Vagina Jenkins, Atlanta 2007

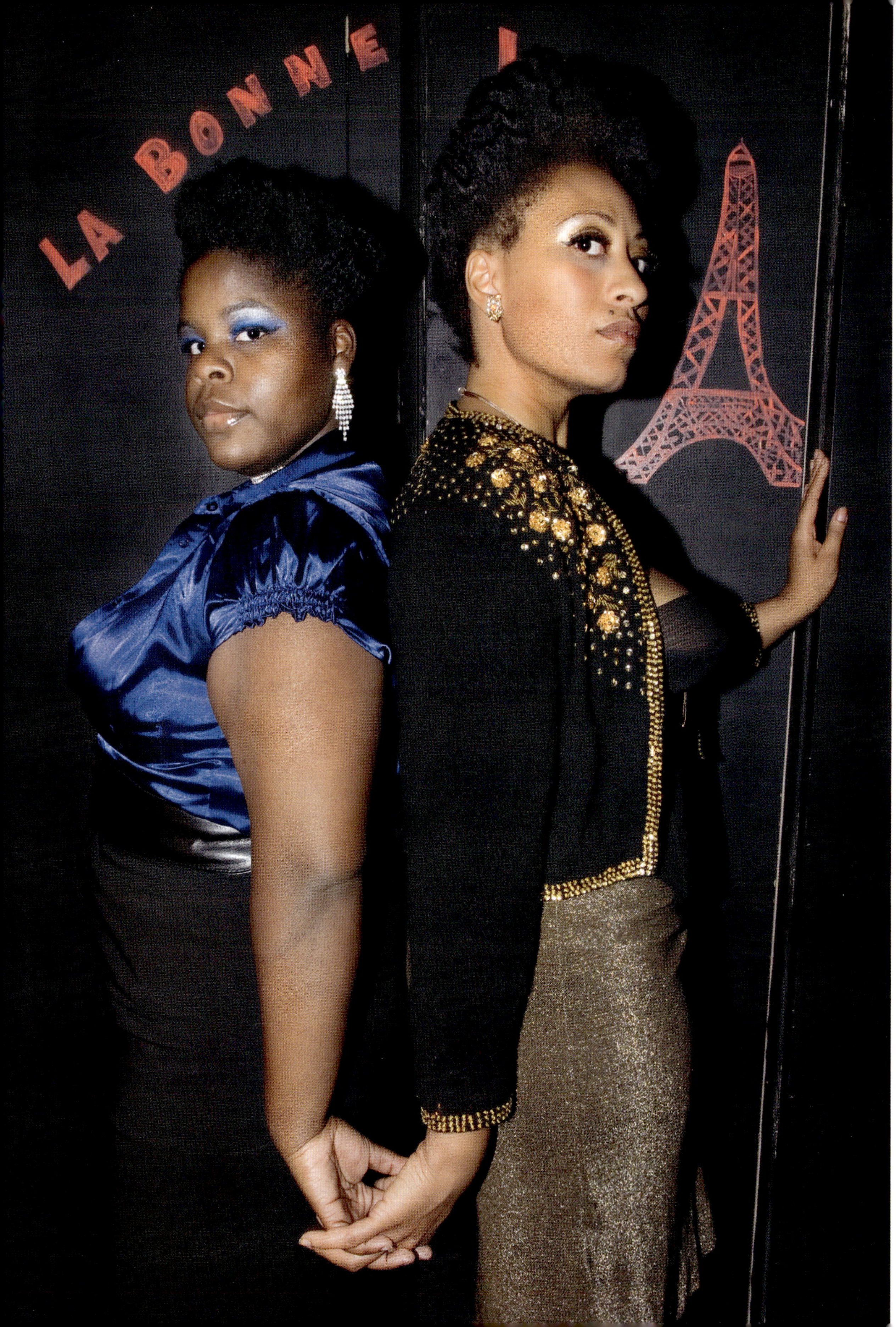
LA BONNE

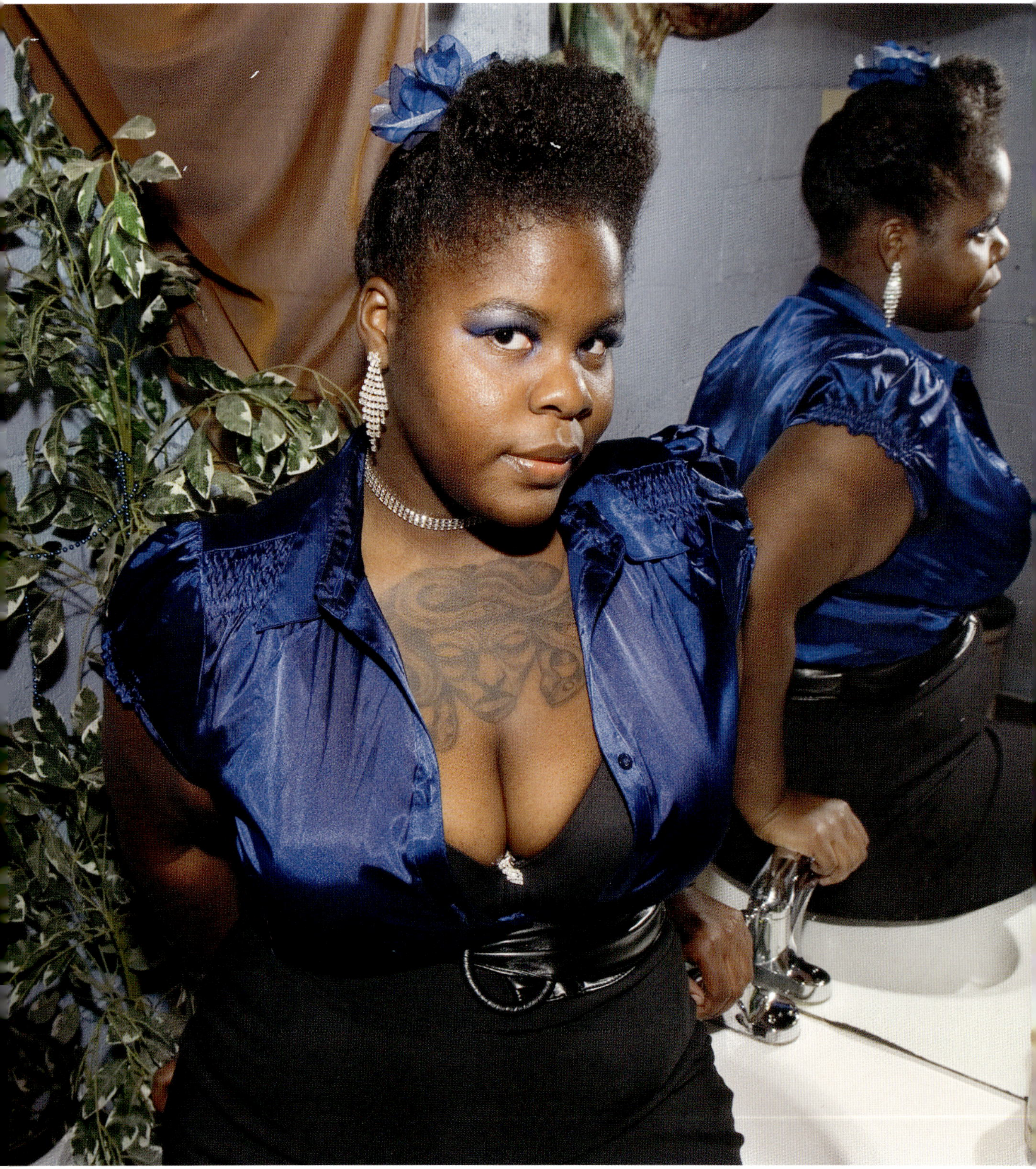

movie – they do it in different ways for me, because their presentations are so intentioned and put together just-so. It makes me want to deconstruct it all with tears, bites and buttons flying every which way!' Mm, deconstruction is indeed a carnal act.

So what about femme? 'That's a hard one, part of me thinks it's a dirty word and what's with all the boxes, yo?' you wrote back. Like others in this book, you then cited your own tradition and made up your own definition: 'I'm femme like my mother and my grandmother are – hardworking, handywomen who can repair a leaky faucet or change the spark plug in a car, who curse like sailors, who get dressed up for church, who can cook like gourmets when moved to do so and order pizza when they aren't. Femmes who like reading waaay to much to be attentive mothers to toddlers, who clip their toenails in the living room and will ask a girlfriend to pop the whiteheads on their backs, who know how to cornrow and plait and make a scene when it's necessary – yeah, that's the kinda femme I am.'

On your best friend, Clover, and on sisterhood, you said: 'I love her like the sibling I never had and always wanted. My childhood girlfriends understood my socio-economic background, my college girlfriend from the Black Student Union understood my racial politics and my queer girlfriends understood my sexuality stuff. I love those friends for the gifts they've given over the years. But Clover is the one person who gets it all without explaining any of it. We can exchange a glance that's a whole conversation. We complete each other's sentences. If I were in trouble, I know she'd have my back without question and that goes both ways. I respect and admire her politics, her warrior spirit, her great personal style, her open heart, the way everything she thinks shows on her face, her surliness, her intensity and the way she loves me no matter what. That girl is cool as hell and I'm glad we get to be sisterfriends.'

Dear Clover,

Your femme role model is the sexy, sexual Shug Avery of Alice Walker's *The Color Purple* because 'she is everything a woman isn't supposed to be'. Upfront about your opinions from the moment we met, you said you 'shamelessly admit all of my flaws and freak people out with my intensity because I'm so passionate about everything'. To you femme is not about clothes, and you could think of a million better things to do than to buy and discuss designer dresses. About Veronica, you in return wrote:

'Even though there is an age gap between Veronica and me, we've such similar lived experience, it's like I've known her all my life. Because we both grew up black, poor, fat and awkward, we know what it's like to be invisible aside from our sexual orientation. She encourages me to take up more space and exaggerate my beauty. We understand each other's past and present and love each other for it. Veronica is a femme inspiration because she knows exactly what she wants and never has and never will compromise that. It's amazing and something I struggle with all the time. She is my best friend and I trust her with every detail of my life.'

Clover X, Atlanta 2007

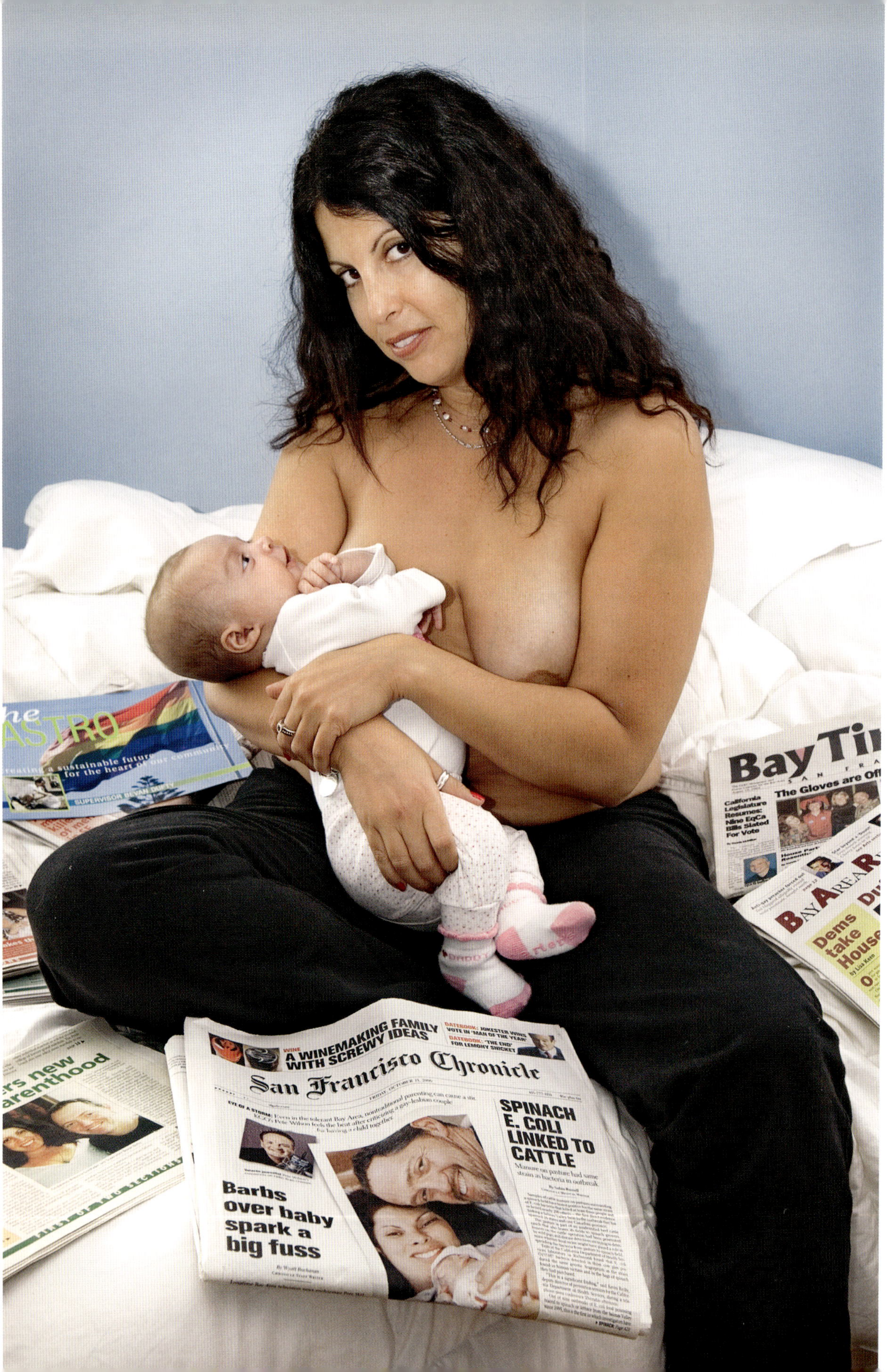

Fierce Maven Femme

Dear Goldie,

You were, along with burlesque performer and bearded lady Amelia, among the first femmes I befriended in San Francisco. While drag kings were the hype in 2001, your brazen presence on the scene was hard to miss. Years later we met again over cholesterol-free eggs one sunny morning in the Castro to talk about queer baby-making.

Playing with familial terms and reinventing family remains a central feature of queer community, be it the African-American tradition of families and houses, the dirty play of daddy-girl and mommy-boy or the endless variations of queer kinship adopted by the rejects from 'biological families', there are reasons for the gay slogan 'we are family'. Family metaphors are ways to make our relationships and identities known to each other. That said, motherhood is both an intensely feminine institution and a site of controversy. While some of us seem born lacking a biological clock many femmes, like Mafia Femme Aly, Jaheda in Manchester and yourself, yearn to be mothers within and against particular traditions.

'I'm a fiercely intelligent Jewish East Coast femme who loves to drag up with the queens and I've always known I wanted to have kids,' you said. For a queer femme who, as you put it 'has no queer markings and is usually only outed by the company of a partner', being pregnant was both exciting and terrifying. You chose to make queer family with your old friend Bevan, an out gay supervisor and as the newspaper headlines attest, it caused immense controversy. 'I came out when I was twenty-nine after having been reared and geared to be the perfect wife,' you said. Now, at forty you camp out with your Jewish femme friends around the idea of the Maven mother and of bountiful, generous family-making. 'I'd recently split up with my lover and was afraid, even though as an OB/GYN nurse I have helped numerous women deliver. What if I was alone when the water broke?' You invited twelve people to share Sidney's arrival and chose to have a natural birth – which to you meant 'no make-up and a simple French manicure'.

While some might argue that there is nothing more 'natural' for a female-born woman than becoming a mother and making a commitment to the child's biological father, Sidney's arrival became a public spectacle. A local radio host announced that children should be the result of romantic love, not friendship, and thus, even in the queer city by the bay, it didn't matter that the two of you planned on living in the same house and raising Sidney in your shared Jewish tradition. In matching leopard coats, amidst the gifts of five baby showers, no doubt Sidney's arrival is a joy of immaculate conception. You're no Madonna, rather, you're making urban queer family and giving Jewish motherhood a femme twist.

Goldie & Sydney, San Francisco 2006

Bird La Bird
– A Tweet with a Coverchick

Web designer, femme fashionista, blog tweeter about town, Bird La Bird is an overall crafty chick who likes to ruffle feathers and engage in courtship rituals and matings with geezers and Arthurs. With nests in and routes through Liverpool's outskirts and Derry, Northern Ireland, Kath Monan is London's lead singer of the Bird movement for the femininely plumed and plucked and their companion species. We first tweeted after the Bird Club had opened its wings at Transfabulous Festival of Transgender Arts. Since then this mistress of bird propaganda has produced warbly tracks like 'Supertaster' (a courtship ritual to Arthurs) and 'Do you know what kind of club this is?' (on how gay club bouncers cannot spot a queer bird). A believer in cross-breeding, acutely aware that birds like to flock and shit on borders, Bird has generously shared her watering holes with this northern Swedish mockingbird on more than one occasion.

Bird of all birds, what's with this term anyway? What's wrong with femme?

– The most important reason to call myself a Bird is to be cheeky and really just to have a laugh. *Bird* is loaded with queer connotations and I like the specificity of it. In post-war UK it's been a term for an-assigned-female-at-birth woman and used to describe someone of a feminine appearance, as in *Dolly Bird*. It also has sexist connotations, which makes many UK women not appreciate being called *Birds*. But to me it is also a white, working-class, British phrase and a term of endearment. I am a bird! I don't identify as a femme primarily because it is so tied to *butch* and the couple hegemony. *Bird* is more ambivalent and perhaps it can break down this binary? And why do we need American terms when we have our own? Since terms like butch and fem(me) have come into currency, the sexual and social landscape has changed, surely our names and warbles can change with it? For me Bird is British and it's camp, harking back to the *Carry On* films era. Sometimes the debates around identity politics get too earnest. We shouldn't take ourselves so seriously! I'm experimenting with how to use *Bird* on feminist terms. I may not be right, but I think if a term has a lot of power, that power can be re-appropriated.

I really love the idea of 'plumage' as a metaphor for queer femininity and the kind of excessive dress-up and ruffling of feathers that many of us marvel in. But given the heterosexist history of the term *Bird*, in your mind, are there limits to the use of this term?

– 'The fifth rule of Bird Club is Anyone can be a Bird!' Birds are not born. We are incubated in beauty salons and hatched in hairdressers! It's also a homage to one of my heroines, Angela Carter and to Fevvers in *Nights at the Circus*. 'Is she a woman or is she a monster?' 'Is she fact or is she fiction?' When I came up with the idea for Bird Club I didn't do any research into the term beyond my own experience of being one and the dozens of expressions like 'the early bird catches the worm' and 'eating like a bird' I came across. I had done bits of Women's Studies at college and I'm a lifelong feminist. I like using a non-human term, inspired by Donna

Kath Moonan, London 2006

FINGER-LICKING GOOD
STONE BUTCH BLUES
SEX CHANGES
SKIN SHOWS
Practice of Love
Female Fetishism
TALKING BACK
lynn breedlove
William Pope.L

Haraway, it's about affinities between feathered and non-feathered birds and creating loose alliances between those who wear lipstick and feathers and those who don't.

I love it! So what is the Bird Club?

– Bird Club brings you live Bird on Bird action and a bird's eye view of major social issues such as how long it takes us to get ready to go out. Bird Club believes in diversity, our numbers are great. We have many species with unique habits, plumage and breasts. We like to flock in large numbers making patterns in the sky. We call that art. I like to muck about with language! Also, Bird Club is about savvy, sexy entertainment. The purpose was to have a laugh. A tweet. Show off our plumage. Have courtship rituals with cocks and each other. It was started in 2006 by myself and Maria Mojo (Dyke Marilyn). We performed several shows together and I organised a couple of Bird Club nights. Like a flock, Bird Club will morph and change. In the future it may take the form of a loose collective of performers and artists dedicated to sexiness without the sexism.

– In 2007 Bird Club moved from comedy burlesque to organising a march. This happened due to the level of marginalisation and invisibility of femmes at the London Lesbian and Gay Film festival. Anna Dunwoodie's *Femme* strand in the festival was the first non-online UK debate and forum for discussing queer femininities and femme. Erica Roberts also wrote several articles for *Diva* that inspired the March. Bird Club used images that were a direct homage to the Lesbian Avengers and Pam Grier in *Cookie*, because she was their poster girl, along with a mythological African bird. I like my graphics to have many layers of meaning and enjoyment. Bird Club fits very neatly into queer and feminist contexts but we don't let ourselves get tied down to one tree. We have many places we perch and can fly away whenever we wish.

Your slogan was 'Femme invisibility – so last year!' To me this cheekily captures the attitude of femmes in queer contexts in recent years. How did you come up with this slogan?

– It's about using the language of fashion (because it's feminised and aimed at a feminine audience) as agit prop. I'm also interested in playing around with graphics and slogans, using media techniques, like from *The Socialist Worker*. In the UK this paper is seen as important but a bit boring and holier than thou. I used the same graphic style but changed it to *Specialist Warbler*. It was bloody hilarious to find comments on Flickr afterwards about the involvement of *Socialist Worker* in Femme Pride! Who says plumage isn't political? Collaborating with the amazingly talented illustrator Cyan I created posters with slogans like 'Birds shit on the shoulder of ageism'. I wanted the march to be celebratory, not a moaning about how marginalised we are. A big sound machine, great decor and high camp costumes. We marched with the trans section of Pride because above all it is really important to us to be in solidarity with transwomen. And of course our cock admirers... I'm a Martha for my Arthur.

I hear ya, sister, so what do you reckon, are Birds endangered? Is there a Bird movement – aside from some of us privileged with wings to migrate across large watering holes?

– Bird movement – you mean like a poo? Ha ha. I came out as a bird when I was twenty-five in Liverpool and then it was pretty isolating, so I flew to Manchester – that's not very far! But things have changed. I'm definitely seeing femmes becoming more vocal here on the gender queer scene in London. Club Wotever and Transfabulous have given people places to go, to come together and dress up, be out in many more gendered ways. A lot of femme articles, performances and so on, are being produced. New Burlesque has opened up doors for queer feminine performers. I do want to point out that this scene is subject to economic/cultural class structures and it's often very white. Personally, I don't go to the straight burlesque nights in London anymore, as they're about as interesting (and expensive) as a stock-broker's luncheon.

Right. I have to say, I love the pin-up with books. It's one of my favourite images of femme-inist theory, which to me is a stacked way of straddling the presumed contradictions of sexy lingerie and 'science'. What are your thoughts about this?

– I would be dead without feminism. I read all the time and I'm really into theory. I've also always been into dressing up, I was sad – everything around me was sad – when I tried to look like a dyke. I'm very into 50s burlesque style, tight lace corsets, very high heels, hold-ups, red lipstick. I'm a tough bird, I stand on my own two feet and aim to take care of myself. I want to push femininity and point to its artifice, as constructed and plumed, beyond the strict gender codes I grew up with. Also, there is a lot of ageism tied to femininity. What is always celebrated in the capitalist centre is young, able-bodied, white femininity and when it 'deviates', it becomes Suicide Girls, which for me doesn't represent a very interesting vision of what other femininities might be. Ageing marks the feminine body differently. As lipstick wearers we should challenge the negative imagery that dominates western media. All reality TV 'experts' will be severely pecked!

– Me, Del and Shanti Freed, who helped with costume and make-up, came up with the pin-up theory shot together. It's me on a good day! It's about the things that make me feel at home: too high heels and big fat books. Being photographed is a show-off's dream! I like that the books are teetering, as if everything could fall and nothing is stable. I'm also very pleased with my titties. Something to show to someone else's grandchildren, isn't it?

Bird La Bird & Sam, Club Wotever, London 2005 | Bird La Bird, London 2008

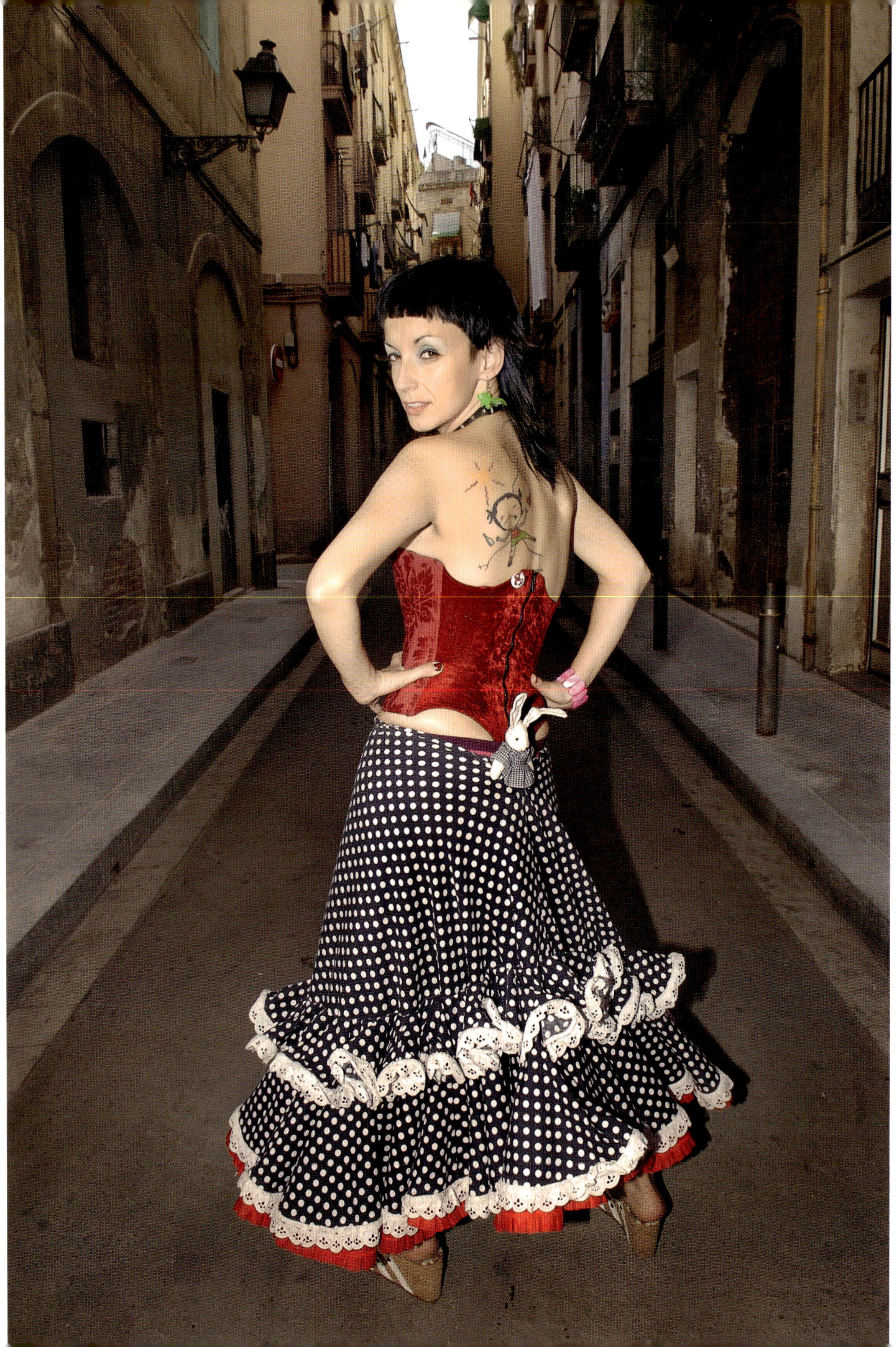

ITZIAR ZIGA | Playing with Our Latin Female

MORE THAN ONE Barcelona party night I've ended up exchanging clothes with my punk-butch friend Flori. With her trucker mannerisms she drags my black dresses over the grungy floor as I spin in her camouflage pants. I love these improvised trans-vest-sessions where both of us lighten the weight of our own identities. We parody that which we never wanted to become and have fun with the games that were stolen from our childhood, when she was called marimacho (tomboy) and I would raise my working-class princess chin high in the face of neighbourhood taunts.

My mother married in 1969 wearing a white leather hooded mini-dress, a goddess from the working-class suburbs, just like me. She, born in Pamplona (birthplace of the Opus Dei) in 1939 – the year Franco won the war – would pick me up at school erect on her 9-inch heels. *Itziar* is the name of a Basque Virgin, which comes from the ancient goddess Ishtar. I was raised in an industrial city on the Cantabric, between toxic clouds and fluorescent green fields. I have a degree in journalism, am a writer by passion and a waitress by necessity. I now live in Barcelona, the city where I am possible. I'm thirty-three years old and faithful only to my precariousness.

I started to research and write about extreme radical femmes (my bitchy girlfriends and myself) ten years ago. Neither I nor my sisters of corset and struggle have references for who we are in this Franquist Latin Catholic culture. We've constructed ourselves together, reinventing Saint Agueda and Madonna, Tura Satana and Maria Jimenez, Frederica Monseny and Alaska. Exuberant femininity distinguishes them from the heterosexual Latin female who apparently delights in the roles of woman/wife/mother. This fantasy place seemed unliveable then, but is now my lovely Barcelona bubble. Allow me to clarify: I'm speaking about an imaginary femme community, a place where we have common spaces and affects but we are not willing to be rallied around for our hyper-femininity.

I have to say, I've always been surprised by the mothers of my European friends, and from where I speak, Europe starts north of the Pyrenees. At first they all looked like dykes to me. The Spanish woman is, or was, often something else. Commonly found at weddings, their own and others', surrounded by lace suspiciously similar to the curtains that seal the windows of their houses, the Latin female is, indeed, *very* female. Perhaps because of this, butch–femme play in the Spanish lesbian community is as strange as paella on Mars. Don't forget that forty years of Franco dictatorship and isolation deprived us of external references and provided some interesting limitations. For whatever reasons, dykes in Spain are really dykes.

I remember the first women-only parties I attended in the mid-90s in Bilbao. Three styles dominated: the Basque camionera

Itziar Ziga, Barcelona 2007

(bulldagger) with highwaisted pants, shirt and vest; the hippies with their long hair reddened by henna and the punky-borrokas. My college girlfriends and I stuck out like sore thumbs in our pretty frocks. Around then I was investigating a look that would reflect both my politics and my desire. I recall lots of indecision and change.

I still have a photo of myself sporting very short shapeless hair, unplucked eyebrows, stretch leggings and slogan T-shirts. Even *I* thought I looked horrendous. I also tried to live without a bra, but with a size 90 it's hard to look androgynous. It was around that time I started fucking girls.

More than ten years have passed. I live in a city with one of the largest populations of queer fauna in the world and I don't feel impossible anymore. *Still*, Carmela, Majo, Helen, Bego, Laura and myself are asked at girl parties: 'You're straight, aren't you?' We don't complain, this confusion is interesting. For three years I worked for a feminist newspaper where I took a fancy to appearing for interviews dressed like a whore. I marvelled in the surprised faces and sometimes even in the rejecting ones. These days I no longer shrink before the looks of strangers. I celebrate having held on to what I've always dreamt of becoming: something like the character Agrado in *All About My Mother*.

Myself and most femmes I've interviewed were frustrated princesses as children, our spectacular femininities reprimanded by our families and peers. Some because they were labelled boys, others for thousands of other reasons. My case wasn't that terrible. My hair was cut so that my mother's life would be easier and none of the girls wore party dresses at my elementary school. But I felt like the mirror reflected an image that wasn't me. I ardently desired long wavy hair and the exotic life of an adventurer, far from the unglamorous desert of my neighbourhood apartment blocks. I ask forgiveness from the saintly feminists for this: I'm still totally turned on by sequins, feathers and ruffles and the vertiginous bodies of actresses and television hostesses that I admired in my asexual childhood.

IT'S TRUE, I'm a poor western Catholic suffering from bipolarity like all the rest. No matter how hard I try I've never been able to escape the duality of masculine/feminine. Since I can't escape, I'd rather laugh than punish myself. There is nothing more sacrilegious, or more fun, than reciting a prayer backwards, at least for this humble sinner who delights in being a bitch who personifies male desire but refuses to satisfy it. I will never be a possession, this product decides for itself with whom it will go, for how long and under what conditions. To top it off, some of us who've chosen femininity prefer getting it on with another woman, a tranny or a fairy... that really fucks men up! To me, it's this fraud that radicalises the potential of femme on the heteronormative map. My stomach tingles with pleasure just thinking about it.

Those who enjoy their femme fatale seductive powers without critical reflection and are capable of nailing a stiletto in my eye if I get too close to their hunting grounds, don't interest me in the least. Believe me, there are loads of them around here. Perhaps we steal clothes in the same stores, but we don't go to the same places or inhabit the same (psychic) spaces. It amuses me to think that at first glance I could be mistaken for one of them. As drag-queen Gina/Jordi Burdel proudly affirms: 'I'm a caricature of what men have tried to induce into women and women have refused.'

The femmes I interview share some common denominators: their relationship to queer theories and feminist activisms and their tendency to use

Itziar, Barcelona 2007

75

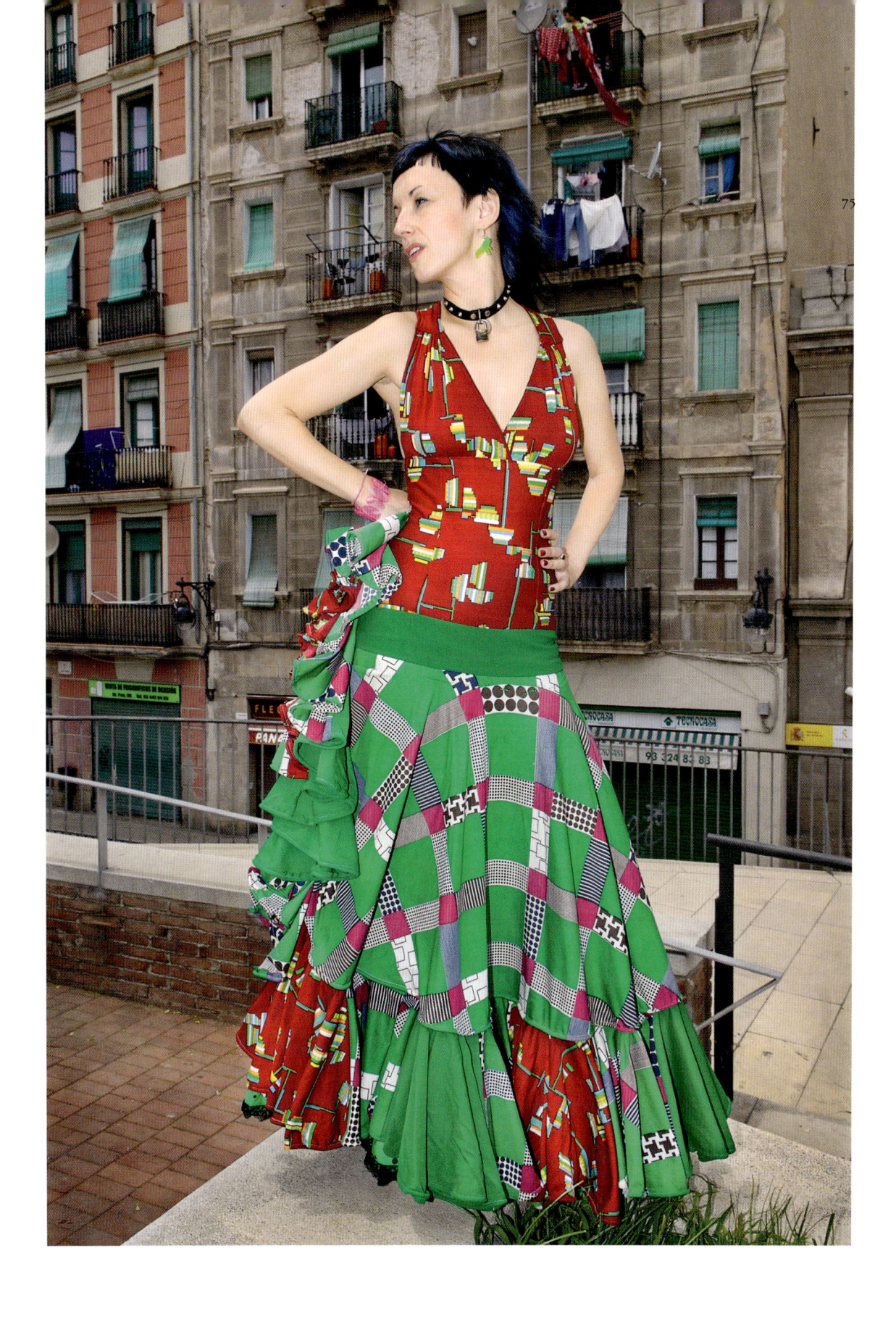

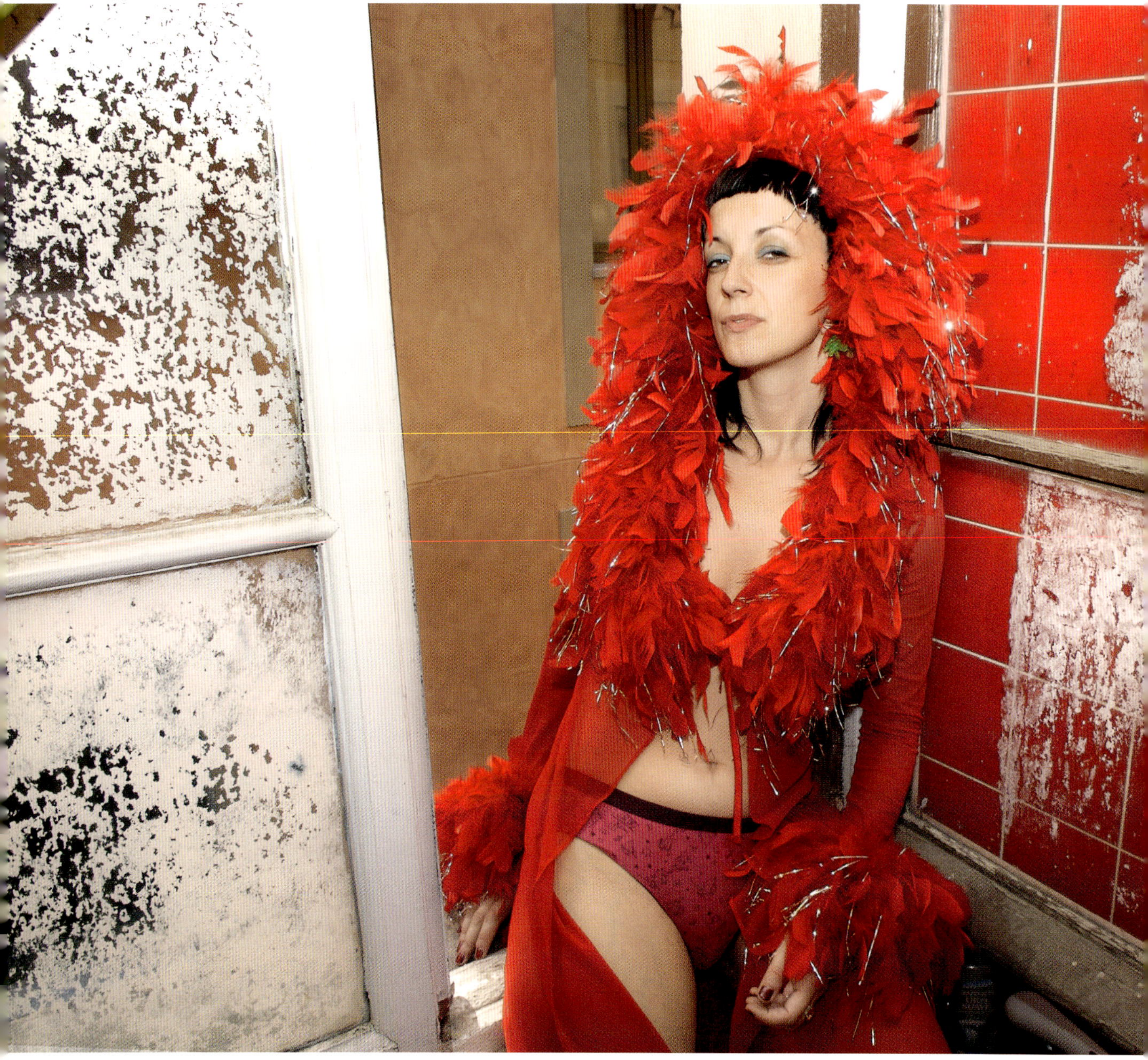

eye shadow. It's curious how in our initiation into feminism almost all of us abandoned the signs of our princess identities. Hey, we all did our time as truckers' apprentices hoping to avoid getting the evil patriarchy's shameful mark inscribed on our bodies. 'We've taken a round trip with femininity and our choices shouldn't be undermined,' as Paula, an Argentinian friend, said.

Why is a woman's reputation inversely proportionate to how low her neckline is? I've never understood how one can defend women's rights while judging those who slip on clingy miniskirts, climb onto the frightfully highest heels and walk around swinging hips or with their faces *pintadas como una puerta* (heavily made up). When my years of college militancy in Bilbao – feminist, libertarian, antimilitarist and so on – gave way to times of precarious and nomadic living and indecision, anything that even smelled like a banner made me break out in a rash. I was exhausted by so much dialectic and seriousness. It took a while to get the appetite back for making politics.

For the last five years, warrior princess Monica and myself have called ourselves *ex_dones*. We are *ex_women*. The missing link between feminism and histrionics, a group both ghostly and lazy. We spend enough energy on our never-ending searches; for a job, a flat, emotional stability, sex and drugs. Our project has centred on what we've christened *Pantojismo*: the attempt to get aesthetic and political profit out of drama queen fits. We've borrowed the name from Isabel Pantoja, a notorious Copla singer (who's incidentally currently involved in torrid real estate corruption allegations and is rumoured to roll about with other females). We are inspired by the heroines of the Coplas our grandmothers and mothers sang while cleaning the house, women who were eternally cheated, scorned, exasperated by Love and Fate.

Pantojismo is a fun and absurd tool to exorcise that suffering Latin female stuck like an alien in our entrails. Her larvae were inoculated by an emotional education that prizes self-loathing.

The flamenco imagery of the April Fair comes quite handy. If you've never slipped on a great ruffled dress you won't know what inspires one to parody a woman's rage. Martirio, a post-Copla singer, once said that the *peineta* was the continuation of the spinal column. A total cyborg-flamenca! We use the expression 'my *peineta*'s rising' when we feel the alien drama queen taking us over, when we're invaded by an unstoppable Pantojismo attack, those fifteen dumb minutes in which one is capable of perpetrating the lowest of emotional blackmailing. We invite participants to create their Pantojlike character through costuming. For us, Pantojismo is a game where we can investigate the unfathomed dangers of extreme femininity which we all carry inside us.

In our workshops we parody the most pathetic moments of our love lives. We add dynamics to television's goriest scripts to laugh at our pathetic sides. We dig into our soap opera miseries with irony. Just because we are college graduates and postmodern feminists don't assume we keep our composure when things don't turn out as desired. We're the heiresses of that old feminist wish to transgress the borders between the political and the intimate.

Now, as I look at myself in the mirror wearing my impossible heels, my bosom sweetly strangled in a corset and a dildo dangling between my legs, I smile. Come on, does anyone really think I look like a slave of patriarchy?

Itziar @ Home, Barcelona 2007

Epistemology of the femme closet

TOWARDS THE END of 2007 Del and I did some work in New York and stayed with Kate Bornstein and Barbara Carrellas in East Harlem. Kate had invited me to go shopping for punky gear in London's Camden Market after the Transfabulous Festival earlier that year but I left with bigger sartorial bounty after visiting her fabulous closet. Furry jackets, a dress worn for a book photo, some crazy striped bell-bottoms, hats and gloves. I was thrilled. It's true, many femmes like shopping, but more for bargains than labels and closet stories are often cast in low price triumph. While the love of feminine trappings can be a sore spot and occasional cause for disagreement among femmes – does the outfit make the femme (queer)? – it's less about consumption than about relationships, offerings and legacies. Femmes both marvel in and are ridiculed for what Indra called 'the borrowing, stealing and trading. The collective rituals of dressing up, doing make-up, making hair.'

Femmes dwell and nest in closets, dressing rooms, femme spaces and beauty parlours, not (only) because of the pleasure of the transformation that might take place there, but because of the sheer personal joy. Sofie Wahlström, flicka (girly) femme in Stockholm, declared her own room a femme space. 'To enter it is for me always cheery and affirming. Being in my room, my own femme space, confirms my idea of what femme is, what queer femininity is, and what excessive femininity is and it gives me a femmy solace from the rest of the world.' Often the public and the personal merge, like for Andy Candy who works in a Stockholm vintage store, in Jun's Malmö Miss Juniversum empire of 'kitsch and bad taste', or in Sossity's travelling box of remade diesel femme wear for big girls.

Making femme house calls invariably takes me straight back into the closet, a fairy tale place filled with stories of extraordinary experiences nestled

Jun Wizelius, Malmö, Sweden 2007

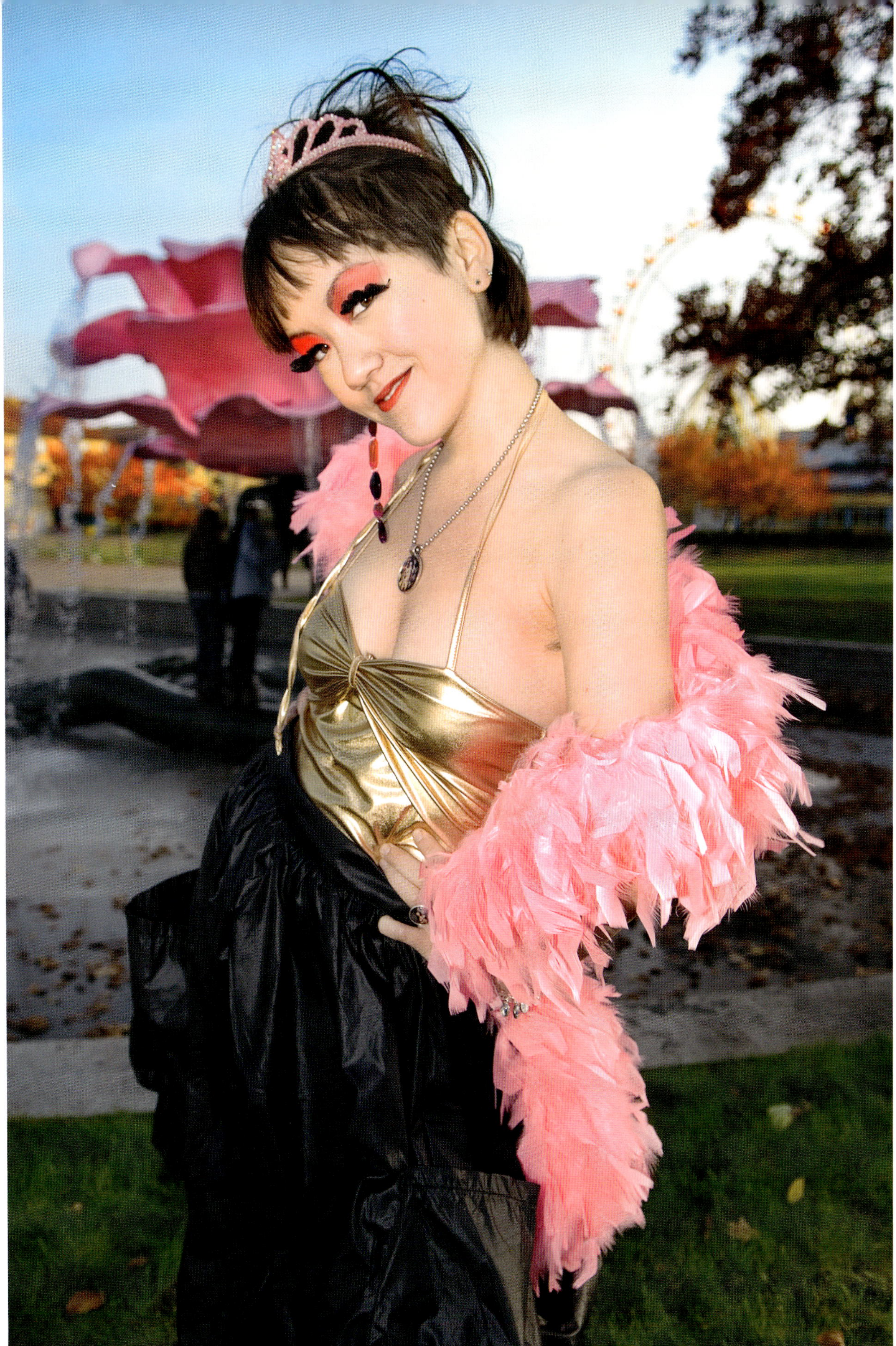

80

softly within the folds of outfits worn to events, performances and meetings. Andi's Atlanta trolley house closet full to the brink with shoes, bags and tales of every Femme Mafia costume event. Indra's feathery attire sprinkled across every flat she's had, dresses decorating closet doors and corners, a material record of life as drag. Diamond Dagger Amelia Hess's Oakland home dressing room, complete with mirrored vanity table, vintage hat boxes, costumes and a poster homage to her lineage of bearded ladies.

The sheer visual pleasure of a over-loaded closet is itself a topic. Bird La Bird mused that 'mine's full of tight lace corsets, 50s stockings and frilly knickers, very high heels, pencil skirts, big knickers, hold ups, opera gloves, nurse and waitress uniforms, East German women's army uniforms, boas, fake Vivienne Westwood, punk 70s – not Kelly Osborne but Siouxie Sioux.' Maria, a København writer, sex worker and queer feminist agrees. 'Yes, corsets, always corsets, and shoes. I love dressing up for me, I put nail polish and lipstick on when I'm just at home writing. I'm older now and I don't care that in the world I'm probably not visibly queer.'

Wearing lipstick 'to make yourself feel better' as Del puts it, is a thorny issue. Over tea in a London hotel lobby in a rush hour between rehearsals, actress Deni Francis said that she 'wore very little make-up as a college radical feminist' but since then she has held onto her love for a femme-inine wardrobe, even if it tends to make her 'always assumed to be straight'. It could be the hair, Deni notes. 'I'm British-born and mixed race, my mother is Irish and my father is Asian/Anglo-Indian. I can't imagine being without my long hair, it's part of my identity.' Married to long-term partner, Crin, she sometimes chooses not to wear her Indian gold wedding ring, as a subtle marker of queerness in the straight acting world. On fashion Deni says: 'I dress in the way that I do because I like it. I don't try to look queer, I am queer. This is what it looks like. I've always liked dressing up and fashion. From being a glam-punk in my twenties with lots of black, ripped leggings and odd stockings (one sheer, one spotted) to more grown-up glamour now with lots of vintage dresses and shoes. I love high heels... and wedges are really practical in a busy city. They have to be well-balanced though. I never wear shoes that I can't walk in – or run and fight in if I had to!'

Varieties of femme are indeed about shoes and frocks. 'I've never been a high femme but now I love the occasional foray into it,' Caroline declared. 'It was a major thing to get my toes out in sandals after years in boots. I was a ferelle femme for years, a bit crusty, I didn't shave and I've had dreads since I was twenty-two. I am still very attached to my combat boots and to leather. On

Sofie & Felicia, Stockholm 2006 | *Maria Dixen, København 2007*

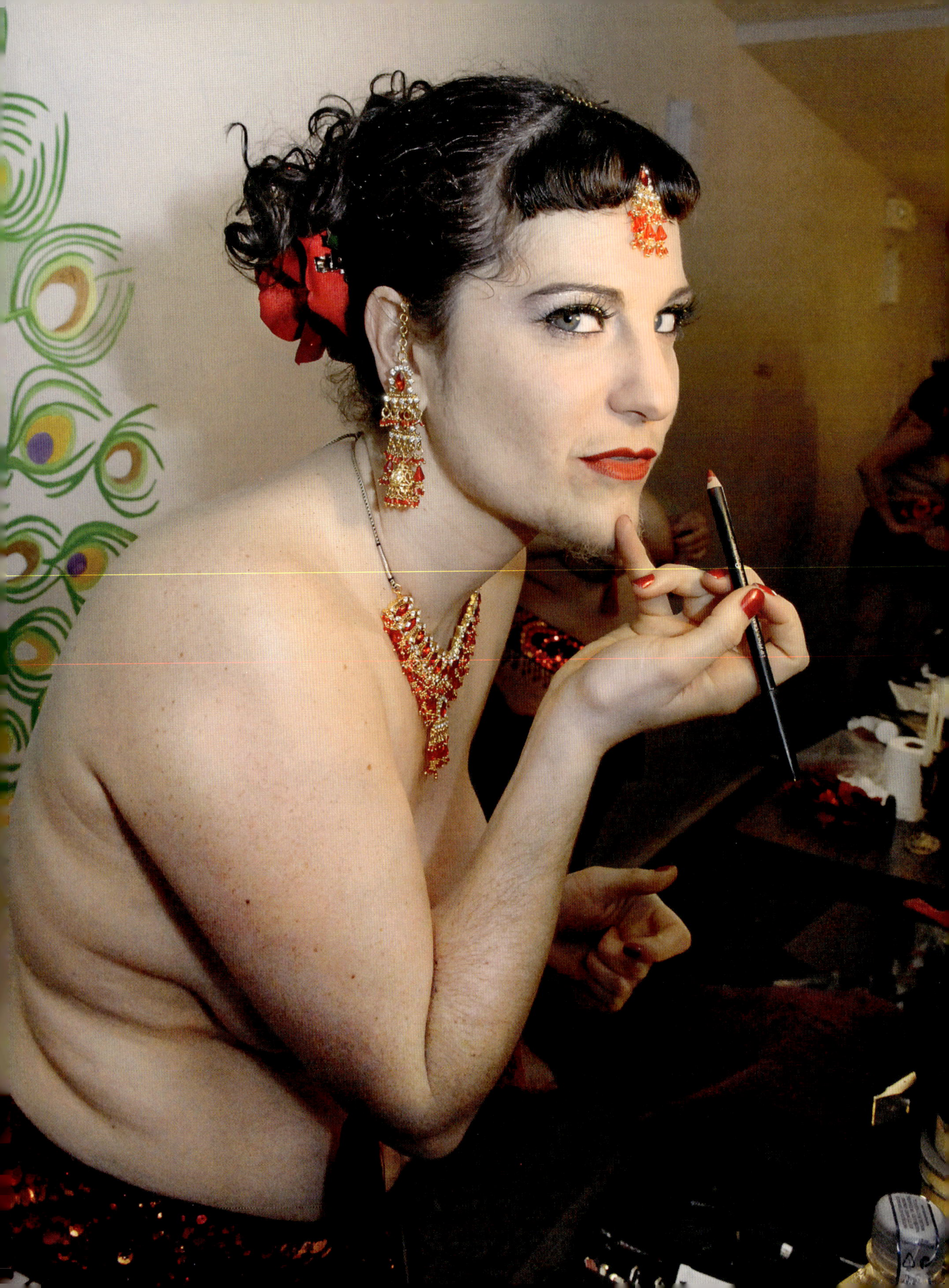

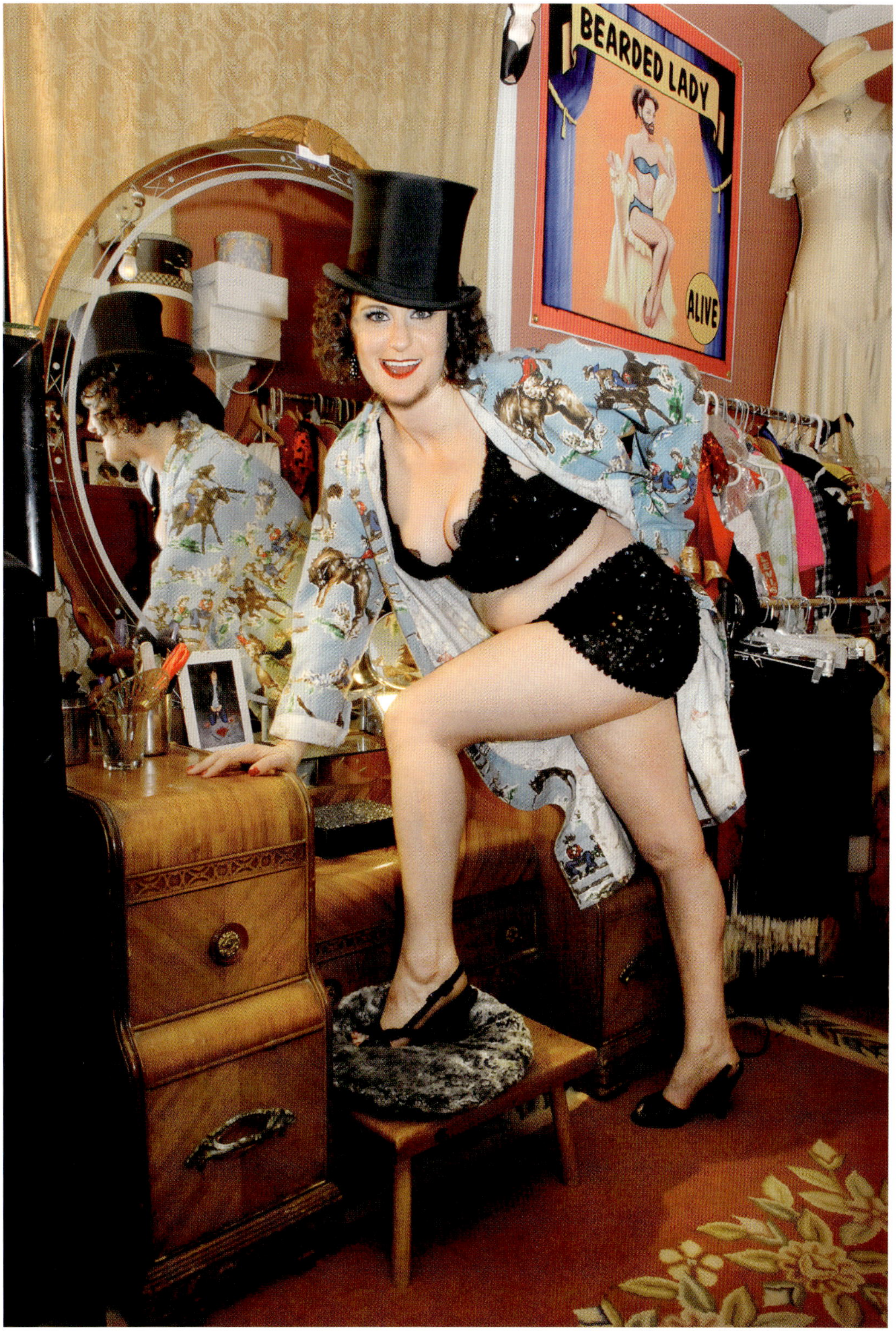
BEARDED LADY
ALIVE

the bike or behind the decks I'm definitely a butch femme, tough and streetwise. I dress practically for the bike and being high femme isn't. Then I dress for my butch lover and that's a different matter.' Recalling how she was a tomboy through her teens and twenties, Caroline added, 'I didn't get nail polish and make-up. It felt fake and like it would make me weaker. The older I get the more I dip in and out of femme dress and the more I get off on it. As a forty-year-old I don't feel vulnerable anymore, it's like it sits better in my skin now and I love the subversion of reclaiming lip-stick and heels, seamed stockings and the newly found rituals of waxing and shaving.'

TO SOUTH BEACH BORN, Cuban-mixed heritage Atlanta Mafia Femme Debby, femme-ininity is intimately tied with her personal history of sexual abuse. 'For a long time I thought if I wasn't pretty and "made" myself ugly he would leave me alone. I ended up being 200 lbs and unhappy. Eventually I reclaimed my femininity, because it was doing my hair, getting dressed up, buying new clothes, taking care of myself that made me happy and want to be me. I still have body issues, but accepting who I am, queer and femme, has helped me heal some of the wounds, to be stronger and to like myself.'

Over fish tacos in Atlanta Solange spoke of how in her college feminist days in Chicago, she stopped shaving, plucking and wearing make-up because, as she put it 'I needed to deconstruct my femininity to find what I truly enjoyed and wanted for me. I also felt pressure to conform to the "dyke look" in the only queer community I knew then, on a liberal, mostly white campus. But I wanted to feel the sense of rebellion that I saw in that aesthetic too.' While it was lovely and liberating Solange said, 'I missed my plumage and didn't feel quite myself. I was thrilled to find others who shared my aesthetic and dilemmas with making these choices'. 'In the end I did not feel un-femme, I just felt unplucked and without plumage.'

Malmö-based Jun also felt pressure of a required look. 'When I hit the dyke scene at nineteen I dressed down. While my fag friends always love a glamorous dyke, looking like a glittery queen doesn't work if you wanna get laid. Either dykes are too afraid to talk to you or they just think you're weird. Over time I got more comfortable and could carve out space for my own style. My pink sequence tutu dress, bought for my ninth grade graduation is still one of my favourites, along with gold and leopard print. Anything that's kitschy!'

Is there a femme fashion? It might be better seen as a series of dress acts that acquire (queer) meaning in particular spaces. And as Reina Lewis, queen of lesbian fashion (theory), reminded me the first time we met, 'the competencies needed to perform and recognise (queer) dress acts are complex and historically specific, both to personal histories and to the wider historical moment.'

At this moment, many femmes note that especially in white, middle-class dominated feminist contexts, a different and distinctly un-feminine uniform has been required but that ultimately, femme is forged in resistance to multiple norms at once. Lisa Walker [2001], femme theorist of race and desire, reminds us that celebrating visible markers of difference remains a key tactic of identity-based political movements and those not readily 'seen' according to such logic of visibility remain under scrutiny in racialised and highly gendered ways. In that light, it's worth noting that the femme figuration emerging from closets and changing rooms in this book does not share a dress code and that the bodies adorned femme-ininely here, do so for ever-shifting personal, sexual and public enjoyment. Above all, while some femmes' 'straight-seeming' closet of shoes and frocks may make them suspicious in queer contexts that privilege gender deviance and incomprehensibly queer in the straight world that follows the same logic, in femme-centred invisibility is hardly the main issue. And there are many closets left to come out of and to dwell in.

Solange Garjan, Atlanta 2007
previous spread: Amelia Mae Paradise, San Francisco 2006
Amelia Mae Paradise, Oakland 2006

The Face of Swedish Transfeminism

Candy Darling,

I have so many great dress-up memories with you! Your leopard Tina Turner homage, the cherry outfit, the swan dress you wore for your birthday, the first time you came to LASH, Stockholm's S/M dyke club and wore hold-ups... Your closet and your work place, a vintage boutique, have a way of merging and you always give me style tips.

As eating disorderly femmes, we've bonded over years of dieting and you've written about how as a transgirl you had few role models. Finding points of identification in the fierceness, body politics and gender deviance of Tina and Oprah, you noted that, 'in a society where norms of whiteness, middle-classness and gender conformity are interwoven, trans and brown bodies that take up public space become threatening. To be accepted, we're told to shrink and conform to ideals of femininity that were never ours.' Weight-watchers is one of the heteronormative institutions you've taken on.

Born in Sweden to a Greek father and Austrian mother, you grew up with German as your first language. 'Many think I must be upper class because I speak like them,' you explained once when we watched old queer activist documentaries. 'It's because the woman who taught me Swedish was from Östermalm (a posh Stockholm neighbourhood). Language can betray you.' As a regular contributor to *Kom Ut*, Sweden's queer paper, your critical writings about gender norms in Sweden's system for sex reassignment and your refusal to be pathologised has made you the face of transfeminism in Sweden. In front of Huddinge hospital's gender investigation clinic you noted that 'collaborating with Del means that one leaves the role of the model and becomes a subject through his camera. The images are not documentary because Del steps into one's life, but because they are the result of conversations with Del in an intimate setting where one gets to be part of and control the process itself. For me it has always been nice to collaborate with Del. Herm shares my vision and is very understanding.'

A goddess of low fat cooking and birthday cakes, you are a crafty chick who loves making versions of the femme accessory you always wear, the bonnet. 'I like to make them out of bow ties, especially the really big velvety kind from the 70s. I love taking an emblem of masculinity and turning it into a femme attribute.'

I love how you never back down from pointing out sissy and transphobia in the LGBT movement. 'It's ironic that I am not welcome in feminist separatist spaces, because I am probably the biggest man-hater in the feminist movement. I despise gay men who hate women and femininity. Why would any woman want to be a fag hag? To be ridiculed and made fun of by gay men is horrendous, I know,' you said.

Feminism became home away from bullying. 'I am a feminist, and above all, a girly one. Since puberty I've struggled with my body, like all girls and certainly many femmes. I'm a feminist because I'm sick of the disrespect I get for being

Andy Candy, Stockholm 2007

Infektionsgatan

a girl. The *Darling* generation (Sweden's equivalent of *Bust*) really sought to politicise this.' Trained in Gender Studies at Stockholm University and a seasoned feminist activist, you explained that 'transfeminism is for me a form of feminism that primarily objects to the 1970s heteronormative essentialist radical feminist view of human nature, making it possible to change both identity category and biological sex without that affecting one's feminist analysis'.

You lecture regularly on transpolitics around Sweden and have been part of femme organising, but find it hard to talk about solidarity. 'It's hard to say what part of me is femme and what is trans, because femme is a kind of femininity that is dissonant, clearly distinguishable from the straight kind. There is a strong connection between femmes and transfolks, because femmes have reflected on body image, identity and above all, gender expression, which of course us transpeople spend a lot of time doing as well. Also, femme organising is often trans-inclusive. At times solidarity is more a theoretical issue than a practice and that makes it rather useless. But there are a lot of femmes who are trans-identified, both MTF and FTM.'

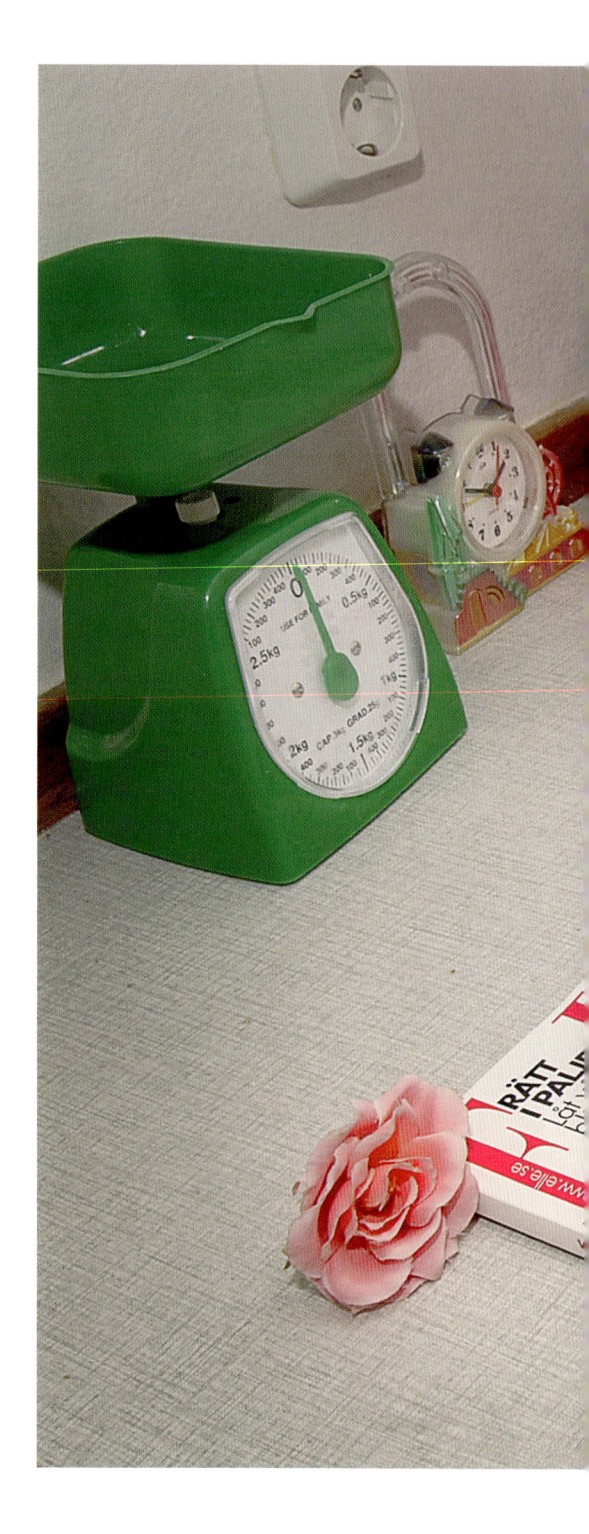

Andy Candy @ Home, Stockholm 2007

89

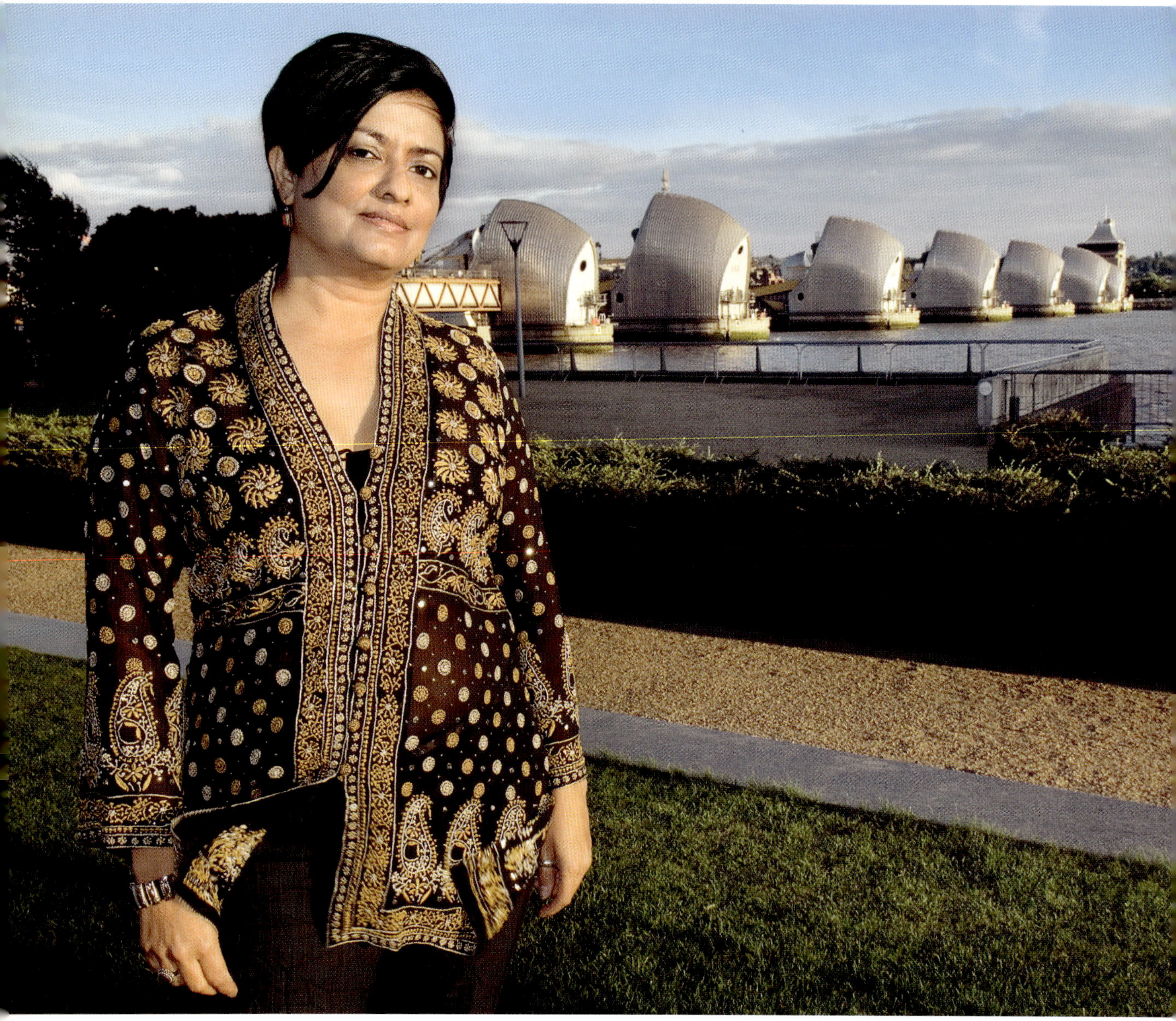

PRATIBHA PARMAR | Pocket-sized Venus

AS A QUEER trans-national, desi femme-inist, whose experience of dislocation and belonging has been shaped by a history of diaspora, *fierceness* has become, of necessity, a part of my DNA.

Fierceness: a way of being, a survivor's modus operandi for a femme Indian girl exoticised by white heteronormative culture. I'll confess: the lure of *Fierce* before femme seduced me to write this.

The day I was called 'a pocket-sized Venus' was a crucial turning point in my politicisation as a feminist. I was at university in a Northern Yorkshire town in England, first time away from home revelling in my freedom and learning to drive. A rather creepy and rotund white driving instructor called me 'his pocket-sized Venus' while putting his hand suggestively over mine on the gearshift. I was angry and speechless. I went to my first ever women's consciousness-raising group and complained about the violation I had just experienced. I wanted sympathy and righteous anger from my newfound sisters – instead, I was reprimanded for being too feminine: 'Why don't you stop wearing lipstick and those tight, tight purple velvet trousers?' Another woman said it was difficult to be around me as I was 'oozing with femininity', as if it was some kind of a pus to be cured lest the patriarchy find it desirable.

No pretty red colour tainted my lips for fifteen years after that. Well, not until my desi queer sisters encouraged me to put on lipstick and blusher as we sat around looking for fleeting lesbian moments in Bollywood films. And we found them in films like *Razia Sultan*, a historical epic where legendary actress, Hema Malini, who plays the first female ruler of Delhi in thirteenth-century India, is sung to, stroked, caressed and then kissed by her lady in waiting (Parveen Babi). It didn't matter that Hema was fantasising about her absent male lover while being kissed and that the kiss was masked at the last moment by a white feather. *Parveen Babi* was kissing a girl and that's what made us all wet with excitement, yes, we exist and we exist in Bollywood films – if only in homoerotic moments such as these.

This desperate hunger for visibility in our own cultural frame bonded us in that first thrust of desi queer grrrls coming together to plot, plan and party. Oh how we fantasised that it was us our lovely Hema was bending down to kiss, as we replayed that clip, eating samosas dipped in hot chilli chutney, trying out different coloured duppatas over our leather jackets or silk shalwars over our scuffed Doc Martin boots.

Yes we were mixing it up – leather with the silky smooth, colourful Delhi bought scarves, flowing pants over hard-core, skinhead, lace-up boots.

So what did these sartorial experiments make us? How did it define us? We didn't really care as we finally found ourselves coming in from the cold, from the marginalisation in the white lesbian communities to discovering and recreating our new families, our new identities with each other.

Pratibha @ The Thames Barrier, London 2007

There was a sense of relief and freedom – the butch girls who had always fantasised about playing femme and the femme girls who never really wanted to play at butch could now go back to being princesses. And the dykes who never desired that duality/straightjacket of femme or butch felt free to experiment.

We were now giving each other and ourselves permission to create our own queer identities in whatever way we wanted to express them. To borrow the sentiments of the poet extraordinaire June Jordan, for us, 'We are the Ones We Have Been Waiting for'. And while June Jordan was saying this in a whole other context, it felt like we had finally found ourselves in finding each other as desi queer gals. Identity politics had these wonderful epiphanous moments before its inevitable disintegration and demise.

Sometimes when I sense envy rising at the current proliferation of desi dyke groups and wish I'd had this ready-made support when I was 'coming out', I remember that first flush of discovering other desi dykes and our instant mutual love and then the envy vanishes and I thrill at our 'history' making.

CHANEL NO 5 RED glided on to my lips oh so smoothly as if it were a long lost friend who had finally returned to me. It's a vivid memory and it was my desi queer sisters who boosted my confidence to reclaim and re-envision my femme identity, to rejoice in colourful clothes, take pleasure in make-up and play Bollywood dress-up in that hyperfemme way that only Bollywood heroines know how!

Don't get me wrong – I am not blaming white feminism for decimating my femininity because I learnt a great deal from their critiques of patriarchal femininity. Some of these women opened up a revolutionary way of looking at the world. No question about it – my femininity at the time was unreconstructed, it was bought wholesale without any critical understanding of patriarchy's wily ways of keeping women powerless and at their mercy. I went on Reclaim the Night and Right to Choose marches and both my anger and my consciousness grew. I learnt fast to decipher the myriad ways in which white patriarchal femininity was constructed, imposed, continuing to devalue, dehumanise, de-throne our sense of self-determination.

But a dilemma was birthed – the push and pull of pleasure in my own femininity and the simultaneous need to resist proscribed rules designed to destroy my agency. But there was no choice – I had to start that journey of disowning my femininity and later, much later, circle back and reconstruct it in my own colours and shape.

However, at that particular pivotal moment of personal transformation, entwined so inextricably with the feminist movement, I had to visibly mark my emerging feminist identity – eyebrows were no longer tweezed, legs were no longer shaved and of course not a touch of make-up. On came the dungarees and off went the cleavage and the figure-hugging trousers. I tried desperately to look less feminine and ended up looking a bit soft butch, a bit androgynous and a bit bland and amorphous.

As I also learnt too about the long history of European, white male construction and consumption of 'exotic' Asian femininity, it became urgent that I discard any marker that would be mistaken as exotic. The most symbolic act of banishing my Asian feminine marker was to cut my hair. For an Indian girl to cut her long silky tresses was tantamount to a complete loss of femininity and her chances of wedlock. No man would marry a girl with short hair... so it was not all bad news!

There were mixed feelings of liberation but also sadness in this ultimate act of sym-

Pratibha Parmar, London 2008

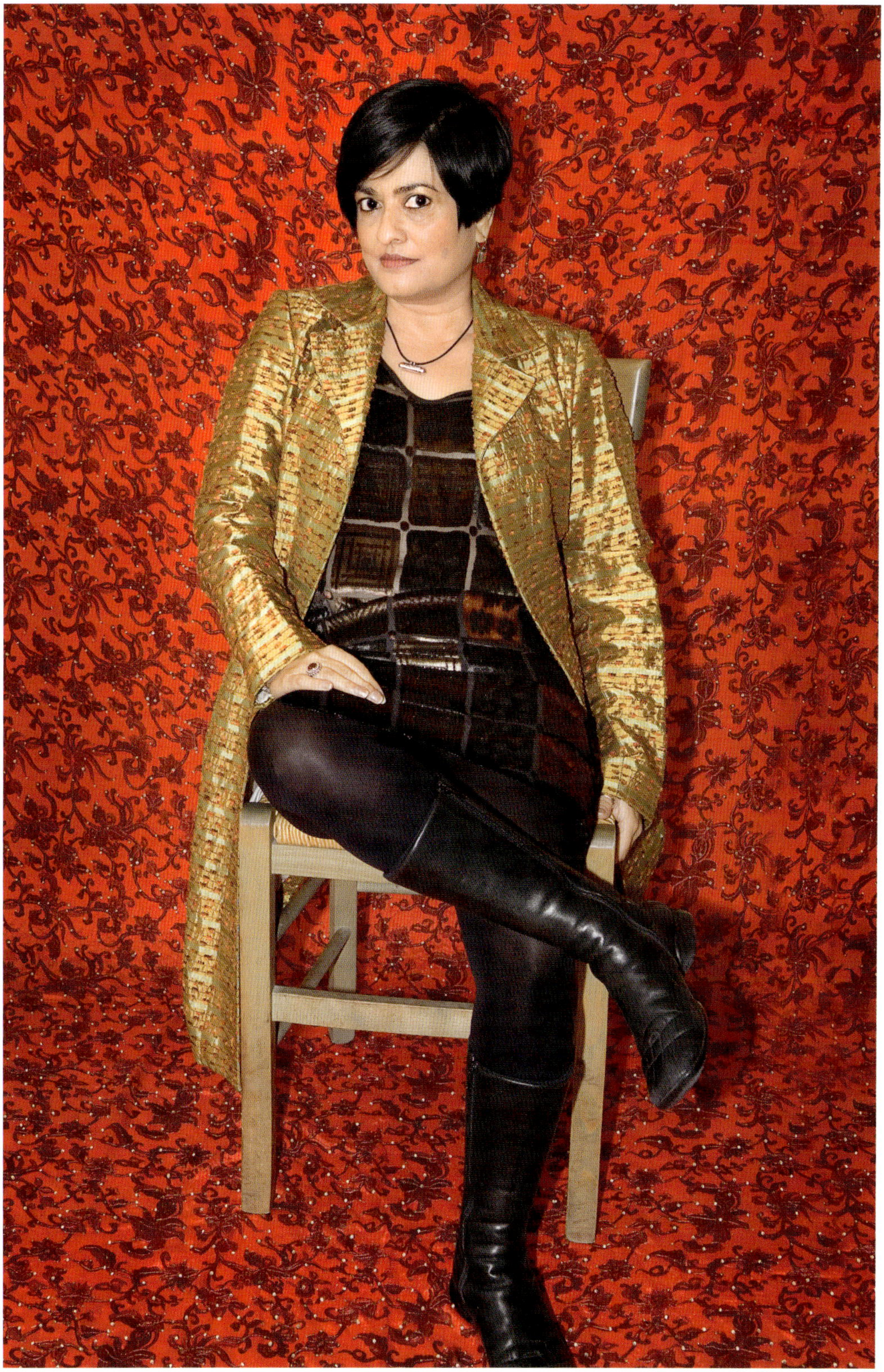

bolic divorce from my family and my community. My beautiful long black hair that came down to my waist had for so many years been lovingly oiled, brushed and cared for by my mother. There was the sadness of that lost connection to my mother through my hair... That childhood memory of her hands rubbing oil into my scalp while gossiping with the next door neighbour while I sat between the folds of her sari.

Liberating my femininity from multiple cultural constraints and expectations, from the demands of white heteronormative culture that thrived on Asian exotica was key in giving me balls and a loud, feisty voice. This was also a time when I was starting to claim my sexuality and define my racial identity.

While many of us women of colour, began to question our post colonial subjectivity and resisted/critiqued whiteness and its attendant privileges in its various guises and disguises, we didn't see/read many white women, be they feminist, queer or not, interrogating the privilege of their whiteness.

I felt compelled to interrogate the lily-white feminist landscape where far too often the stereotype of the meek and mild submissive Asian woman was accepted without question. I co-wrote an article, 'Challenging Imperial Feminism' [1982] in an attempt to both critique and start a dialogue around race and racism in the white, middle-class feminist movement.

From across the Atlantic came the embrace of other women of colour that gave me another kind of homecoming: Audre Lorde, June Jordan, Alice Walker and Angela Davis, whose writings and lives became lifelines in immeasurable ways. I took to heart Audre Lorde's wisdom that it was crucial to our survival to define ourselves for ourselves on our own terms and not let others do the defining.

The collective literary outpourings by women of colour in anthologies, books and articles at the time gave me a sense of shared sisterhood and belonging that I hadn't experienced before, a language to describe and understand my otherness as a woman of colour and by now a lesbian. They showed me routes/roots back to my whole self, to reclaim my culture and my race on my own terms and finally map out anchors for my queer, Asian femininity.

It was later, much later that I translated my imaginative desi femme yearnings in my film *Khush*, a documentary about South Asian lesbians and gay men. *Khush* celebrated the emerging confidence and community of South Asian queers across the diaspora. For many of us, our ancestral home was India yet we were born in another continent and lived in yet another continent. For instance, I was born in Kenya, East Africa and as a child came with my family to the UK as immigrants where we made 'home'.

Pratibha & Shaheen, London 2008

Many of us were dealing with homophobia prevalent in South Asian communities and at the same time challenging racism in the white lesbian and gay community. This web of experiences found expression in my filmmaking practice. In *Khush*, the multiple subjectivities that many of us inhabited as we forged our identities out of experiences of displacement, were captured through personal narratives. In an explicit homage to Razia Sultan, I wanted to reframe Hema Malini's 'forbidden' kiss and so I filmed a fantasy sequence between two women where the kiss is neither masked nor alluded to. Instead in a deliberate act, one of the women turns the other woman's face towards her and then they kiss. A fitting final signifier of our 'coming of age'.

MY LIFE HAS BEEN shaped by the intersecting structures of race, class, gender and sexuality, I've learnt that these are transitory constructs with shifting meanings. But it's precisely this fluidity that I find exciting in its potential to disrupt fixed, essentialist socially constructed categories. We all have choices in how we present ourselves to the world. My most profound learning has been to own that I have a choice even as I continue to fight/strategise/regroup to keep my right to choose. There is power in creating an image, a self-identity that can never be possessed or defined by the oppressive gaze of the 'other' if only because I refuse to give that gaze any agency.

It's no coincidence that I've called my film company Kali Films, inspired by the fierce Hindu goddess whose gaze withers any who dare to malign her power. Like Kali, my values, reverence and love for women and the way I express my femininity is my own – outside the bounds of conventional patriarchal orthodox culture – Indian or Anglo-Saxon.

A mother who worshipped Hindu goddesses brought me up. As a child in Kenya, I sat with my mother in ritual prayer at her makeshift shrine in her bedroom and I would gaze at the images of goddesses like Kali's sister Durga, a fierce and graceful embodiment of 'femme-ness'. As a child I wasn't fully conscious of their power but now I can see how their essence seeped into me, guiding my journey.

As my dear sister-friend, Laura Amazzone, a Yogini and devoted Priestess of Goddess Durga says, '"Goddesses" like Kali and Durga embody the full spectrum of the female psyche and experience – they are sensual and wrathful, fierce and compassionate, beautiful and terrifying. Terrifying because they will not succumb to patriarchal definitions of what it means to be a woman!'

My childhood heroine was Rani Ke Jhansi, an Indian warrior queen who fought the British colonial rulers and won! This female freedom fighter in her royal femme finery, sitting on horseback with an army of men behind her, brandishing her sword against the white man, evoked Kali's fierce energy and she too planted the seed of a fiery femme in me. Especially as I fantasised about her in her royal femme finery.

Which brings me back to my brazen, ballsy, feisty fierceness, without which I couldn't, wouldn't want to be a femme. My femme identity is ultimately about coming home to my own fabulous, wild, irreverent self!

For Campbell, my 'fag daddy' whose charming insistence that I write this was hard to resist, and Shaheen, my handsome butch who only ever allows lipstick on her lips if it comes from my lips.

96

Femme Anti-War Activism

Dear Leah,

To me you are undoubtedly one of the most significant femme poet theorists and activists of the third wave generation. Your essay 'On being a bisexual femme' in the quintessential anthology *Fem(me): Feminists, Lesbians, Bad Girls* was one of the first femme texts I read and it brought together so many things for me. You quarrelled with feminist theory, argued that femme is a queerly constructed girlhood and proudly declared that it is the opposite of being oppressed by the standards of white middle-class propriety. That piece remains a beautiful affirmation of femme-inine solidarity, a critique of beauty ideals and a sharp analysis of the forms of oppression that multiple femmes face. It helped me see that I didn't have to fight my femme, but also that I still have to own where history has placed a Northern Swedish white girl. In the same book you dialogue with Amber Hollibaugh about the pains of ageing, the different struggles of femmes at different historical moments and the importance of bringing strands of activism together. Now you blog about how you love being called an elder at thirty-two, which after more than a decade as a radical

Leah Lakshmi Piepzna-Samarasinha,
San Francisco 2006

femme of colour and a queer Sri Lankan writer, you are, in many respects.

We met at Femme 2006 in San Francisco, only one day after the world had been informed that all you need to blow up an airplane could be found in a beauty product. The gender coding of yet another wave of terrorist-panic was hard to miss: it seems make-up remains a highly political issue. As Amber noted in her conference key note, femme activism is hardly reduceable to make-up. The texture and growth of hair on our differently-hued femme bodies is, however, a political question, as you and Jewelle Gomez both point out. 'There is a tendency among some white femmes to argue that they face oppression solely on the basis of their queer femininity,' you said when we met up later at a coffee shop in the Mission. 'For femmes of colour it's hard to know why one is stopped, harrassed or questioned. Many of us choose to live in our own hoods and focus on other questions.'

As a spoken word artist who's always part of multiple activist struggles, your contributions to the femme conference were, as always, crucial. Aside from reading in the show, you organised a workshop with Minal Hajratwala for queers of colour on the theme 'Femmes in Times of War', to discuss what it's like to be Arabic, South Asian, North African or Muslim femmes in a post-9/11 world shaped by Islamophobia and racist terror at every border crossing. Later you wrote: 'It was a place for femmes of colour involved in anti-war activism to talk about our challenges in working in the mainstream anti-war movement and the ways we've found to resist as queer women of colour, in our cultural, political and sexual communities, and in coalition groups. We talked about balancing our needs for self care with our activism and organising, and shared our various tactics – ranging from being involved in women of colour/queer of colour/people of colour affinity groups, to doing stickering and street art, and working against military recruitment at schools.'

After years of living in Toronto, you are now in the Bay Area, when you are not touring America with your queer of colour cabaret troupe Mangos With Chili. You continue to point to how activism is always charged with desire, about the connections and clashes between different forms of identity and different forms of survival and about how being femme is about tracing a feminine lineage of resistance and getting one's girl body back. In *Brazen Femme* you write: 'Is my fem body fake? Pasted over a raw wound that will always be there? It was not a cut that can be stitched up. What does gender performance mean when you need a rock? I build this body, this gender, layer of silk over steel skeleton.' [2002:139]

Yes, you speak firmly from a femme-identified place ('being as much of a femme at a self-defence workshop as at an anti-war demonstration', always 'stomping into the room', as you put it) but you always prioritise alliances with women and queers of colour. 'We need to create our own community institutions and affinity groups, our own organisations based in our communities to find ways to work within our communities while being out', you said once and I hear ya. You bring the strands together, as an invisibly disabled, radical abuse survivor and anti-violence worker interested in creating community accountability strategies that actually work and I remain convinced that your work moves mountains and that your poetry heals the world.

Bandit Queen of Manchester

Dear Jaheda,

I've loved our passionate conversations since we first met around queer art scenes in Manchester. You consistently question the need for labels and boxes and put your life on the line for your beliefs, much like one of our sources of inspiration, Bandit Queen Phoolan Devi.

'I've never thought about if my femininity is queer, but if we were going with my aesthetics (long black hair, long nail polished finger nails, lipstick, and outfits that cling to my curves) I guess I'm femme. Delving deeper, the possibilities are endless,' you said.

A freelance artist who expresses yourself, your thoughts and politics through performance, rap and spoken word, the Sphere project is your pride. 'When I first came to Manchester I felt that as an Asian Lesbian I was pretty much on my own and it seemed stupid and illogical. How could I be the only Asian in the Village? I decided to set up an arts project around the lives of South Asian LBTQ women. With artists Maya Chowdhry and Shanaz Gulzar I began a two year search for women and finding – eventually getting both.' Based in stories, Sphere has since done an installation for Queer Up North, devised

Jaheda Choudhury, Manchester 2007

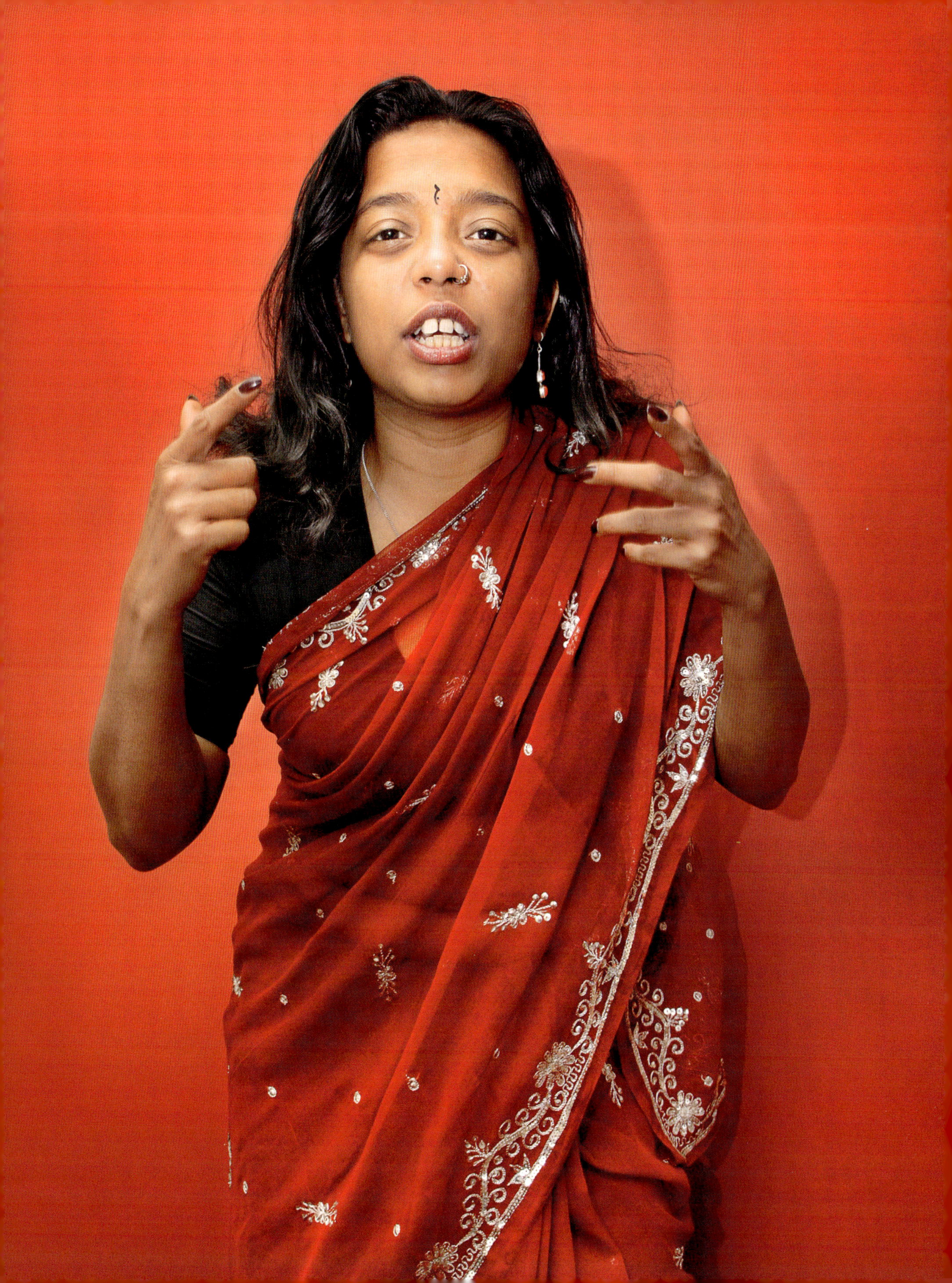

Air Conditioned
Fully Licensed
Live Music
Function Room
224 6443
LAL QILA
Indian
Cuisine
OPEN

a play for Black History Month and a short film for Mixing it Up, all in the city you call 'Gotham City without Batman'.

You belong to and engage many communities that all share stories of struggle for collective and individual survival. 'My bloodline is from Bangladesh, specifically Sylhet. I'm connected to it through the stories my parents and other elders told me growing up: Islamic stories of kindness, stories of independence and three fights for freedom – from Empire, from India and from Pakistan. Despite all that, my life's in danger when I express my love for my girlfriend. My sexuality puts me in the LGBTQ community, which has also had to fight to exist. Yet, when I wear my sari or my kameez to a queer event/night, I'm told I'm in the wrong country. The artist community sometimes feeds my ego, yet artists are killed and persecuted too because of how they tell a story. My arrogance and self-belief keep me writing and feeding audiences' hunger to learn and be entertained.'

Like many of us, you are driven by fierce desires. 'I'd like to feel a child grow in my womb, give birth and become a parent. I desire masculine women, the smell of the soft leather when they put on their harness; the attention of an audience as I share my world through music and poetry; acceptance and acknowledgement from the wider Asian community without having to hide the existence of my beautiful girlfriend. And one day I wish to go into the Gay Village in Manchester and not have my sexual identity questioned.'

Jaheda on the Curry Mile, Manchester 2007

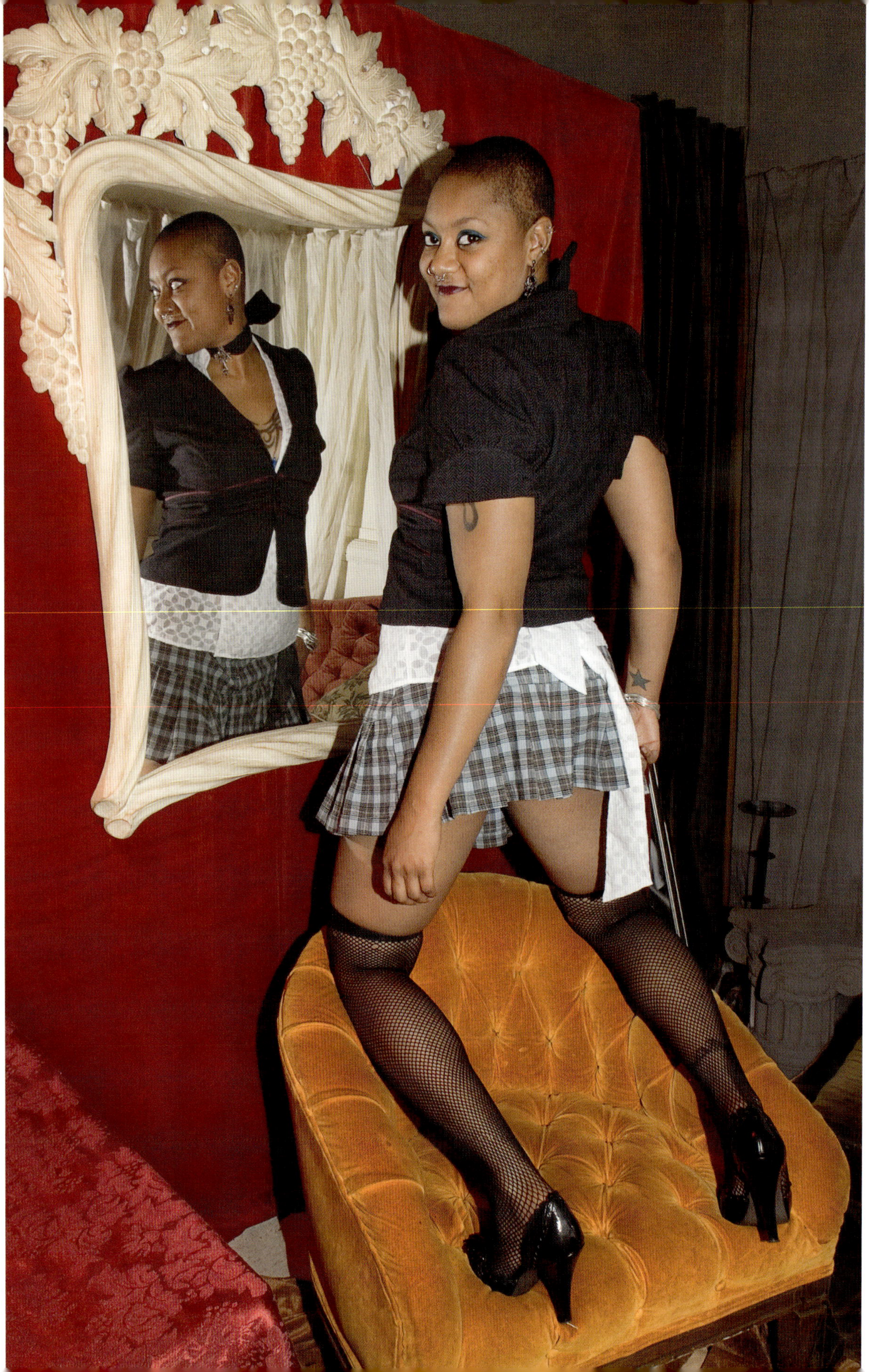

To Be Young, Pretty and Queer

I vividly remember Miss Stewart's mohawk when the Atlanta Femme Mafia talked about how to organise at Femme 2006. Marla had recently left the Bay Area to get a PhD in sociology at Georgia State, and she was the perfect guide for the southern girls around the city where she had ruled many dance floors. With an innate fierce confidence and an unapologetic femme sexiness, Marla showed up for her femme sisters who were not getting respect in Atlanta's queer communities. After a year of virtual chatting, Marla generously helped Del and me plan our trip to Atlanta and while the photographer rested before a full day and night of photographing the Mafia, she went out of her way to show the Swede around. Bonding over feminist stakes in academia and activism, shared research interests in female sexuality, race and queer popular culture and a joint pleasure in having a rockin' good time, I eventually had to admit to not keeping up with a basketball star's stamina on the dance floor...

Marla Stewart, Atlanta 2007

After going out with you in Atlanta, both to My Sister's Room and to a Mansion dance party with Miss Hedonism, girl, I must say, you sure know how to work a dance floor and a bar crowd!

– Being feminine has its benefits, but being a pretty femme has major privileges. Sure, beauty is in the eye of the beholder, but we can all generally acknowledge that pretty people have it easier, simply because most of the time, they get what they want.

– I feel like that's where most of my confidence comes from... the validation from other people. I don't think it's necessarily about bodily features as much as attitude. It's about the confidence of knowing that you look good and taking control and ownership of your sexiness. You may be objectified from the outside, but for me, that ultimate sexiness depends on the confident energy you give off. Although having the ability to pass as straight and the ability to avoid questions about your sexuality comes in handy, especially with regards to safety, being fashionable and pretty help you to get what you want. Entering the queer community I immediately knew I was femme and saw this identity as powerful, as well as sexual – something that I thoroughly enjoyed. I loved dressing the way that I did and being conscious of the way I walked and talked to people, piquing people's curiosity as they walked past me. I controlled their every stare and comment and I knew it. To purvey my sexuality and perceive this sexuality as powerful, was (and still is) a gift that keeps on giving.

It's interesting that you talk about controlling how people look at you. This seems to be a site of controversy with regards to femininity. Is it possible to be in control of one's 'objectification', so to speak? Also, could you say a little more about what you mean by being pretty? According to whose standards and in whose eyes? Has it anything to do with being young?

– I feel like there is and there isn't control

over my objectification. I use my sexuality to my advantage – feminine, visibly queer (to most), and fierce. When I present myself as sexy, I make sure that everyone in the room can see just how sexy I am. So in this sense, I really do feel like I control their looks. In the American colonised mind, there are certain features that most people consider beautiful. It's the 'exotic' look – a look that says that I'm not from here, even though I am. I'm usually considered exotic by most people – doesn't matter who they are… they could be black, white, queer or straight and yet I'm still tied to something that's not what they are used to seeing. It's because I've medium-brown skin and large eyes, but I don't have typical black features, such as full lips and nose. Everyone thinks that I'm mixed race. People from Ethiopia believe that I'm Ethiopian while others think I'm Indian or East Asian. Sometimes I think pretty is shaped by all the 'isms', but in my world, it's really dependent on who it is. A fat black queer woman is not going to have the same standards of beauty as a straight white male. So I guess it's about whose lens you are seeing it through. Are you seeing it through the patriarchal white male lens or are you seeing it through a black/other queer lens? Is it through a colonised mind or not? Being pretty has somewhat to do with being young, but not necessarily. In our youth-obsessed culture, we correlate youth with sexiness, but I believe that you can be sexy at any age. My basic attitude is 'I don't give a fuck who you are. I'm beautiful and you better respect that.' I know that I'm going to be old and sexy and loving it!

You were queer in high school but as you put it, 'ran out of the closet' while an undergraduate at San Francisco State University. After being part of queer communities in the Bay Area for years, you relocated to Atlanta. What are the main differences for you as a queer femme in these two cities?

– Atlanta is a lot more segregated, at least on a social level. When I moved to Atlanta for graduate school, I went to all the clubs and was immediately recruited into a lesbian, almost all black 'family'. I was familiar with how these families worked; it's like in the film *Paris is Burning*, but I'd never come across anything like this in the Bay Area. In Atlanta, it seemed everyone belonged to one. Mine was the House of Buchanan, a relatively small house at the time. They were loving, supportive, took me under their wing and exposed me to a brand new world. There was the mother and the father of the house, aunts, uncles and all their children. We met up once a month and did things together including pageants, lip-synching performances, holiday gatherings and family reunions. I eventually left because the commitments were too great for a full-time graduate student who was also working full-time, but I miss the familial bond and support structure they offered.

Why did you join the Femme Mafia?

– I never ran into such a thing in the Bay Area. I knew of no femme politics when I was there from 1998 to 2004. In Atlanta, the Femme Mafia formed because of the harassment they were getting from other lesbians and queers about how they emulated straight women and often weren't served drinks at the bars. Although I'd never had that problem because I look visibly queer, with piercings and shaved head, naturally I wanted to stand up for those that 'looked straight' and show them that femme comes in all shapes and colours. The Mafia was made up mostly of white women, but a few black women from my school recruited me. We were already a part of a black queer activist group called BlackOUT and I was excited that I could go to a bunch of femmes and not only speak about fashion and make-up, but also discuss femme-inism, activism and community building in the queer domain.

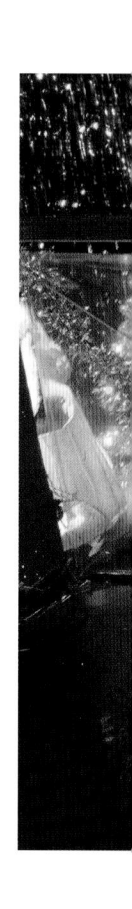

family were powerful. We demanded and received all the respect we deserved. We were pure divas and the studs catered to us like the true chivalrous gentlemen they were – and yes, they referred to themselves and were referred to in male pronouns. So to hear that the white women were getting harassed seemed absurd and strange. I could see why some of the femmes needed to take action. The Mafia is there – fierce and unapologetic about who we are.

Wow. You make it sound like white femmes are worse off than black femmes… is that always the case do you think?

– Atlanta has a strong black femme presence compared to the Bay Area and I feel this is because of the need for organisation, given the history of the South. The Bay Area is more liberal by far, so I believe that the presence isn't as strong because people are more accepting of the way we are. That said, black women have been objects of sexual curiosity and this history pervades our present in every which way, particularly for black femmes. In Atlanta, black femmes are often invisible in mainstream or straight communities and to fight off homophobia and heterosexism it's necessary to band together and show off our queerness, as well as our fierce and powerful capabilities surrounding queer organisation. I know I'm a subject of curiosity. But whether I have on my basketball gear or a short mini-skirt with some fierce heels, I control the way people perceive me. My femmeness is captivating. Once 'others' see what black femmes are capable of, this will help facilitate acceptance in the South and slowly deter racist, homophobic and heterosexist comments.

Yes, Mafia Donna Rachael told me that femmes used to get cigarettes thrown at them in lesbian bars. Solange Garjan, a Tennessee-based femme, made the point that while femme seems to go in and out of fashion in white-dominated queer communities, they have a more appreciated, permanent place in black communities. Would you agree?

– Yeah, this happened in primarily white lesbian/queer spaces. At the black clubs, the vibe is different. As a femme, you will always get served. You're in a space of women loving women and that's all that needs to be said. Joining a family, one of the things I first noticed was that you were either a femme or a stud. The femmes of this

Joelle & Marla, Atlanta 2007

Quatrième Génération Fem

Chère Wendy,

It was a very hot July day in Paris 2006 when we first met at a cafe by the Seine. Del knew you through your lover Lynnee Breedlove of the San Francisco queer punk band Tribe 8 and insisted we should meet. It was and remains, an explosive and passionate meeting of Leos. I remember our texts to each other that day: 'I'll be the tall fake blonde in the polka-dot dress,' I said. 'I'll be the fake blonde with the tiny top reading *The Ethical Slut*,' you responded. Each of us a queer version of white European femininity.

Within moments, I was moved by your articulate views on dyke politics, pornography and feminism. 'We need Fem solidarity,' you said, 'to get over our inherited self-hatred and trust issues, because in most societies, women are raised to think they are worth nothing, aside from beauty. You need a fem friend to talk to, who tells you that your dress looks fantastic and matches the colour of your tattoos. Someone who buys you a vibrator for your b-day, fists you at a playparty when you both feel like there's nobody there who surpasses the sexiness of your best fem pal. And to talk about politics, teach you about female ejaculation and pet you when you have love drama, feel sad, wrong or ugly.' Indeed, heteropatriarchy feeds on self-hatred and competition between feminine subjects and sisterhood remains a queer act.

Like me, you found your queer femme dyke identity through relations with American lovers and allies and we bonded over shared desire for butches and trans masculinities. 'Here people are not so much into categories. We have a long tradition of being in a universalist country, where nobody wants differences to be labeled because they don't want to acknowledge people's specificities. Labels that are reclaimed are important, because if something doesn't have a name, a label, then it is not visible,' you said in a later email exchange. In racist fortress Europe, universality is a marked category, while whiteness gives privileges, queerness has a price. The first to talk about femme-ininity in France were your idols, 'the smart and adorable Ingrid Renard and Christine Lemoine who published the first book on butch–femme dynamics in France,' you said.

We were joined that day by Poppy Foxheart (who you describe as 'my high-femme-friend-top who rides her bike up the steepest San Francisco Hill, wearing a tight Victorian corset, incredibly high heels, carrying a basket full of organic food while telling me the best way to bake vegan macaroons') and femme photographer and filmmaker Emilie Jouvet, whose film *One Night Stand* has visualised femme desire in French queer pornography. In your flip-flops you called yourself a 'lazy femme'. Later you wrote 'now I'd call myself high femme, after getting a few more huge flower tattoos, buying three more expensive corsets and growing six more inches of bleached blonde hair.' Marilyn Monroe, Colette, Leslie Mah and Michelle Tea are your icons and heroines along with your friends.

You've done much to politicise queer femininity in France, including through your recent book *Quatrième Génération*, a novel-biography-manifesto in femme theory tradition. You use the

Wendy Delorme, San Francisco 2006

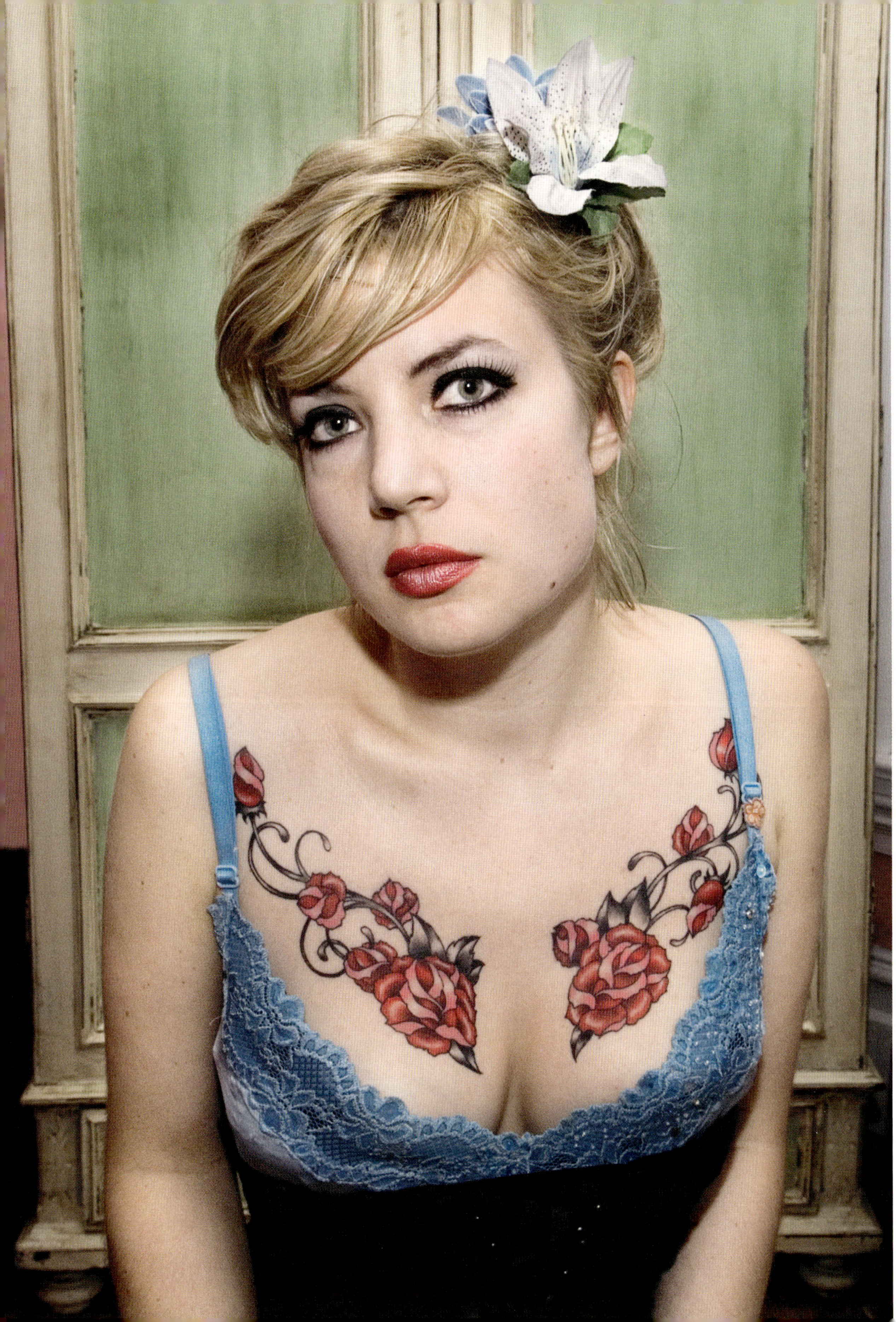

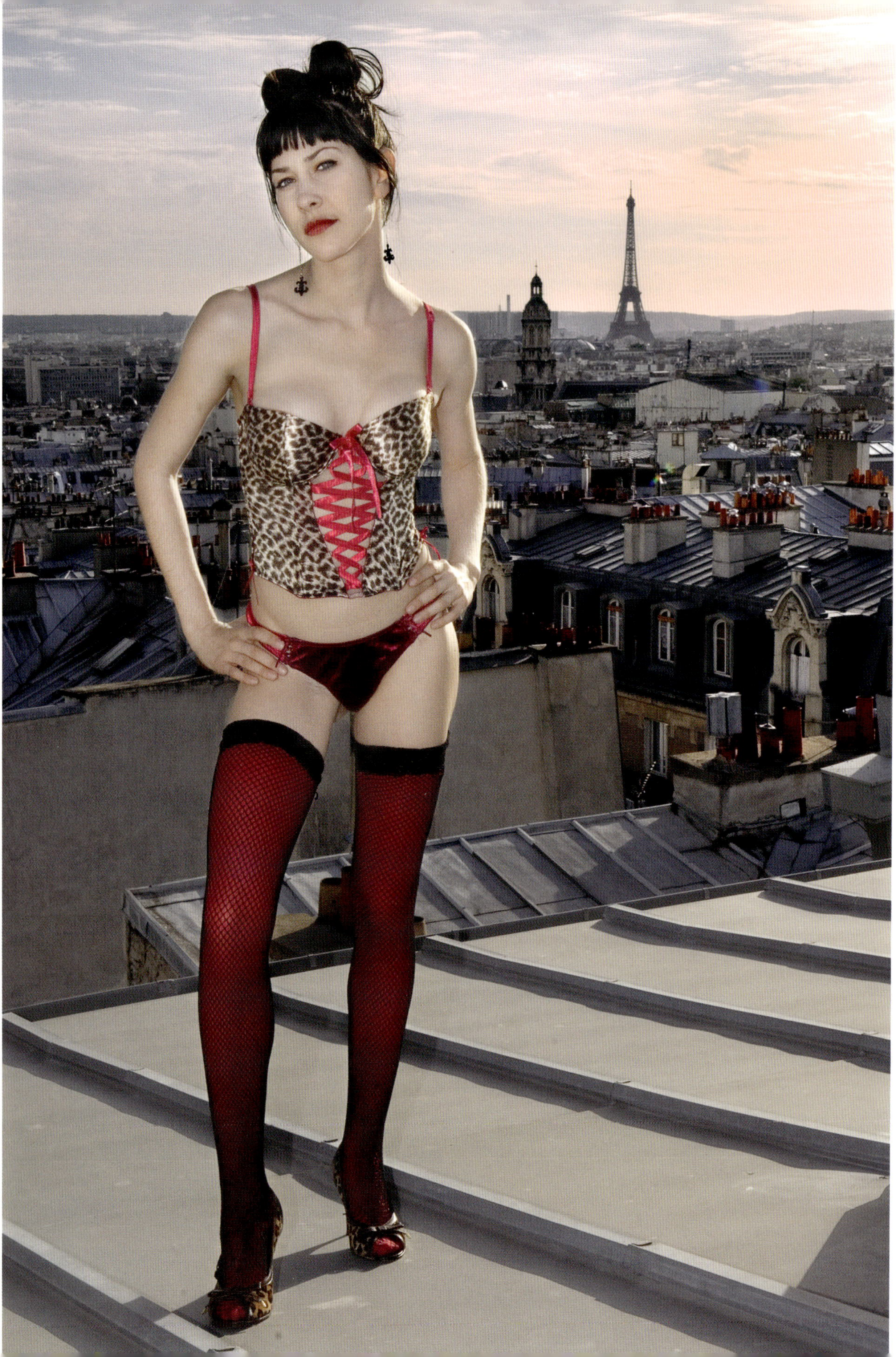

spelling 'fem' to distinguish it from the French word for woman. With Louis(e) deVille from Kentucky, fellow performer and good friend, you started the Parisian Fem Menace because, as you said 'we wanted to find other femmes! The main purpose was to create links between femmes, to make art together and create visibility. The Fem Menace is a very informal organisation, dykes in France are not yet strongly reclaiming the "fem" identity.' This involves saying out loud that butches and transboys are sexy, because, as you put it, 'in France it's rather difficult to feel sexy when you are a butch, both femmes and butches get dissed for being either too feminine or too masculine. So we decided to promote each other's visibility and sexiness. That's where we are at.'

In the cold of winter 2007, you came north with your burlesque troupe Drag King Femme Show to queer up Stockholm's The Hootchy Kootchy Club along with Rosie, Dyke Marilyn and Miss File. 'Being in front of a camera, writing books, talking to students in a classroom, getting naked on stage, it all has the same purpose for me: deconstructing gender stereotypes and creating visibility and awareness about multiple gender identities and dynamics of desire that many people ignore or have prejudices about.'

Louis(e) deVille, Paris 2006 | Wendy Delorme, Paris 2006

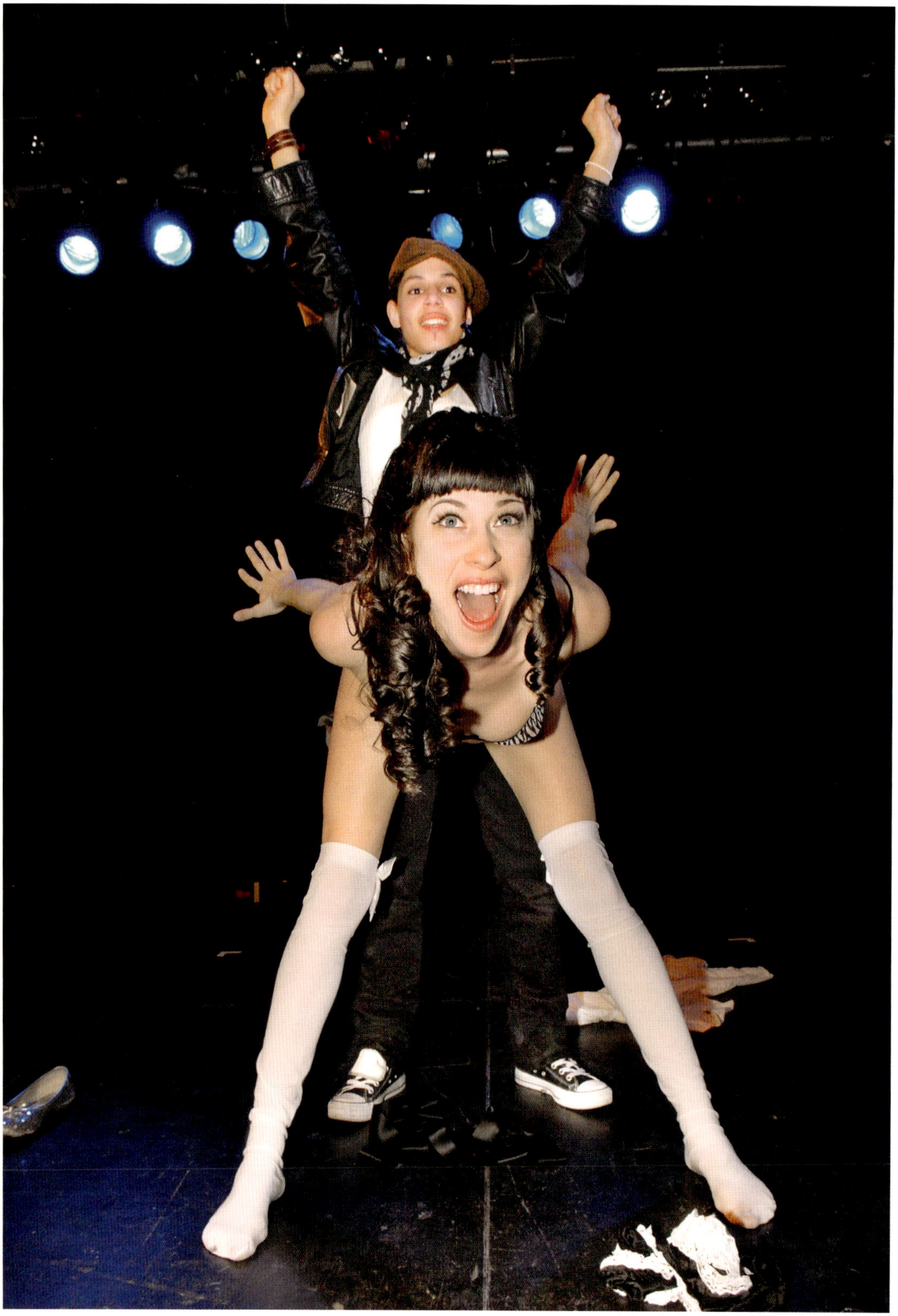

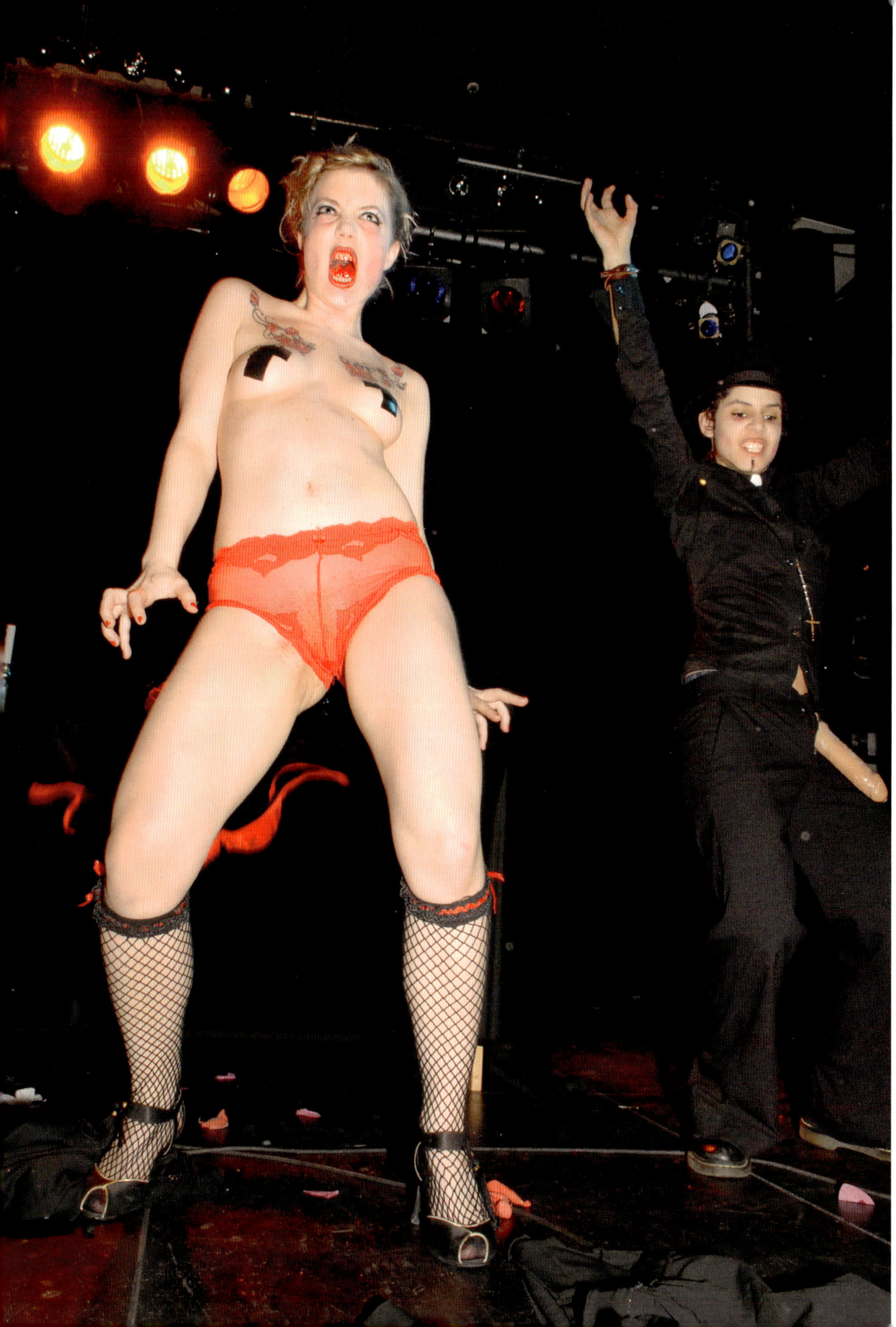

The bad girls' genealogy

WALKING THE STREETS as femme-inine subjects – whether we stomp in boots or click in stilettoes – femmes experience misogyny on a daily basis and it makes us as angry as the next girl. Still, as Solange, Pratibha, Itziar and many others note, many of us have had to defend the pleasures in plumage and plucking in feminist contexts. Sisterly betrayal hurts more, especially if all you want is to play with the girls. Dossie Easton's 1986 poem 'Radical Femme' chronicles the pains of contempt that she faced for enjoying six inch heels:

Let me tell you: We are violated by those / Who would contain our largest spirits and / Confine our greatest passions / Into the small image of chastity / We are raped by those who / Would have us believe that / Nice girls don't like sex. / They harm us more, and harm more of us, than / All the violence / of meat shot on split beaver.

In a heterosexist world which both glorifies and resents 'artificial' feminine trappings, feminist sisterhood has often demanded its own form of stripping – reducing the pleasure in a tease to a simple objectifying matter of please, basing politics in rejection and fear of erection both in ourselves and others. At times, feminists seem to dream of purity and authenticity even as we know that nobody's hands are clean and 'natural beauty' is for sale in every health food emporium. If girls are taught that femininity is one's most viable resource and dangerous quality, it's no wonder that many reject it and that its pleasures cause controversy. Yet, in the fight to become propertied citizens with rights of subjecthood, the good, respectable feminists at times reproduce patriarchy's oldest trick: the line between the good and the bad girls.

As the anthology *Femme: Lesbians Feminists Bad Girls* [1997] states, femmes have a long legacy of identifying as and with bad girls. Many of us continue to be feminine subjects whose sexual practi-

Dossie Easton, Marin County, California 2006

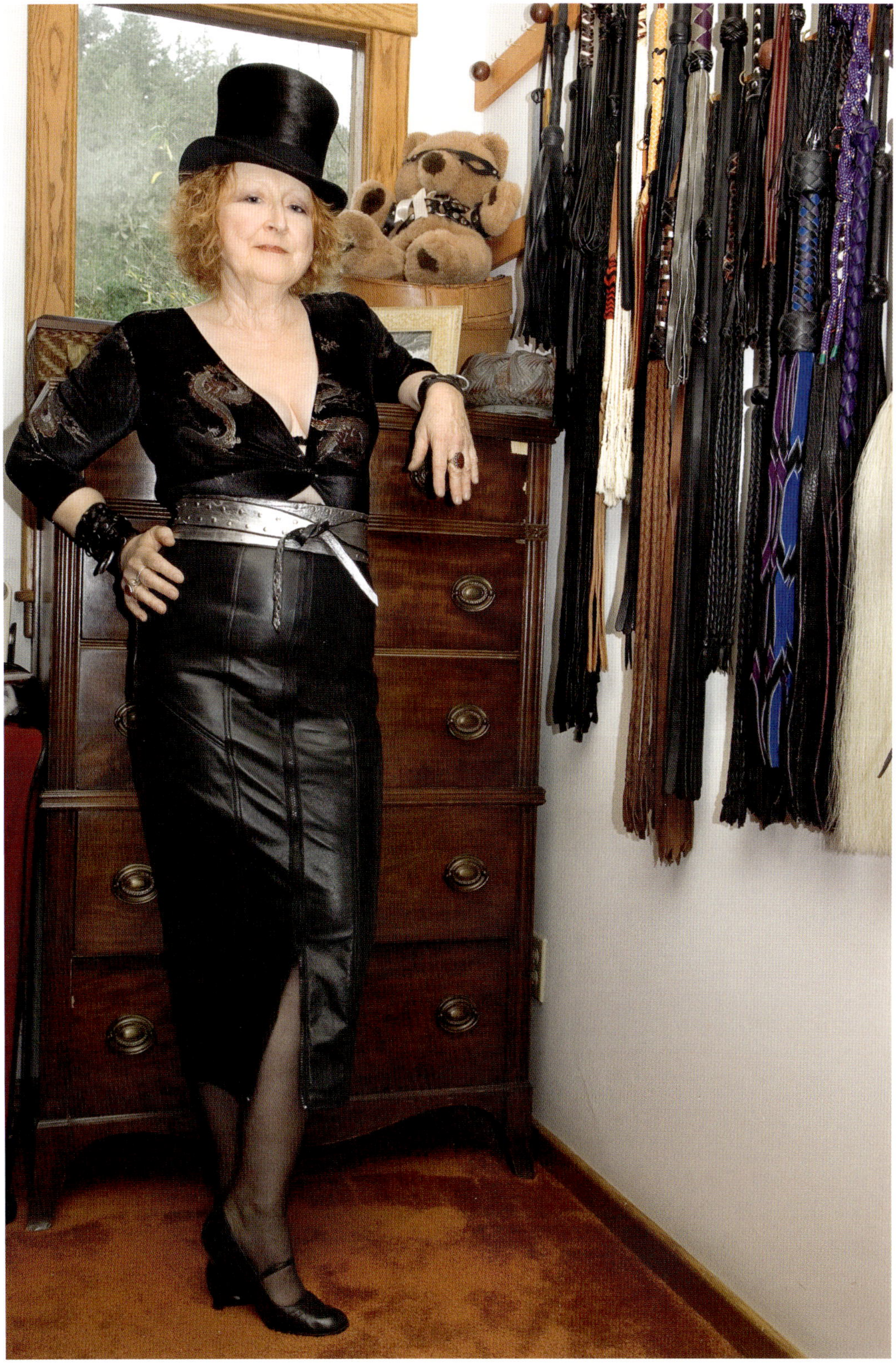

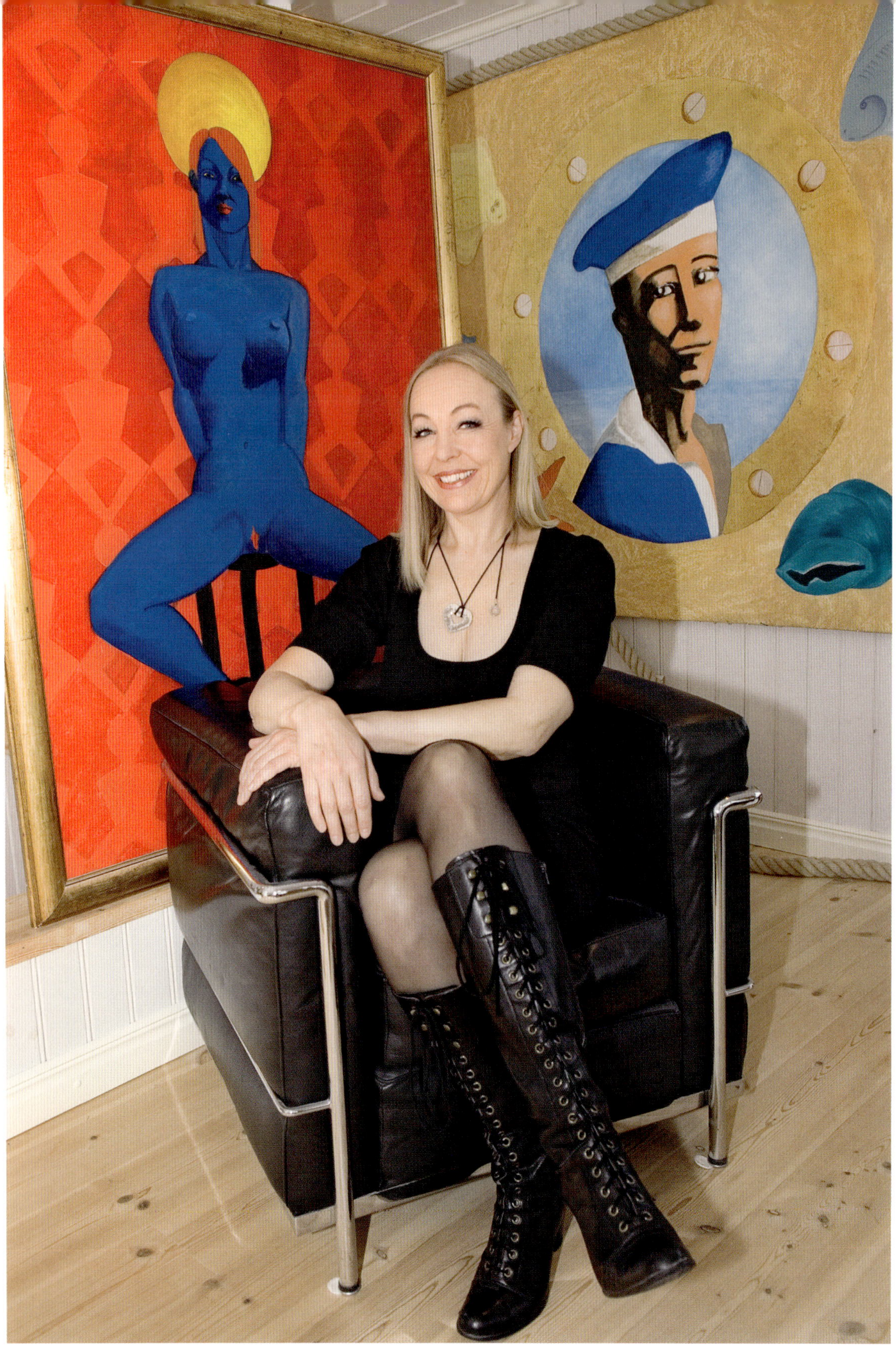

ces and gender expressions fall outside of societal conventions of respectable womanhood. In *Brazen Femme* Kathryn Payne [2002] speaks up for this lineage, noting that femmes, sluts and whores often shop in similar stores and wrestle similar demons. Many of us have occupied all three positions, and if not, certainly been bad girls or been mistaken for one. Refusing to reproduce for the father, fucking for pleasure or pay – because it's sometimes no more demeaning than breaking one's back scrubbing floors for the good girls and walking proud in the high heel steps of what Joan Nestle [1987] called 'the historical sisterhood of lesbians and prostitutes', femmes still insist on the right to be feminists. As Virginie notes, bad girl sisterhood is that of public women, outcasts and deviants. We are (loyal to) the bad girls ideologically executed or taken hostage with the rest of the working class, queer and feminists of colour in the ongoing sex wars and its longing for purity. Beyond shame, cattiness and catcalls lies a promise of solidarity.

Aside from being activists and theorists of stage and screen, sex work is a common occupation for the queerly feminine. Whether this means BDSM and sexual education, like for Dossie, Barbara, Laura and Morgana, being a pin-up making art with vaginas like for Ylva Maria,

Ylva Maria Thompson, Stockholm 2007 | *Kate & Barbara @ Lesbian Sex Mafia, New York City 2007*

or if it means stripping, pissing, dominating and hooking like it has and still does mean for so many femmes, it is clear that in a capitalist world where sexuality has always been commodified and deviance is at once rejected and desired, sex work is as viable an option for survival and subversion as anything else.

Here is the thing: queer femmes are unruly unwilling participants in what Bird La Bird calls 'the gentrification of the lesbian body'. We are rarely the liberal L-word lesbian chic, the tattooed waif of *Cosmopolitan* or the best-selling writer of tips on how to please your old man. Sex in our time is more commercialised than ever, but whether your appearance in the pornographic and erotic was mainstream, like for Ylva Maria, or is coming out of counter culture, like for Wendy or voluptuous vixens Jukie and Celestina, femmes are driven by visions of change. And when Lady Monster, Simone de la Getto or Vagina Jenkins perform big burlesque or any of you speak of and from cunt, it fuels us with hopes of a future where feminine sexuality continues to exist and change, cheeky and courageous, in the complex field of pleasure and danger [Vance 1984]. As Ylva Maria said, 'calling oneself a bad girl is a conscious stand. A bad girl experiments with and challenges the image of how a woman is supposed to act in different ways, above all she does it publically and does not care if it provokes.' These are our bad girl contributions to sexual theory.

Kate Bornstein & Barbara Carrellas,
New York City 2007

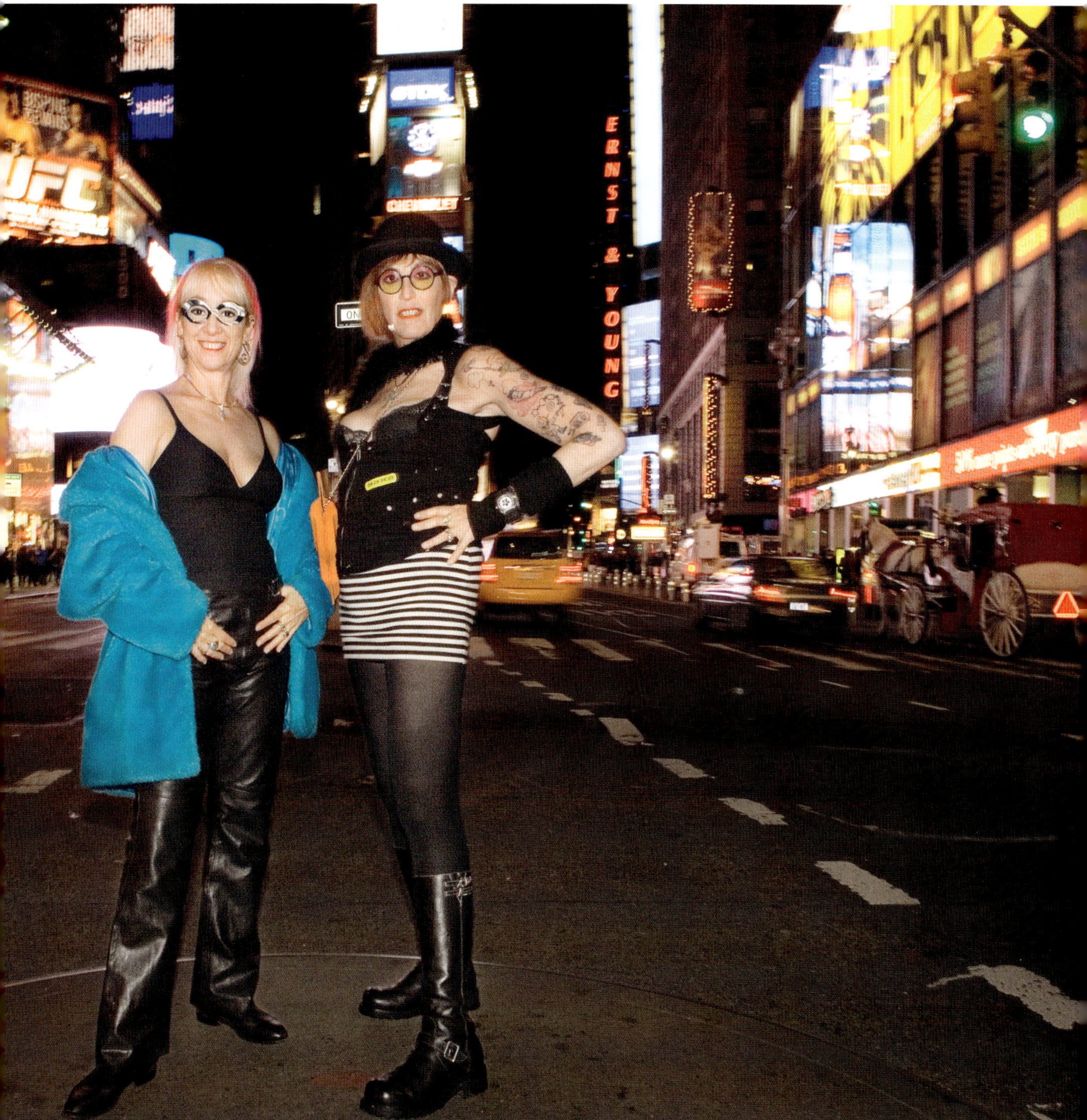

Berlin's Feminist Sexpert

Writing to the esteemed Dr Laura feels a bit like writing to an advice column because we haven't actually met. Like her femme allies in this book, Barbara Carrellas, Dossie Easton and her inspiration, and Annie Sprinkle, Germany's own feminist sexpert has a passion for art, sex and communication work. A writer, workshop leader and lecturer, Dr Laura also runs Sexclusivitaeten, a female sexshop and Club Rosa, a lesbian escort service, and organises a Friday salon in her home. Her American sisters are widely known in the world of radical ecstasy and urban tantric sex and Ylva Maria's bad girl art is well known in Sweden, but to still my own perverse curiosity I've let Dr Laura be the leading voice of sexperts in this book, offering her own European perspectives.

So Dr Laura, your old friend Dr Del is always raving about you. Who are you?

– I am a lusty, laughing lady who wants to share the joy of love and living with the people who visit me. I love to play around and switch roles in daily life, I love to laugh during sex and in any other situation. Laughing is so orgasmic, a huge release and can *invulve* everyone. That's the energy I work and live with.

That reminds me of Barbara Carrellas' powerful *Urban Tantra* that we got the privilege of sharing with her and Kate Bornstein in New York. So are you femme-identified? What does that mean to you?

– I confess that my femme was more visible decades ago when I had long blonde hair and I dressed like a killer lady with long legs under a mini skirt. These were the days of offensive and demonstrative politics and I promoted the pub(l)ic femme/feminist/lesbian/sex worker image to show we can be both, 'sexy' and intelligent.

The lesbian crowd found me suspicious, assuming I was hetero, bi, a slut and not a real lesbian. My girlfriend and I – both sex workers – cross-dressed during strip shows as the first lesbian strippers in Berlin in the early 90s. Help! Circumstances made me change and cut my hair. Now I am even more into cross-dressing than before and play with different images or combine gendered accessories. I still love to turn things around, but the femme is not as omnipresent as before. I still claim the underestimated 'femme' qualities and love to go out in little nothings or negligées with boxer shorts or gloves. Now the girlz live their femininity and experiment with different outfits and identities, which is great to see.

I hear you. And no doubt, like Dossie Easton and other femme-identified sex radicals, you have done a lot to enable and celebrate that. So what are the pleasures in femininity for you? Are there particular garments that you like?

– I love to dress up as a man in silken underwear with a cock in my slip. I love the leather outfit of a domina femme, a corset and chaps to show a beautiful ass. I love to express the loudness and vulgarity of a femme with esprit. I also love to show up as a whore with her pimp and use clichés to shock. As a sex worker I often remind people that in the sex industry, the butch–femme duo has been around for centuries. Whores were told to wear men's clothes to distinguish themselves from bourgeois femmes. In the 20s in Berlin, butches

Laura Méritt @ Home, Berlin 2007

WOMEN
SUSAN SONTAG
femalia
KLITORIDE EXTRAVAGANZ
CRAZY NEW YORK
LINDA GRANT
BAUSTILKUNDE
DAS GEHEIME WISSEN DER FRAUEN

120

had to provide for the life of the couple just like heterosexual males did. So they went to work as male dominants in high boots while the femmes were the pimps in the bar managing it.

That is a fascinating part of the legacy of public women and the queer affinities of sluts, whores and femmes… So what about your own desires?

– All my longer relationships have been with butches. I know how to treat a stone butch and surrendered for a leatherman in the 90s. I still enjoy the qualities of well-educated sirs charming their ladies, especially when they do the housework! And I love symbolic actions, like when my new butch partner received one of my worn slips from my old butch as a rite of passage.

What a sweet and an interesting twist on kinship rituals! Lately it seems that half of Stockholm's queer artists have migrated to Berlin, but I have never been. Is it true then as they say that 'high femininity' is not very common in German dyke/queer subcultures?

– There is a small butch–femme culture in Berlin but the scene is less highly gendered than say in Southern Europe or USA. Thanks to the trans and queer movement, which comes out of the women's movement, we have more options then ever before. In the trans movement which is hip now – especially for tranny boyz – there is a higher acceptance of femininity. The feminist movement in Germany has also developed a bigger acceptance of genderplay. *Gender Trouble* has lead to many gender differentiations and essentialist arguments are hopefully out. In the metropolis and in my salon I meet many different people, some are gender free, others find their one identity once and forever. There is more respect, acceptance and experimentation.

Polly @ The Pregnant Oyster, Berlin 2007

Danish Pillow Queen Femme

Dear Frøken Signe,

Ever since Del met you at a København queer event, he's been talking about how charmed he is by you. Looking at the images you seem to ride the lion in more ways than one!

'I view my own femininity as well as my femmeness very much as a subject of objectification, when viewed by heteronormative society, in my own frame of politics and sexually speaking,' you wrote before we met up one chilly December day in Nørreport, you sporting a turquoise rabbit fur. We joked about what kind of planet such a bunny might have come from and what affinities she might have with a self-declared kinky femme with proletarian and leftist activist roots in a rural Denmark village.

That enchanted afternoon we compared notes on the contradictions of femme in a heterosexist world. 'If I can get a discount, I don't care if I pass as straight,' you laughed. Compared to how people used to spit and scream at you during your mohawk-adorned punk years in leather and spikes, being femme is rather easy. 'I don't care much for bio boys and certainly don't dress to get approval from men. But sometimes I'm afraid of men's aggression,' you said. 'Often I look a bit cheap but I do have outfits that make me look like I'm going horseback riding too,' you explained, adding that old ladies are the worst at policing femininity and that returning to your studies has proven that looking too much like a girly girl does get in the way of being taken seriously.

Like many femmes, you feel that naming an identity is important. København's dyke community is pretty androgynous you said, its butch–femme tint amounting to 'one part of a couple having slightly longer asymmetrical hair'. At the same time, when your friends in the European s/m community visit, they often note that København's scene seems to be full of femmes. 'Among others, a femme friend who is older than me has fought hard to create a space for femmes which enables me to claim this identity,' you said. 'I'm lesbian-identified, but rarely get read as such, as my current partner is a transman. I've always been femme, except for at fifteen when I was a baby butch. My mother says my excessive femininity's probably a result of my disappointment when I didn't get the lacquered shoes I wanted at five!'

Femme roles which play with feminine stereotypes amuse you. 'Mostly I'm a pillow queen. I'm happiest when I don't have to take responsibility for what's done to me, always within a clearly negotiated context of play, of course,' you said, looking mischievous. 'A psychoanalyst would have a heyday with me. Maybe I've internalised our culture's dominant ideas of femininity, but this works for me.'

After years of working and taking acting classes, you're preparing for theatre studies at the university. You posed in the supermarket (see page 24) because 'it's a commentary on being both consumer and consumed. My outfit's me. A bit vulgar, a bit *Fame*, a trashy housewife and pin-up in one. It's also my working-class roots. You can aspire to be middle class, but if you're proletarian you'll never quite pass, just like as a woman you'll never fit into a man's world. We can play around with stereotypes and think we're in control of what we do, but we never fully are. It's never simply a performance.'

Signe Flysk, København 2007

SLOT

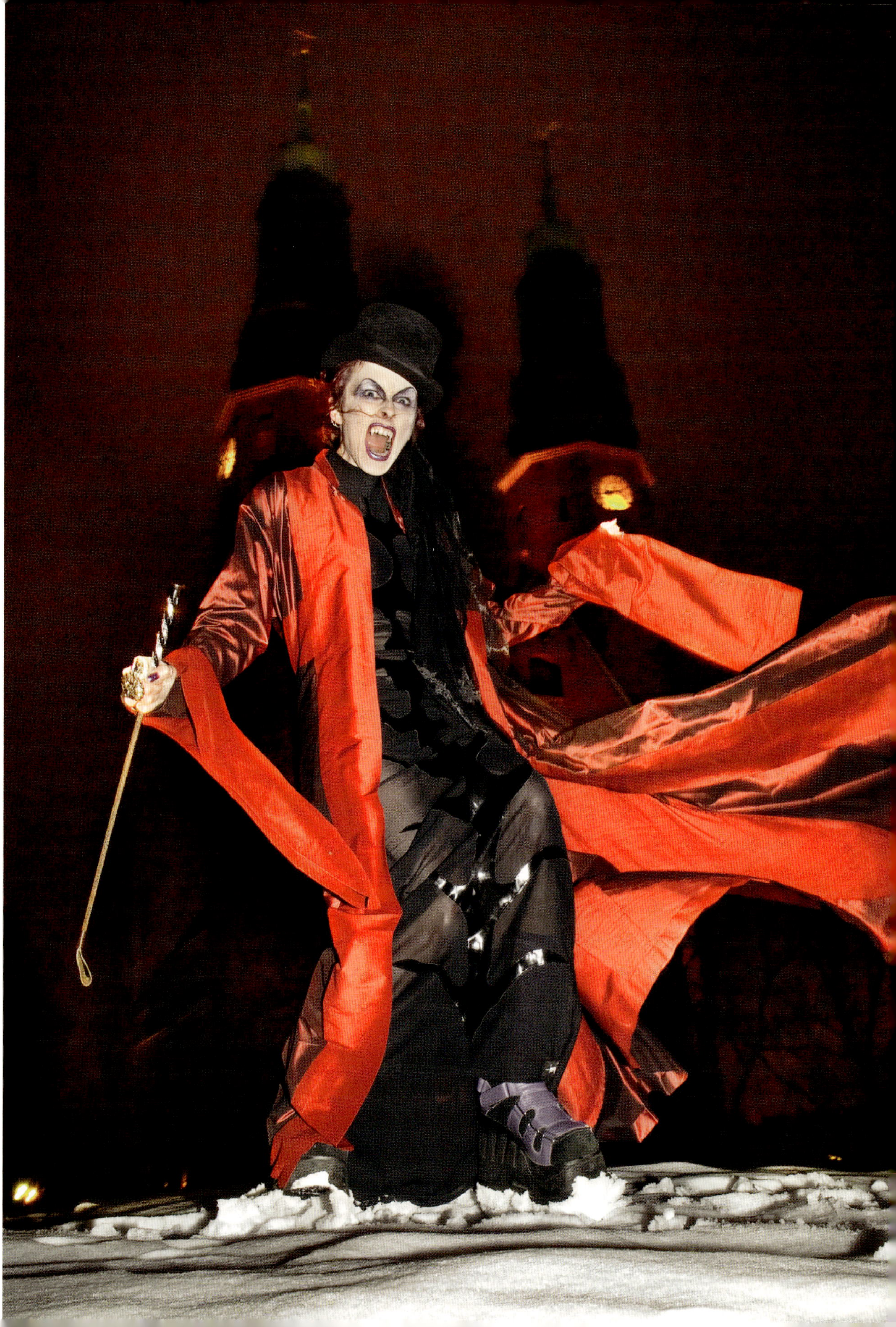

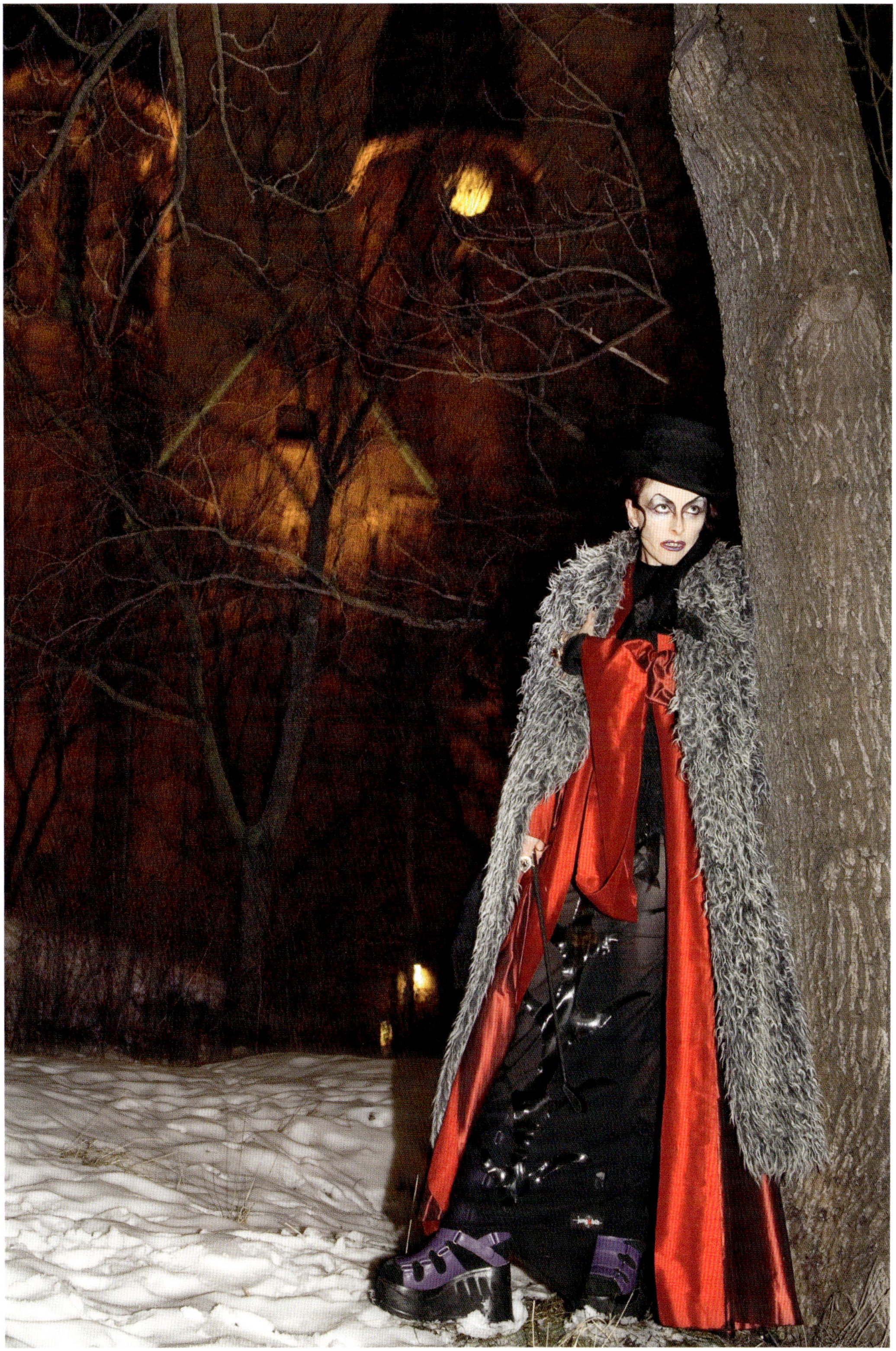

Interview with the Vampire Queen

I met Rosie Lugosi in 2004 on my first visit to Manchester and she was the hostess of CLUB LASH, a women-run S/M club. In my virginal white slip I wanted to kneel at her royal mistress boots and offer my neck. Since then I've seen her read, sing, perform and MC queer events in Manchester, Stockholm and at Femme 2006 in San Francisco. Rosie's an accomplished writer and when she's not performing she manages a crisis hotline for queer youth. With her fiercely funny phantasmatic femme-ness, she's become a mentor, an ally and a sister. After having invited, introduced, hosted and feasted with Rosie many times in many places, this mortal femme dared to ask the vampire queen some questions. As always, Rosie responded with poetic prophecy.

Dear goddess, do tell, who is Rosie Lugosi?

– Rosie Lugosi is a perverse deployment of fem(me)ininity. A caricature who also parodies songs and plays with femme. She's liberated and consciously femme. To me femme is a woman with balls, brains, tits, ass and intelligence on show and Oh My Goddess, how it terrifies! She doesn't do it to be difficult – but because anything else would be slow suffocation.

– As a performer, Rosie Lugosi's a (unique) creation – a female drag queen. People often say, 'no real woman would ever act like you', that is, be loud, vulgar, sexually assertive, wear such exaggerated make-up and make such exaggerated gestures. I'm only mistaken for a man when I am dressed/dragged up as Rosie Lugosi. Rosie Lugosi doesn't draw on ready-made femme icons. She invents herself as her own model. She's a vampire, she doesn't reflect in a mirror… Rosie Lugosi's the original article, not a reflection.

Wow. So what's a femme vampire queen exactly?

– Rosie Lugosi links the horror of vampires with the horror of older sexually active women. She physically embodies the monstrous-feminine through the outward trappings of the dominatrix-vampire-crone. She transgresses age boundaries (for instance, how women are supposed to dress at a particular age), and challenges the tensions that women feel about how 'real' women are represented in society/media. This femme does the unthinkable: she grows old. The worst betrayal and monstrous thing is for a femme to be crone and sexy. To kiss the magic mirror that shows each new sag and wrinkle. To say, I am still beautiful. This is the hardest road a femme will have to walk. As her eyesight starts to blur she doubts anyone has ever trod this way before. We must dance wilder, sing louder, wear brighter clothes, redder lipstick and bigger wigs so young femmes can see us growing old disgracefully and take heart. Rosie Lugosi is old, over 900 years, and yet not a mother. This is the queerest a gal can get: she knows only too well the social ostracising of (femme) women who actively choose not to have kids. She challenges the pressure on all women, whatever their sexuality, to produce children. Vampires create family in an alternative fashion… As a femme she revels in the dance of saying yes to life; all it takes, all it gives and all it costs. She yells out the question, 'how long will you be dead?' and measures all her daily desires against the answer. Femme grabs life by the throat and kisses it crimson.

Rosie Lugosi performs for a variety of audiences, including on national television. What is her message?

– As a dominatrix, Rosie Lugosi is interested in

sado-masochism and laughter. She uses comedy to subvert notions of normative sexuality and gender-specific behaviours. Rosie Lugosi terrifies because she's intelligent yet performs 'slut'. Her drag's not about the female fear associated with dressing/acting like a slut. A vampire's always taking back the night. But she doesn't limit herself to preaching to the already converted. Spend a night with her and who can guess what her bite might turn you into...

– Through performance she also undermines the slander against feminists that we have 'no sense of humour', that politics are 'boring or unfashionable'. Rosie Lugosi embodies what Lisa Duggan and Kathleen McHugh [2002] have called the 'howl of laughter at any notion of feminine that takes itself seriously'. As a high-femme performer, Rosie Lugosi invites the gaze of the audience... and then stares them down.

A vampire always takes back the night – a great metaphor for femme-inism! Speaking of, you hosted the show at Femme 2006 with Bubblin' Suga and your Victorian vices were a huge success with the Americans. Having been a femme for decades, what are your thoughts about femme/movements?

– I feel the femme movement is new but it also has a long history. The newness is in discovering this network, this diverse group and that we now have something fresh to articulate. The ancient side is that femmes have always existed – but haven't always had a context other than in relation to others. We've always had a voice but it's not always been heard for what it is. Femme has sewn on all her own sequins. Each one fought for; battle scars she wears like beautiful flags. Maps of where she's come from and where she'll not go back. Her body's her own Remembrance Day of trench warfare years, for those who stood and those who fell and those who kept going over the top.

– To me, femme dares to stand at the boundary of what's normal and what's queer. At first glance she might pass. But she's the double-take. The square peg in the round hole. She doesn't fit but will not wear her soul out trying. She will not force her foot into Cinderella's slipper, isn't waiting for her Prince to come and whisper, to be happy ever after. Femme's afraid, but it never stopped her from doing it anyway. She doesn't force others to wear the shackles of her fears. She will not weigh others down to make herself feel lighter. She doesn't tie herself to either/or. She doesn't fit with binaries of male/female, man/woman, dyke/straight, girl/boy, masculine/feminine, left/right – not even butch/femme. She doesn't like the word *bisexual* because it suggests there are only two genders to choose from, only two sexual stations to shuttle back and forth between. Being femme's always about sexual politics, which for me is about being sex-positive and therefore radical. It is about welcoming the energy of desire whilst accepting the responsibilities that come with it.

Rosie Lugosi, San Francisco 2006
previous spread: Rosie Lugosi. Stockholm 2007

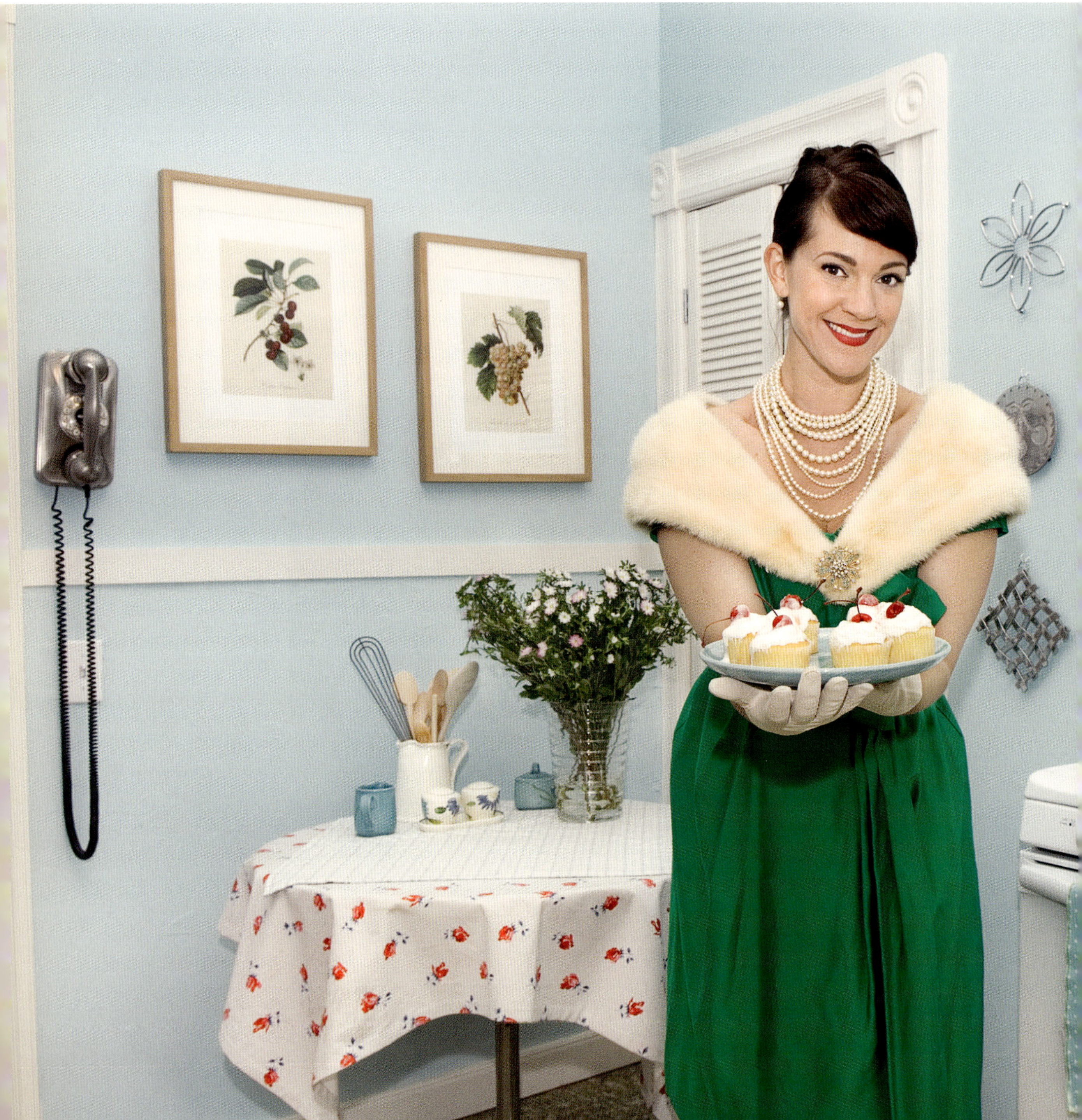

Mommy Far from Heaven

Dear Mistress Morgana,

Meeting you made me understand the power of mommy and of domestic discipline. I found myself wanting to get on my knees and scrub your kitchen floor, because, as you said, 'there's something kinky about everyday objects and settings.' The stern but warm, loving yet strict dominance of the fully clothed and 'mature woman' is intensely powerful in that it's both so queer and so strangely distant and ordinary. Your satisfaction comes from unlocking kinky passions and taboos, and your dominance is fuelled by your gentle smile. Cohabitating only with your chicks, Rita Hayworth and Sophia Loren (who lay eggs for the pound cakes to die for that you make for any birthday boy who's worthy), with a fetish for pearls and retro-fashion dresses and aprons that 'capture the essence of traditional female strength and beauty', you're a femininely twisted Martha Stewart – with crafty hands to imprison butch bottoms in your dungeon and femme ethics to keep you from a white-collar prison.

The photographs made with you in your gorgeous Victorian house in San Francisco are eerily out of this world, much like the white suburban fantasy of that part of US history that you, like many other white femmes, queerly twist. 'To me

Morgana Maye, San Francisco 2006

the 50s is the decade of full bodied women and absent fathers,' you noted, stressing that your fetish must be distinguished from your articulate awareness of the racist reality of that decade's McCarthyism and American Apartheid. Gently directing us like you do the couples that seek you out for BDSM education, we ran to Safeway to get you maraschino cherries and fake cream to put on cup cakes, for your wish to stage the image of the perfect homemaker. With Rita and Sophia, you were the pin-up for 'better homes and chickens' and in mommy's room, where I spent two nights as a guest on a bed made for other activities, you were three faces of Eve.

'Many people are drawn to age play because it is a distinctly grown-up retreat into the carelessness (and powerlessness) of childhood. There's great symbolic significance in the image of a strong woman leaning over you and depriving you of your maturity, your agency, your self-determination,' you said. Far from heaven, things are not quite what they seem.

Raised by your working-class, entrepreneurial mother, a Mary Kay lady, you, like another avenger of feminine props, theoretical fashionista Reina Lewis in London, spoke of feminist activism and the pleasures in the rituals of femininity simultaneously. Marvelling in domesticity and proud of the craftiness your mother – who's also your best friend – has taught you, you were clear when you insisted that 'my femininity is not that of the innocent girl, it is the grown woman.' Speaking of the pleasures of domination, you've gone beyond leather into the scents of vanilla and baby powder. 'Spooning is kinky,' you said with that warm smile. While honouring matrilinear kinship, you described gender as a similacrum, a copy that does not have an original. 'To me femme is about taking the things that oppressed me and using them.'

Rita Hayworth & Morgana Maye, San Francisco, 2006

PALAIS DES
POULETS

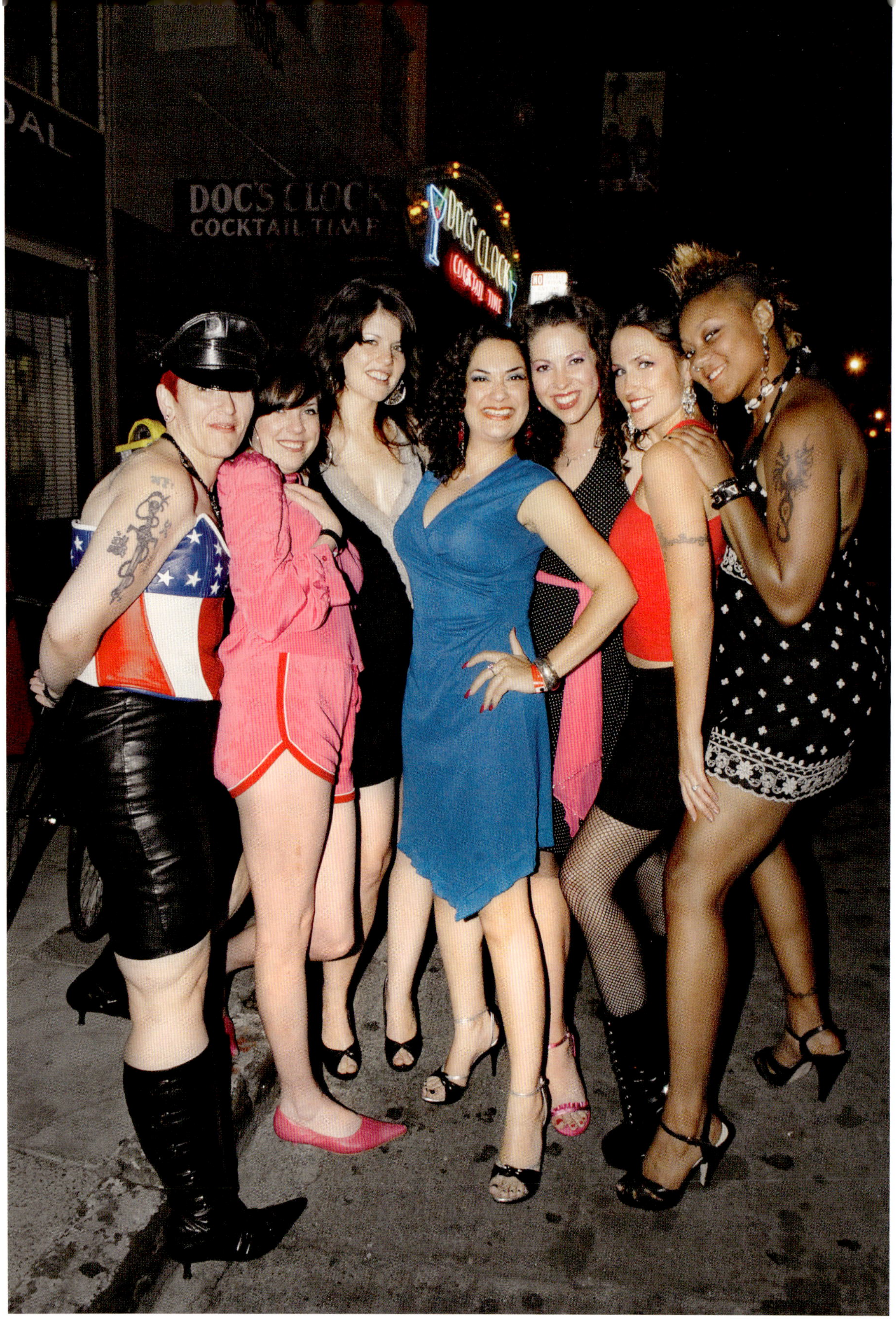
DOC'S CLOCK
COCKTAIL TIME
DOC'S CLOCK
COCKTAIL TIME

Earn Your Reputation

Dear Femme Mafia,

I confess, the prospect of meeting you was a big reason to go to Femme 2006. Stumbling upon your website two years ago and reading the testimonios of a diverse group of articulate and organised Atlanta femmes made my heart skip a beat. At your workshop in San Francisco you explained that after being dissed in local gay press and bars, The Femme Mafia wants to change how femmes are viewed in the world. A fundraiser enabled some of you to go the city that Rachael, proudly Guyanese-Italian, Florida-born Mafia Donna, later called 'freezing cold and with bad food'. You were missing your grits and noted that 'femmes dress very differently in the North. Don't they dress up?' Indeed, you've taught me the importance of regional seasoning in the femme receipe.

The South you all said has a strong butch–femme tradition (particularly in communities of colour), but the Mafia defines femme as an umbrella and welcomes self-identified femmes of all genders and orientations. Rachael, you explained that the aim of the multiracial Mafia is to work against class and race segregation in a city with a long history of both. You hold dinners for femmes 'where drama is left at the door' as you put it, host events in different neighbourhoods, and participate in Atlanta's black and gay Pride. Saliena, you linked finding your inner femme to losing 200 pounds and to you (being in) the Mafia has also reinvigorated the kink community of which you have long been a member. Aly, you explained that after feminism made you put your femininity back in the closet, the Femme Mafia has helped you regain your pride.

Fifteen months later, we visited Atlanta. Another fundraiser contributed to our expenses and you held a 'meet and greet' event at a local bar. Mafia members and allies offered us meals and beds, drinks and rides, because, as y'all kept saying 'hospitality is just the Southern way.' It was a whirlwind of house calls, a queer thanksgiving of 'Turducken', and visits to local hotspots for photo shoots and cruising. Meeting and collaborating with you was a true gift.

Rachael, you're a natural born dominatrix who enjoys getting your heels licked and you 'really' bossed. I don't think I could ever pull off your 'which one of you handsome butches would like to buy me a drink?' routine. A lover of *America's Top Model* and your red-tailed boa constrictor, you're very proudly 'shoulders back, chin up' and 'have very little patience for cowardice'. And Andi, with a certificate in conflict resolution you're cut out to be a vice Donna! You worked your charm on uncle Del, insisting that 'I'm sure as hell not as innocent as I look'. Like Rachael you spoke of being read as white, despite your Caribbean heritage. Cooking in your gorgeous trolley house, you spoke of how 'femme is being free of guilt of liking the apron. True feminism is about respecting all women's right to choose how they want to live their lives. That can include being a stay at home mom and enjoying serving guests. The difference is the freedom to do it in a way that is radical, liberating and queer.'

Saliena, Lindsay, Aly, Rachael, Christina, Carey and Marla, Femme Mafia in San Francisco 2006

Rian, you showed up smiling for the freezing photo shoot in the park and made us all heat up. Like many Mafia members, you're a southern girl and you spoke of how your family lost everything in hurricane Katrina. Recruited by the Donna, your co-worker at Georgia State, you're pursuing your degree in hospitality studies and said 'femme is about learning how to be comfortable and powerful in my body as I maneuver and negotiate my woman identity.'

And Joelle, it sure was a pleasure to meet Miss Hedonism 2007! I will never forget your fishnet dress worn to the 'Mansion Party' you generously took this white girl to. An Ivy League graduate and social worker from Milwaukee with a fondness for ladies and Miller Lite, you called yourself 'a mixed-race feminist nudist and a fat-positive lover of lip gloss and living decadently'. To you being femme is a form of personal activism: 'It is a platform to engage in conversations that stem from people presuming I'm straight. Since I am outspoken enough to regularly out myself as a lesbian in straight spaces I help people understand that queer is not always the way you look, it's just who you are. Besides, my legs and ass just look a whole lot better when I'm wearing stilettos!'

Tina, you wrote us a moving letter: 'I may not stand out in my boring purple top and jeans, but I want to represent nonetheless. I'm very proudly bisexual and had a very strict religious upbringing so my family are not happy about it. Moving to Atlanta was one of the best decisions of my life. I fell in love with the Femme Mafia. They are warm, kind, funny, beautiful, powerful women. I don't have to prove anything and I was simply welcomed into the group and, through it, the rest of the community. I feel comfortable being myself and have a sense of sisterhood. I feel our collective power when we get together and take over any place we go in our stilettos.'

Aly, you're proudly married and preoccupied with baby fever. You offered a manifesto on femme (and) motherhood: 'What separates femme motherhood from straight is the same thing that separates femme from feminine: intention. I'm not femme because I was born that way. I'm femme because I decided to be. Likewise, I can't be a mother by accident or very easily. Femme motherhood is intentional, wanted and worked for. Having a genderqueer partner complicates matters because if someone asks about my child's father, I can't say, "Oh, Johnny has two mommies!" My eating disorder makes me partly afraid of the effects pregnancy will have on my body but I'm so in awe that my little ol' body could do something as brilliant as create and nourish and expel a human being! I'm really looking forward to thanking my body

Carey & Turner, Atlanta 2007 | Atlanta Femme Mafia, Paris, Decatur 2007

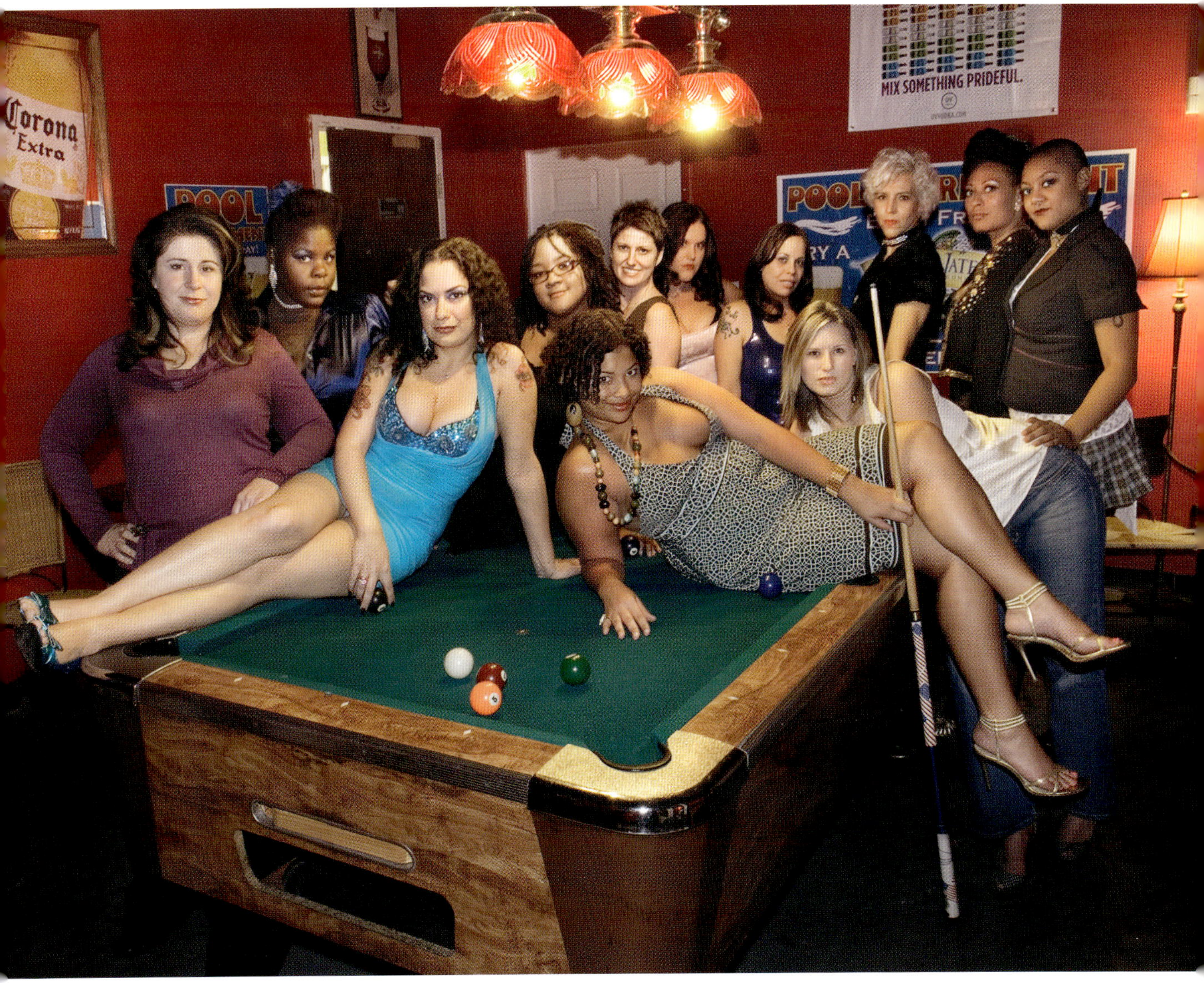
Corona
Extra
MIX SOMETHING PRIDEFUL.
POOL

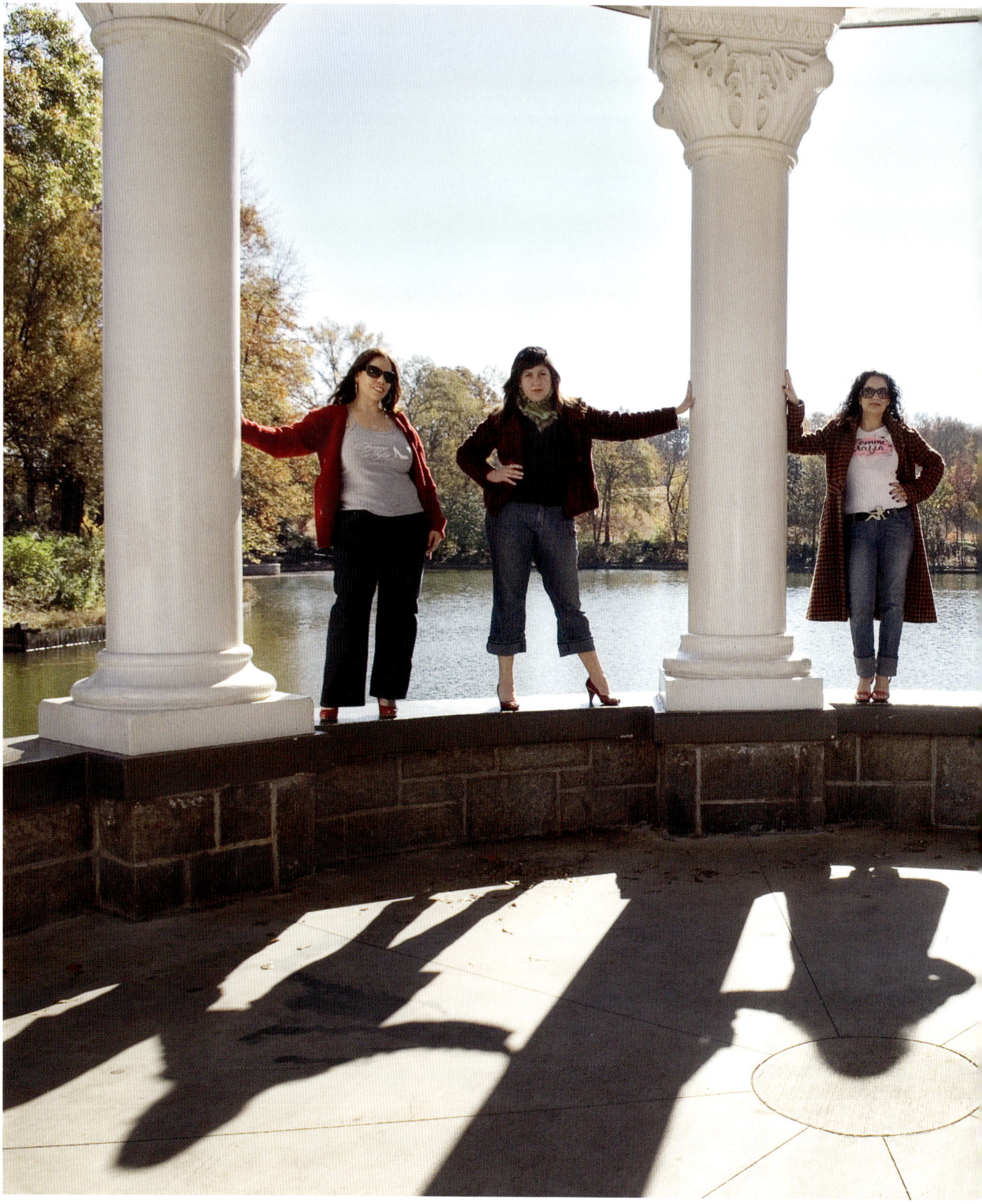

every day for my children. Also, I can't wait to finally have big tits – if only for a few months.'

Yes ma'am, as all the Atlanta butches entitled us. And with Turner as your resident femme-identified FTM happily sitting on Carey's fierce femme activist lap redefining femme-on-femme desire, all in all, you have all pointed to the variety of what femme can be in one location. It's no wonder you all have Maura as your own ethnographer. I predict you will have at least a book of your own.

In the past three years the Atlanta Femme Mafia has received national attention and inspired an additional five chapters at least: Milwaukee, St Louis, Chicago, Springfield and the Twin Cities. In Atlanta you have 175 members and there are two more local femme organisations in the queer mecca of the south, meaning there are so many we didn't get to meet. Through the strength of numbers and 'moving in packs' (and yes, a queer hint of that 'debutante ball' tradition) you have earned your reputation. Rachael, you said that 'the idea of the Mafia – and the pink gun logo has no trigger by the way – is about protection and security for its members. It is about about being aggressive and unapologetic.' No doubt.

Debby, Andi, Rachel, Joelle & Marla, Atlanta 2007

Defying the Laws of Ageism

Sweet Maria,

You are one of the brave and vocal femmes in Stockholm who really has politicised queer femininity. We met in my Gender Studies course and since then we've had many debates about femme, usually with you consuming large quantities of Pepsi. 'It's my body's task to critique moralising attitudes about how one is supposed to act to get approval and access to space,' you once said. 'My words and actions generally do everything wrong but I'm never a victim.' A queen of thriftstore shopping, you style many Stockholm queers and immediately labelled me 'so nineties'. Fair enough. Aside from Audrey in *Twin Peaks*, you are obsessed with 'verbal sluttery, being a brilliant student, looking good in photos and having more friends than *anyone* on Facebook'.

You are entirely unapologetically over the top and will immediately make a dance floor anywhere you can. 'I've been fascinated by feminine aesthetics, loved adorning myself and been excited about ladies as long as I can remember. Still, my femininity has never looked quite right, always too colourful and sprinkled with odd accessories. It's never bothered me, even though people have had the bad manners of noting that it's queer – in the bad sense of the word. Who cares? They have issues, not me. I started calling myself femme, fine-tuned my actions and made them queer feminist strategies. Why not become more annoying, more slutty and more resistant?'

You are often the centre of attention and yet always aware of injustices. Your undergraduate thesis explored femme, ageism and agency. 'Just like there is an essentialist idea about what femininity "is", tied to biologically female bodies, people think about age as a "natural" linear development. Your behaviours and opinions, the way you are in your body, are always measured against a presumed universal idea of "acting your age". Because femininity is often infantilised, to be young and femme makes your chances of getting respect minimal. I get great pleasure from demanding space, in school or in any social situation. I also question who has the authority to speak for femmes. Why do "older" femmes get more space just because they have had more time to acquire such a position? Ageism makes "older" people's stories and experiences more valued.'

On moving in the world as a femme you often talk about strategies. 'You have to trust that you have all the power to fight back. Most people know when they are being oppressive so if you call them on it, you embarrass them. And the femme scores again! Even if my femme companions are not many, they are big in hearts, brains and bravery. Femme affinity goes further, louder, stronger and faster than all those losers who tell us to calm down and shut up can possibly imagine. Maybe it's hubris, but I think everyone loves me and my femmeness. Probably because I am so charming and have such fabulous clothes!' Yes – and because your 'vaginal laughter' is contagious.

Maria Lönn, Stockholm 2007

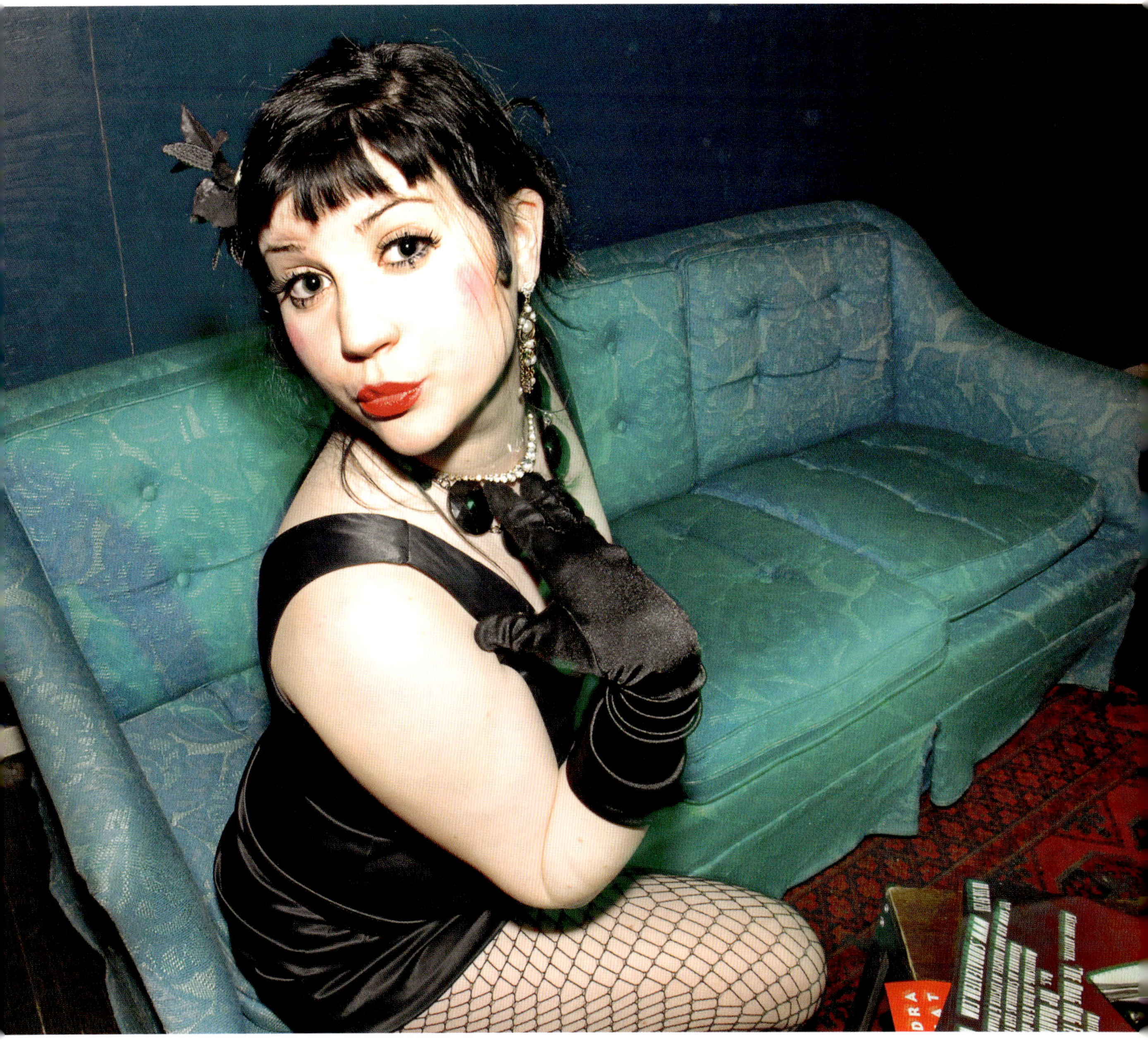

140

LOIS WEAVER | Still Counting

1

2

At 3 I sat in the lap of Virginia and marvelled at the curvature of the earth. Virginia is the name of a state in the Southern United States but it was also the name of my mother and it was in her lap that I felt my girl body lean, lengthen and mould itself against the voluptuous and humid flesh of her Blue Ridge Mountains.

4

When I was 5 I stood on the dining room table, holding the hem of my dress in both hands, and sang 'How Much Is that Doggie in the Window'.

And by the age of 6 I had discovered longing. I kept my lavender patent leather purse in the top drawer of a chest full of Aunt Edna's oversized corsets and Virginia's extra tablecloths. Edna wore costume jewellery, tail-biting neck furs and rode the train with a matching set of luggage. When she came to stay she took me to Woolworth's. Dressed and ready to go one Saturday, I ran back for my purse. I tiptoed and reached my hand into the hiding place but it was gone. Gone and with it every trace of my little girl liberty. Virginia had decided. I was too big for such a tiny purse and it was too dangerous to encourage a love for lavender patent leather.

7

8

Lois Weaver, London 2007

9 was the year I spent most of my just before bedtime in front of the mirror, practising: my kisses, my tantrums and my strip-tease. I wanted to be Miss America or rather I wanted to participate in the pageant and I figured my best shot in the talent competition would be to do a striptease. So I stood in front of the mirror with my pyjamas and a towel and worked on my routine. I was going to *strip* for Miss America!

10

11 was my favourite number, a perfect parallel, impossible to reverse and heaven for a dyslexic who instead of falling in love with God fell in love with the preacher's wife. Her creamy skin, perfectly drawn lips and teased hair teased me, until I had no choice but to sit next to her and softly and tenderly attempt to play 'Just As I Am' on the upright piano in the front room of the parsonage. She coached me and coaxed me from a shining Sunbeam for Jesus to a cardboard crowned and plastic sceptred Queen Regent of the Girl's Auxiliary of the Mount Pleasant Baptist Church. Praise God for a chance to be queen.

12

13

14

15

Sweet 16 and bored stiff, sweet Jesus, with no other choice but to become a cheerleader. I wasn't pretty but they said I had a good personality, which made up for homemade clothes and a complete lack of eyebrows. Plus I had good thighs and a mother who could sew. But as much as I liked the belonging, I hated being the same and was constantly at risk of busting out of uniform. My release came in the form of a job in the Deb Boutique of a local department store where I was outfitted with the first and only Mary Quant mini dress and pair of white Courreges Go Go boots, the Blue Ridge Mountains had ever seen. I took Virginia off homemade uniform duty and put her to work on homemade Mod and vowed never to wear a Villager shirtwaist again.

17

18

When I was 19 I left the world of mothers and sisters but not Virginia. I travelled deeper into the Blue Ridge to attend college with 4,000 women over half of which were physical education majors. 'What do you want to major in?' they asked me. 'Drama', I answered, not realising that most of the drama took place in dormitory hallways where volleyball players wooed the future primary school teachers of America. My theatre training was a conservatory of conversion: converting the Home Economics lab into a theatre, classics into contemporaries and girls into men. I got to play all the parts including Childie in *The Killing of Sister George*. I wasn't a lesbian but I had a 'best friend' who was a soft ball major, drove a red convertible and filled my room with roses every morning. I wasn't a lesbian but my heart skipped a beat each time I heard Sister George describe how she felt when she stepped into the wet and talcum powdered footprints left by Childie after her bath. I wasn't a lesbian but if I had known then what I know now…

By now I'm 20. The faint porous lines of a blueprint are starting to emerge from the developing solution of workshops on collective process, articles on women's liberation in *Time Magazine*, a friend's just on the verge of legal abortion, Antigone's rage against the state, Kent State, bellbottomed cords, embroidered undershirts and *Hair* '…long beautiful hair; Shining, gleaming, steaming, flaxen, waxen; Give me down to there, hair!'

21

22

23

24

At the age of 25 I became a feminist. I took the long road to New York City through inner city Baltimore where I got my hippie hair tangled in the jeans and T-shirts of the peace and justice movement. Virginia forgot to tell me about lots of things. Menstruation was one of them. Another was the unbridled patriarchy of the Left. I soon left Baltimore in search of sisterhood. I scoured the *Village Voice*, sat alone in the Women's Coffee House on Seventh Avenue and on the back pew of feminist meetings at Washington Square Church. I spoke to no one. I couldn't break the code. Finally, I found a group of women who simply wanted to tell the stories of their lives. We became Spiderwoman: Native American, African-American and white working-class women making theatre out of the rags and tags of our everyday. We wove stories of untold violence and family disappointments, appropriated dirty jokes, and wrung new meanings out of the old songs of romance. We were both the princess and the frog. We were liberated feminists for those who had never seen such wanton display and women in need of liberation for those who were shocked when they saw us put on our make-up *after* the show.

26

27

I became a femme feminist at the age of 28, just after Spiderwoman made friends with the drag artists Hot Peaches. We were due to perform in Berlin within days of each other but when Spiderwoman arrived, our trunk of costumes did not. Hot Peaches came to the rescue with a suitcase filled with feather boas, sequined gowns, vast wigs and sparkling platform shoes. This was the 70s and we had become a feminist company who made our costumes from children's toys and cooking utensils. As we began to dress in this finery we secretly knew we would never be the same again. We would never make a show that did not involve glitter, false eyelashes and real attitude. Like Venus from the clamshell, Tammy WhyNot was born from this trunk. I couldn't sing or keep a beat but the great pile of synthetic blonde hair, the push-up bra, the familiar hillbilly accent, the thrill of performing fantasy enabled me to embrace my childhood distaste for country music and my fear of my trailer trash roots. Tammy started work on her remix, 'Stand ON Your Man'.

29

by the time I was 30, I had been pushed up against the wall by a few prominent lesbian feminists asking me didn't I realise that Tammy's push-up bra was offensive, that I was just titillating and tempting the men in the audience and wasn't I *really* a lesbian? I liked the feeling of my back against the wall and knew for a fact that it wasn't the men that I wanted to tempt. So in 'An Evening Of Disgusting Songs And Pukey Images' I created a fake-blood sucking, soft-shoe dancing bouncer in blue lamé who slithered against the dark wall before pouncing into the light and onto the necks of the unsuspecting female audience. This performance of predatory lust and sweet contamination left a blue lipstick kiss on the necks of a long list of victims and the taste of real blood on my lips.

I was finally a lesbian at 31. Cue the entrance of the butch lesbian and the beginnings of my lesbian femme career. She was George Jones to my Tammy WhyNot, Spencer Tracy to my Katharine Hepburn and I was Barbra Streisand to her Neil Diamond. We mined everything we knew: movies, television, rhythm and blues, working-class parents, old-school lesbian friends to find the precious metals we needed to build our altar to the blessed binary and the foundation of a new theatrical company: Split Britches. It was an old formula with a new twist. We played and displayed butch–femmeness in order to disrupt the norm, unsettle the status quo. It was both sex toy and work ethic and the key to the theatrical success of the company. Playing femme mixed my business with my pleasure.

32

33

34

I turned 35 and bleached my hair all over and for good. I sat up in the stylist's chair, looked in the mirror and knew this was what I had been born to be: a blonde femme.

36

37

38

39

Turning 40 wasn't nearly as difficult as being 41, femme and sharing the stage with a drag queen. I loved my drag queen brothers and benefited from their delicious theatricality and femme expertise. But I also struggled with the assumptions that they knew more about being women than women themselves and envied their overwhelming strength and power when it came to taking stage. I could see that their strength was in the performance of resistance. They were resisting society's idea of what it meant to be a man just like butches were resisting the cultural expectations of what it meant to be a woman and the power of both the drag queen and the butch lay in the space between, between the norm and the resistance to the norm. I wanted that space for myself: to both resist and embrace the feminine, to be a woman impersonating a woman and to take stage as a femme on her own, without the signifying arm of a butch. I set about trying to define and create the resistant femme.

42

43

44. After classic and exhaustive attempts at impersonation (Mistinguett, Stella Kowlaski, Marilyn Monroe) Tammy WhyNot came to the rescue. Her love of pink and orange chiffon, her invincible sense of wonder and her ability to fail gloriously and without shame were her super powers and she became my hyper-femme super hero. Tammy's wisdom of Why Not gave the definition I was searching for: resistant femme n. a highly competent woman who just looks like she needs a little help.

45

46

At 47 I got my first real job. Teaching at a university in London was perfect for Tammy's project What Tammy Needs To Know... But while she fed her voracious appetite for knowledge, my roots got longer, my heels lower and my clothes looser. I entered my low maintenance/highly professional femme phase. However, Tammy kept watch, ever ready with sling backs, wigs and lashes.

48

49

Reaching 50 wasn't such a big deal but it was a big number and to prove it I made a performance in which I counted it out slowly, one number at a time, stopping occasionally to reflect silently on one number's story or another year's significance. I finished by pointing out that if I were a piece of furniture, I would be a cherished and valuable mid-century antique.

51

52

53

54

Now let's talk about sex. I was a late bloomer but still, as an ageing femme of 55 I have celebrated 25 years of divine, magnificent, outstanding, assorted and sordid lesbian sex. Listing the brevity and longevity, dominance and passivity would require a separate performance of counting: 1, 2, 3, 4, and counting... each lover, each tender nudge or sharp request, each hurdle of fear that once crossed gave way to safe surrender and then more urgent desire, 5, 6...

56 and I am both hungry and satiated. I crave the violence of the grab, the relentless touch, the soul penetrating thrust and yet I often retire to my gentle and complete solitude. The occupation of my age is to build a graceful bridge between the two. Bridge building is a dangerous occupation. There are always casualties: the lost dreams of a latent adolescence, the bruised butch's entreaty, 'but what about me?' and the femme's stronghold on her blessed and enduring vanity. But I have experience and skills developed from a lifetime of longing. And some tools in my chest: gratitude for those who have loved me well, tenderness for my own fragile and eccentric need, energy that is challenged by the young ones and safeguarded by the older and the belief that I will never be too old for the seduction, the courtship and the descent into the sweat and discovery of passion.

57

58 and still counting.

Tammy Why Not, London 2007

145

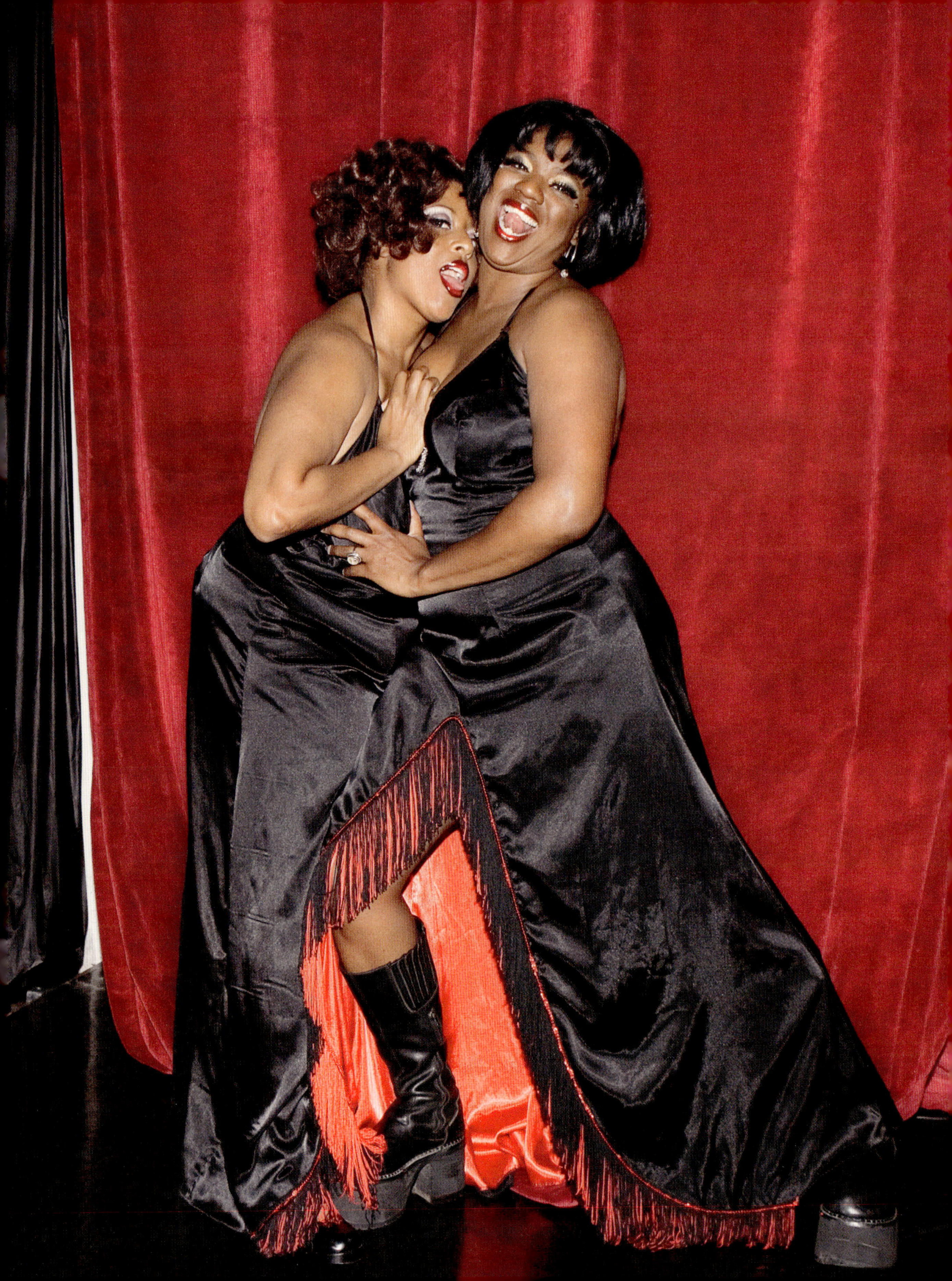

Showgirls queering the stage

DUE TO HETEROSEXISM, both on stage and in the world at large, urban queer communities have a long history of creating their own performance spaces and traditions. Within this gender subversion-centred tradition, queer femininities have a complicated place. Many femme performers argue that bio-queens (women performing femininity), including strippers and burlesque artists, have obvious affinities with the kings and queens of drag and thus deserve space on genderqueer stages. While to the subjects of this book, femme is a lived reality, not 'simply an act', many also use the stage to politicise and render queer femininity visible. As Krista writes, femme-inism is not about an uncritical reproduction of feminine beauty ideals, it's about acknowledging the beauty of all types of queerly feminine bodies, including on stage.

When the second performance night at Femme 2006 was opened by Krista aka Kentucky Fried Woman and Elese Lebsack performing as The Fat Lady and The Bearded Lady, cheekily and seductively stripping to Ani diFranco's song *Freakshow*, it was a commentary and a celebration. The queer audience got two hours of femme-centred spoken word, striptease and burlesque where

Alotta Boutte & Simone de la Getto, Harlem Shake Burlesque, San Francisco 2007

performers both cited and challenged traditional showgirl traditions. By engaging with and at the same time critiquing the growing popularity of neo-burlesque, femme performers demonstrate how showgirl femininities are neither 'natural' nor simply about straight acting. They also stress the importance of addressing the politics of both who is in the spotlight and in the audience.

Simone de La Getto, real estate agent and mother, with a long-term profile in San Francisco's sex positive queer circles, founded Harlem Shake Burlesque, the first all black burlesque troupe of the neo-burlesque era in the US. Harlem Shake Burlesque was started because as Simone says, in the last decade burlesque has 'developed into a pretty white thing' both in terms of performers and audience, including in queer communities. 'An all black troupe causes a stir and the dream was to bring back the significance of Josephine Baker and other early contributors to the development of burlesque. It is still challenging to all white audiences, but they love us,' she said. Harlem Shake Burlesque also performs in areas with predominantly people of colour and seeks to contribute to retrieving a lost history of black performance. In its five years of existence they have inspired showgirls around the country, including Atlanta's Vagina Jenkins.

The hours before a show, in crowded dressing rooms and during rehearsals, are exciting and hectic settings to make images with performers. Here elaborate rituals of costuming and make-up are mixed with showgirl bonding and playful fights over mirror and sound check time. At Frolic in San Francisco Harlem Shake Burlesque shared the stage with among others, The Diamond Daggers, one of the city's several other burlesque troupes, founded by flamenco-trained choreographer and cultural producer Amelia Mae Paradise. An irreverent bearded femme, Amelia cites her own family lineage of Jewish show girls as inspiration and that night her own bearded butch wife Sir Loin Strip aka Sarah Paradise's band Dyspecific were also on the menu.

San Francisco's tradition of do-it-yourself queer production, sliding scale ticket prices and art for political causes is unprecedented in Stockholm. While in London femme performers are regulars on the queer stages of Club Wotever and Transfabulous, Stockholm enjoyed a brief moment of drag kingdom in the early 2000s, but the queer scene is dominated by classic queens, who while entertaining are rarely explicitly political. So what's a queer showgirl to do? In 2006 Stockholm caught the neo-burlesque wave and The Hootchy Kootchy Club began offering titty tassled shows with international burlesque stars. In the Swedish capital where strip-clubs are rare and commercial sex is against the law, the club is regularly packed by an urban mostly middle-class white heterosexual audience that loves showgirls. While the club welcomes queers both on and off the stage and has hosted performers such as the founder of New York's Circus Amok, bearded lady Jennifer Miller, the dildo-wearing zombies of the Drag King Fem Show, Dyke Marilyn and Rosie Lugosi, many queers remain ambivalent about burlesque. The age-old feminist question of whether women taking their clothes off can be subversive ultimately has a lot to do with context and spectatorship. As images of Josephine Wilson's Miss File at The Hootchy Kootchy Club demonstrate, queerly feminine performances evoke a variety of responses from laughter to confusion to disgust, depending on expectations and queer knowledge.

True to the subcultural and activist arts tradition, as the portraits in this book show, many femmes prefer performances based in explicit critiques and commentaries on the world we live in. 'I adore the stage, it's true,' said Solange Garjan, who when we met was getting ready for her first performance as a belly dancer in Tennessee. 'But I've also always done feminist and queer activism and community organising while doing theatre, performance art, poetry and dance. With Black Sphota Cocoon, a women-of-colour theatre ensemble in Chicago, we worked for three

Diamond Daggers, San Francisco 2006 | Amelia & Sarah, San Francisco 2006

149

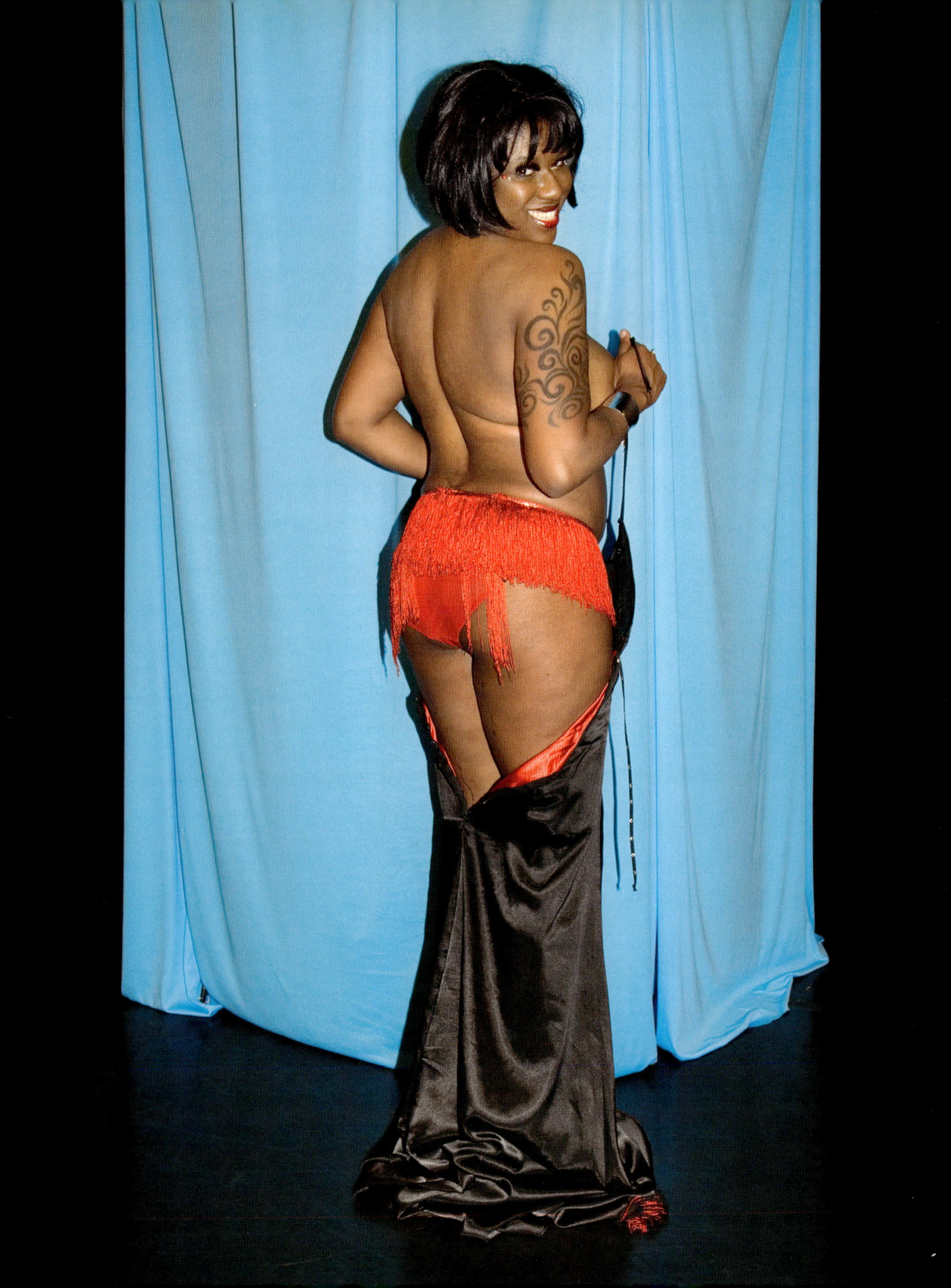

years to represent our experiences by producing our own plays and performance art pieces within our communities.'

Jaheda's Sphere for South Asian queer women performers in Manchester, Leah's Mangos with Chili for Desi queer artists and San Francisco's Liquid Fire, along with big burlesque girls like Jukie Sunshine and Lady Monster, whose work takes on size-ism and racism, sexism and poverty, all actively challenge the white normatively bodied hegemony of most performance and make a femme-inist and anti-racist difference on and off the (queer) stage. Celebrating freaks and diversity as much as classic icons and always begging the question of who is on stage for whom and what it does, femme performance is here to stay. Like Ani DiFranco's *Freakshow* suggests, 'it's about freedom, it's about faking, there's an art to the laughter, there's a science and there's a lot of love and compliance.'

Simone de La Getto, San Francisco 2006

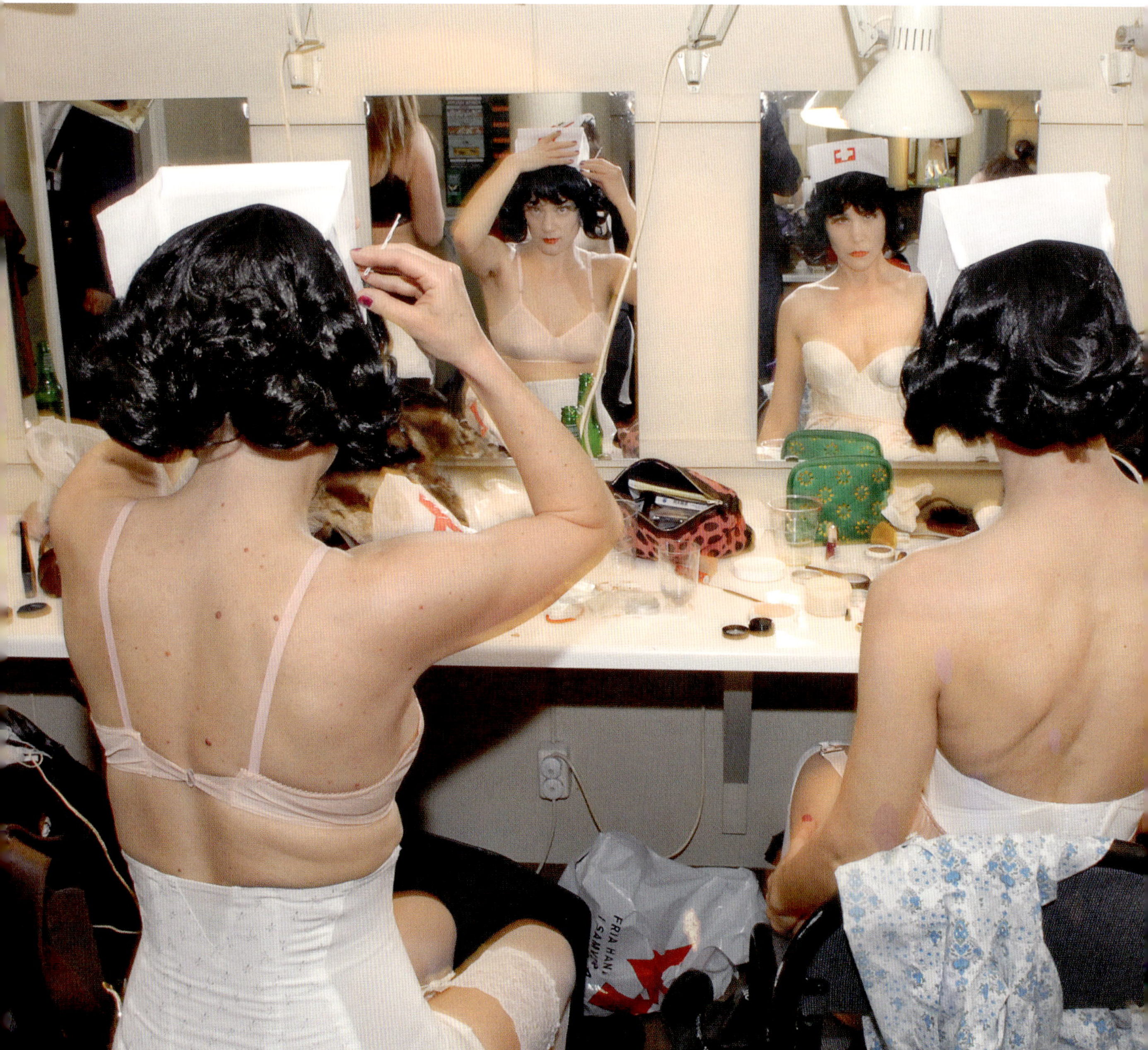

Hootchy Kootchy Hussies, Jorun & Karin, Stockholm 2007 | Jennifer Miller @ The Hootchy Kootchy Club, Stockholm 2007

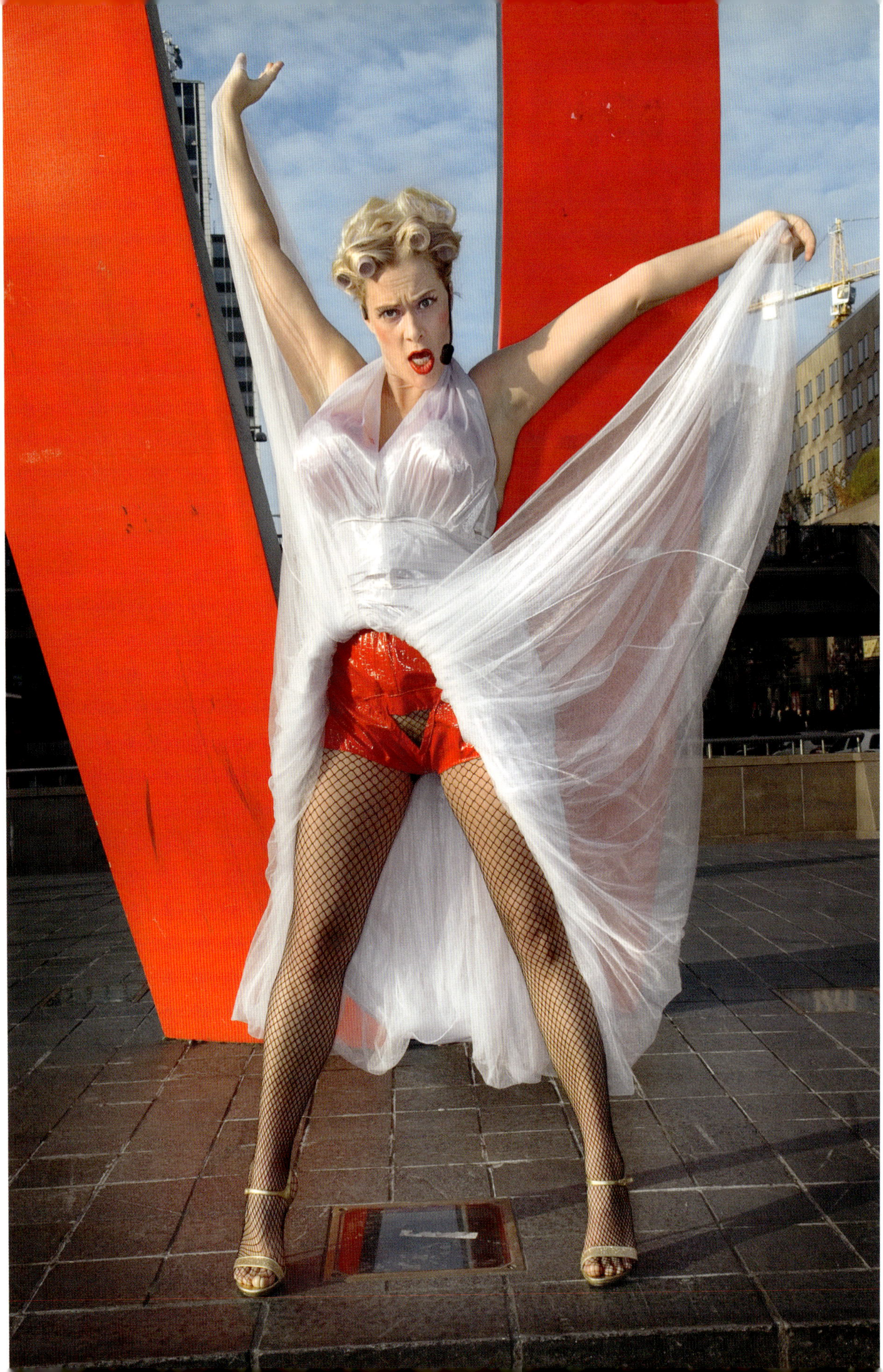

Femme Hag Pussy Power

Dear Maya,

It was party night after International Women's Day in Stockholm when I first laid eyes on the infamous D Muttant, sporting the legendary red hotpants covering all but her pubes, rapping her number one hit 'Lick My Pussy!' to a screaming queer feminist crowd. You later described D Muttant (*mutta* being Swedish slang for pussy) as your personal liberation, a kind of primal scream from a stage: 'D Muttant was my channel to express my anger at society's attempts to squeeze me into boxes. I'd always felt wrong and limited by straight society's views of me as a woman. Too tall, too broad shouldered to wear 7-inch heels, too fat to wear a pearly bikini top, too intellectual to wear a fetish dress. And too nice to holler that patriarchy sucks and that the constant abuse we take in our most private spaces, our identities, must stop. We have to be deprogrammed from heteronormativity. I experimented with being both butchy and slutty, most often I felt like a drag queen. It's fun and liberating to use feminine attributes without giving a fuck as to whether it "suits me".'

Blonde theory indeed.

Maya Hald, Stockholm 2007

In 2007, you were part of the impromptu group we called Blondes Have More Guns as a cheeky comment on the quintessential stereotype of white Scandinavian femininity and to queer up the Hootchy Kootchy Club. Amidst the tittie tassling you also performed as boxing girl Artemis. 'I have a mutable identity. Perhaps I use queerness when it suits me, but I also defend it in the squarest of straight scenes,' you said. As images of Miss File's performance from the same stage show, it was a queer show with a predominantly straight audience that night.

'Femme is a way to question what femininity is. It is expressing a kind of femininity that's a deliberate choice and which in some ways squeaks against standardised femininity,' you later said. 'If that includes being a bit over the top, not being discreet but rather causing discomfort, to allow humour and distance, then count me in,' you added. 'At the same time, femme for me remains tied to the butch–femme binary in lesbian contexts, and even though I'm more queer than straight, I'm not a dyke. I'm more of a femme hag.' When you performed at the demo for a nineteen-year-old girl whose rapists got off because she was known to be a slut into 'ruff sex', you asked your high-heeled sisters to join you on stage as you rapped for sluts against rape. 'I've always felt welcomed in the queer world and it all starts with both the feminist struggle and the ideal world that I somehow still dream of.'

Maya D Muttant's performative politics have always explored femininity. Legend has it that in art school you did a live performance at Sergel's Torg in Stockholm, a commentary on H&M's annual Christmas underwear ads and the beauty industry. Behind a glass window, you slowly shaved your entire body with a razor, ending with all your hair, to point to the labour of 'natural' femininity.

Back at Sergel's Torg, making a feminist spectacle of yourself for the artist's camera, meant discovering new things. 'The original idea with D Muttant was to use girly attributes like a pink tutu, glitter, blonde curls and a lot of make-up while simultaneously being a complete bulldozer spewing sexual politics, venting personal aggressions and not giving a flying fuck what people thought. Bringing her out on the street changed the space; the red vaginal lips competing with the phallus sculpture in the square fountain that seemed put there just for us. We heard a gang of teenage girls discussing whether I was a man or a woman and it made me feel happy and strong. As someone who is most often seen as a woman (here I look like a twisted 50s pin-up) it was a relief to be seen as something in between. D Muttant's mission has become mine: to preach to the world that we must be able to see attributes for what they are, just that. They may define us for the moment, but not in depth or for all time.'

Bitte, Ulrika, Jenny, Ann & Maya @ The Hootchy Kootchy Club, Stockholm 2007 | Josefin Brink, The Vänsterpartiet Office, Stockholm 2006

FÖR
FRIHETEN
OCH
FRAMTIDEN
SKU
40 år
1903-1943
självförsvar för
tjejer i skolan

VÄNSTERPARTIET
PARTIKANSLIET

Parliamentarian Pin-up

Dear Josefin,

Hur sexig är jag nu motherfucker? ('How sexy am I now, motherfucker?') It was Stockholm Pride, maybe 1999 and on stage was Vagina Grande, a feminist ska band, singing about fighting back against sexual harassment. You on your sax with a bunch of chicks who've all been instrumental to feminist sexual politics in Sweden as filmmakers, performance artists and feminist theorists. All of you loud, proud, political and passionate. I was stunned.

At the time you were the editor of the feminist magazine *Bang*, bringing hard-core working-class perspectives to a fairly academic publication. Now you hold the keys to the party office of Vänsterpartiet (The Left Party). When we made this image, you were running for parliament after years of grassroots work. The 2006 Swedish election not only put a right-wing alliance in government, it also got you, an out dyke and a vocal radical feminist in opposition. 'The main and huge difference about being in parliament compared to my previous activism is doing it full-time and getting paid an insane amount of money. Also, the institution makes it different,' you said. 'When I was a journalist I argued for what was important to me. Now I have to represent the party and can't say things I have to eat later. So it's more responsibility but also a lot more meaningful to be part of a movement rather than just having opinions you can't back up.'

You've remained loyal to your own brand of fierce femininity, a 'punk-rockabilly-Marilyn-mix-*Svenne* style (with a white Swedish touch)' as you called it. People in parliament, you said, are so civilised that they never comment on appearance and being a woman in politics is not as hard as on a regular job. 'The woman who cleans my office – how weird is *that* anyway? – digs my high heels and asks how I can walk in them. And sure, slimy old men have sent text messages after TV debates commenting on my looks. When you've buried your soul arguing against unemployment cuts or for abortion rights, it's pretty lame that all they do is drool over you,' you noted. But it won't stop you from giving powerful May Day speeches or standing up at town meetings, always sporting red.

Not one for labels, you said: 'Yeah, I guess I could be femme, but that's not exactly how I introduce myself or what I put in the phonebook. But I do love all the typical feminine attributes and don't see them as oppressive or degrading in themselves. On the contrary, I feel powerful in red heels and red lacquered nails. I don't know how good of a role model I really am, but I guess it means something if a queer girl who's had a pretty rough and messy life actually dares to step forward and take issue with important old men who've never done anything but politics.'

Indeed.

Josefin Brink, The Vänsterpartiet Office, Stockholm 2006

Rock Stars and Riot Grrls

Oh Starry babes,

Ukuleles, heart-shaped gee-tars and electric blues, saxophone ska beats and punk rock – the 90s brought fresh aesthetics and art forms, placing new rock stars in the hall of queer feminine fame. Bitch, Leslie Mah, Shawna Virago, and Michelle Tea, all literary riot grrls, you each femme the queer punk revolution in your own particular way. You call attention to the heterosexism of the art scene with poetic power and femme-inist anger in kickass boots and baby-doll dresses, inspiring queer girls everywhere to embrace girliness and speak their truths and me to write fan mail.

    Bitch, you drove us into the Jersey night to your parked touring RV. Having seen you on dyke march stages and college scenes, it was a special evening of making images and conversation while you sang a soft version of 'Staying Alive' and played your ukulele, 'to relax your face' you said. Posing barefoot, dreamy and hippie-like, you told tales of high school pompom squads and navigating complex loyalties to women and transfolks at Michigan's Women's Music Festival, of Sparkly Queens and Drag King Bars on tour with fellow musician Animal and of growing up learning to perform femininity in your British mother's basement dance school in Detroit. Like Michelle

Bitch, New Jersey 2007

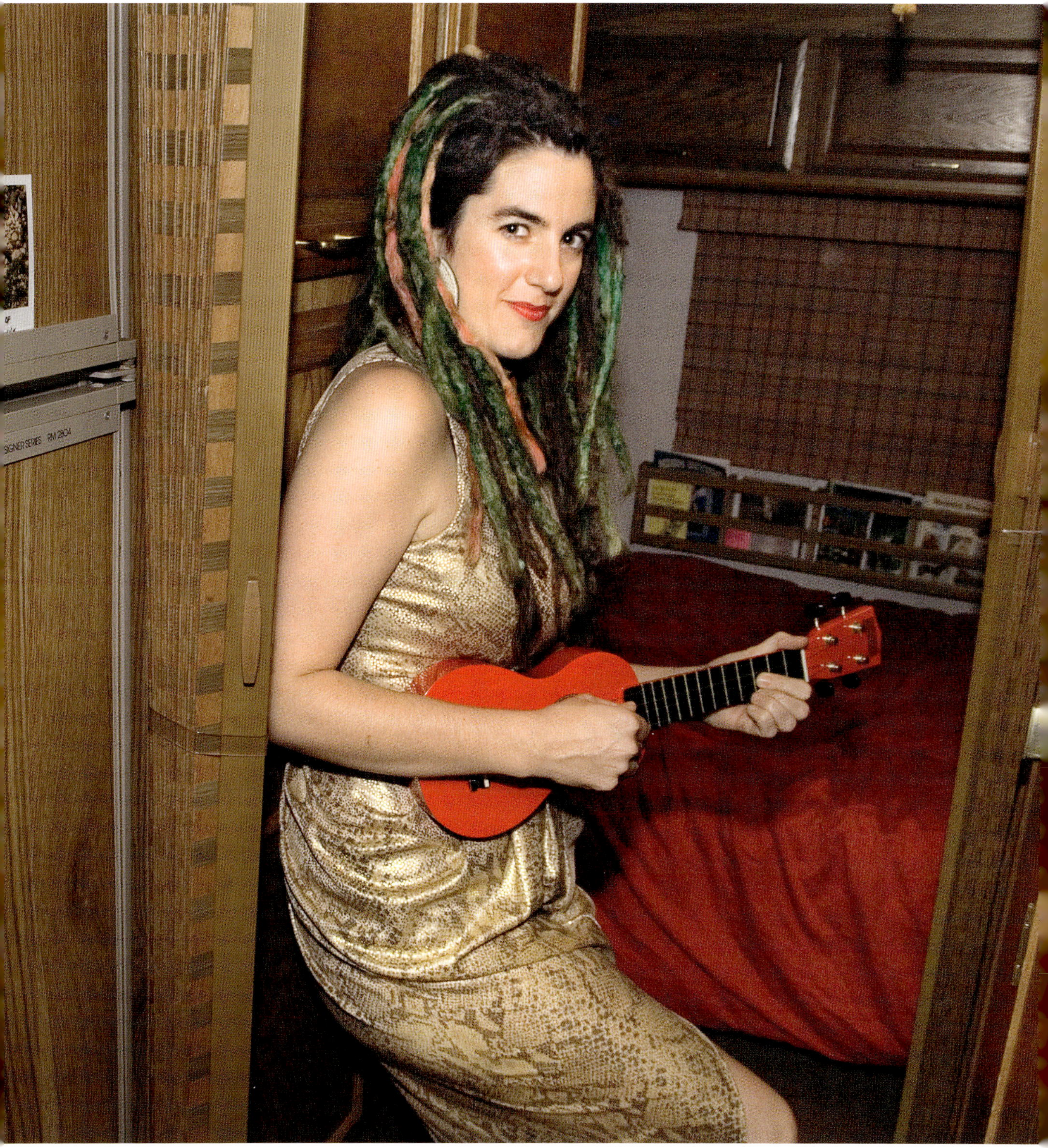

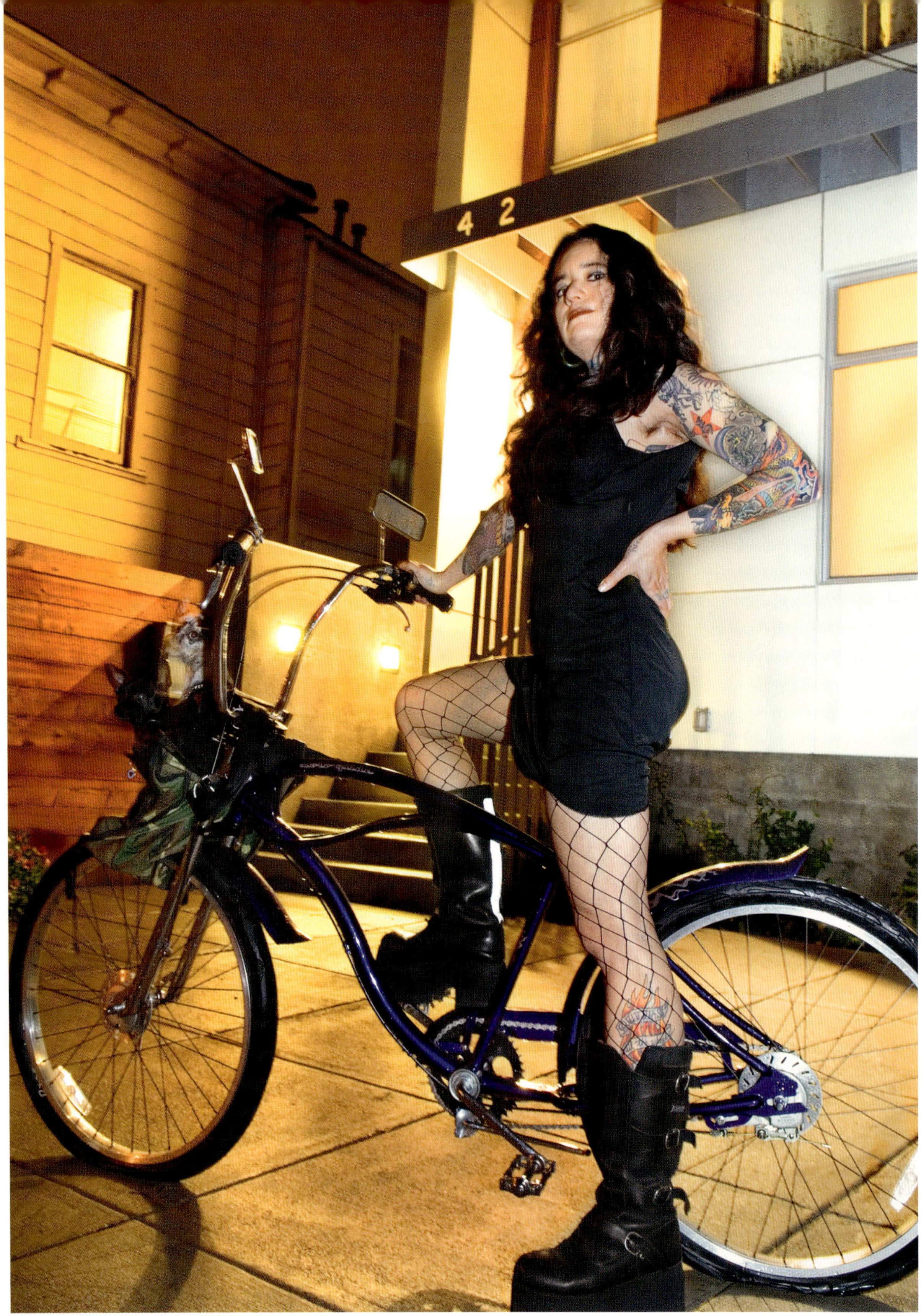
4 2

Tea, you spoke of mixed feelings towards Los Angeles and dressing up for Hollywood parties with your lover Daniela Sea. A '6-foot Bitch' no longer feeling too tall for the world, you're staying true to your righteous babe roots and spoke of your love for dreads and jamming, of exploring your inner stud, and of feeling femme in a hoodie and jeans.

Shawna Virago, you're not only a rock star, but a role model for activist bravery. You brought your electric blue guitar to the bathroom of the Lexington, San Francisco's dyke bar, as a commentary on the continued trans exclusion of many women's spaces – though the Lex has been very supportive of you. You don't call yourself femme but feel sisterhood with Kate Bornstein, even as you 'transitioned before the release of *Gender Outlaw*'. You are both anarchist girls and role models for survival in a cruel world. An articulate songwriter and trans activist, you said: 'Like most femmes, I'm always trying to understand the shifting parameters of my own femininity. I know first hand what it's like to carve out self-defined space while experiencing sexism and looksism. I have found potential for alliances since we're all experiencing these challenges. But does anyone know what gender is? Then please tell me 'cause I'm outta answers. The best I can come up with is that it's a lot like water-proof mascara, which claims to be permanent but actually comes off quite easily. But since I've been on estrogen I've become better at complex math and operating heavy machinery.'

Leslie Mah, you wore dresses on stage in the 90s before it became riot grrl. Yours became its very own tough style as your mixed-race and Colorado femme punk roots emerged in full force in songs like 'Estrofemme' and 'Hapa Girl' during your days with Tribe 8. I'll always remember you opening the San Francisco show for Siouxie Sioux's last tour, and seeing you ride your bike around the Mission. Now you tattoo 'for love, for happiness and because like with music, I can't not do it'. An Oakland homeowner, with chihuahuas and lover, you're a testament to the possibility of staying punk rock when you get off the touring bus. Femme to you is a fuck off to racism and sexism at once, 'rowdy and queer, like a transition' as you and Bitch both said in the film *Female to Femme*.

Michelle Tea, nobody narrates incidents in the lives of proto femme-inist bad girls of all ages better than you. My love of tea began with your hosting Sister Spit, a touring troupe of queer girls with fiery eyes and words scribbled on napkins roaring off stages across America, redefining poetry for a new generation. In the late 90s, you and Sini Anderson gathered the laureates of genderqueer life in the outskirts of capitalism's wasteland, the grey zone between art and prostitution. At the height of dot.com invasion, like now, you still hold on and keep it real. Your books chronicle the passionate mistakes and heroic horrors of everyday girlhood: poverty, abuse, the sexism of underground cultures and more but you never get stuck on victimhood. When we met again, your stories were about to hit Hollywood and, laughing about 'not wanting to look broke', you held up your first ever 'lady suit' bought on Polk Street, vintage, of course. Having never embraced femme for yourself (tho 'placed there by others'), you prefer it as a noun and noted that 'femme power lies in letting go of your awkwardness and seeing yourself as sexy'.

Leslie Mah, Oakland 2006

Sofie Wahlström, like so many riot grrls in the wild west, you've made *flicka* (girl) the starting point for queer politics. You're a poster girl for the Stockholm asexuality movement and you march with pink shock in the black block.

'I often get questioned why I chose girliness as an expression and a weapon, when it's so often seen as a difficult path to get one's message across. The subtext is that girliness is nice and not dangerous and that it would've been "easier" to be read as subversive if I'd used queer masculinity or a loud, ho-like bad girl femininity that can never be interpreted as (hetero)normative. That would have been to surrender. A flicka femme marvels in childish, naïve, crazy girly things and gets insanely happy and cheered up by seeing and surrounding herself by such things. It's not some kind of distanced irony but challenges the idea of girliness as cute and nice. Pushing ageist norms, as a twenty-four-year old (I don't identify as grown-up) I too can use those things that are usually saved for little girls, which are not seen as suitable. I refuse to grow out of being a flicka.'

Miss Juniversum. Jun, you are a fiercely 'half-Japanese' Stockholm transplant to Malmö, where you shake things up with your love for 'bad taste', putting your entrepreneurial skills to work in your kitsch store. 'Swedes have a lot of issues with Asian femininity. I've always wished I didn't look so "small and cute" because that is not how I feel,' you said. 'My roots are punk – at thirteen my dad shaved my head for me and through school my crazy outfits always stood out. At sixteen I decided I wanted to "fit in" but people either talked over my head or infantilised me. I had a feminist awakening and shaved my head again. Suddenly everyone thought I was radical. I grew up with Miyasaki films sent from my relatives and in those films girls are allowed to be many things compared to western animated films. As a kid in a mixed suburban neighborhood, I never consciously thought I was inspired by Japanese feminine heroines but I'm sure it had an impact, along with 90s tough girls like Courtney Love, Björk, and Skin.'

Sofie & Felicia, Stockholm 2006 | Michelle Tea, San Francisco 2006 | next spread: Shawna Virago @ The Lexington, San Francisco 2006

165

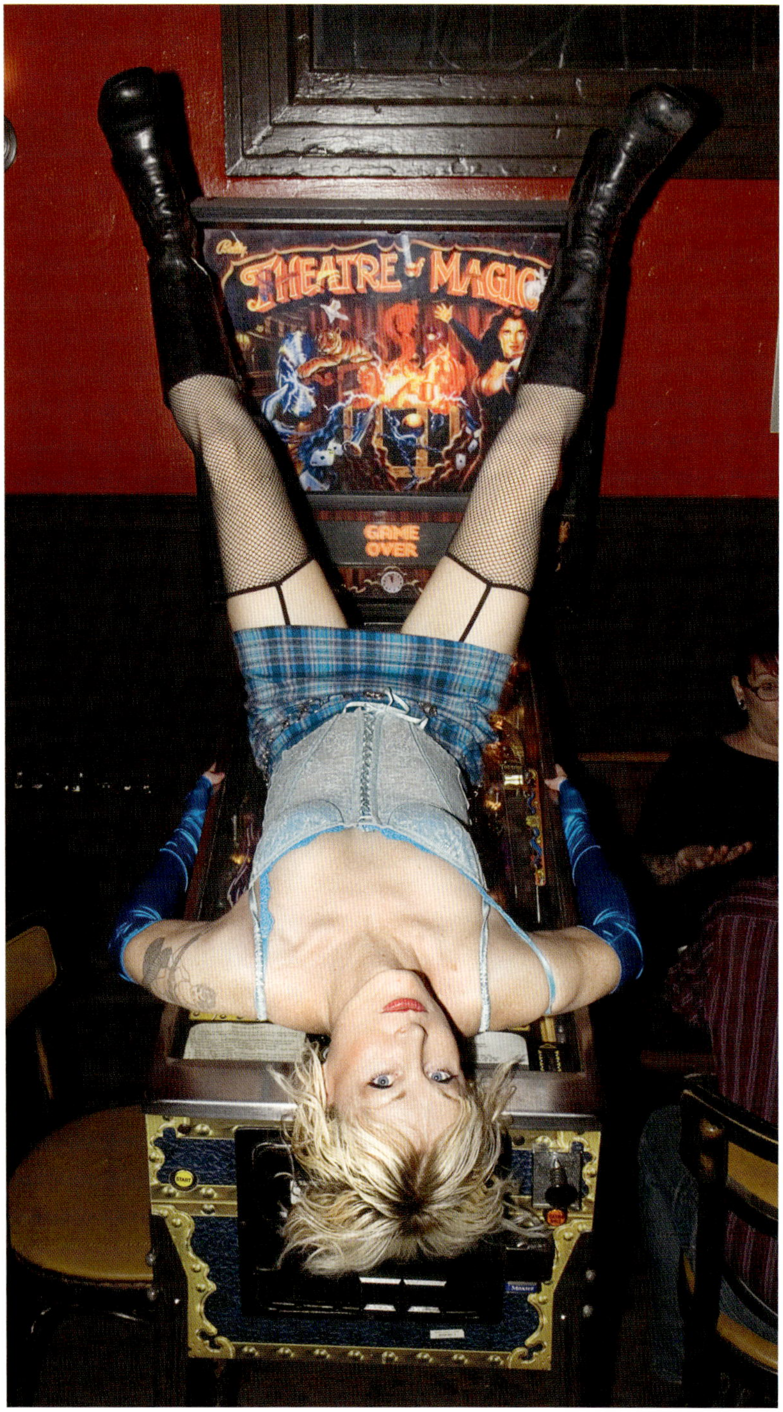
THEATRE of MAGIC
GAME OVER
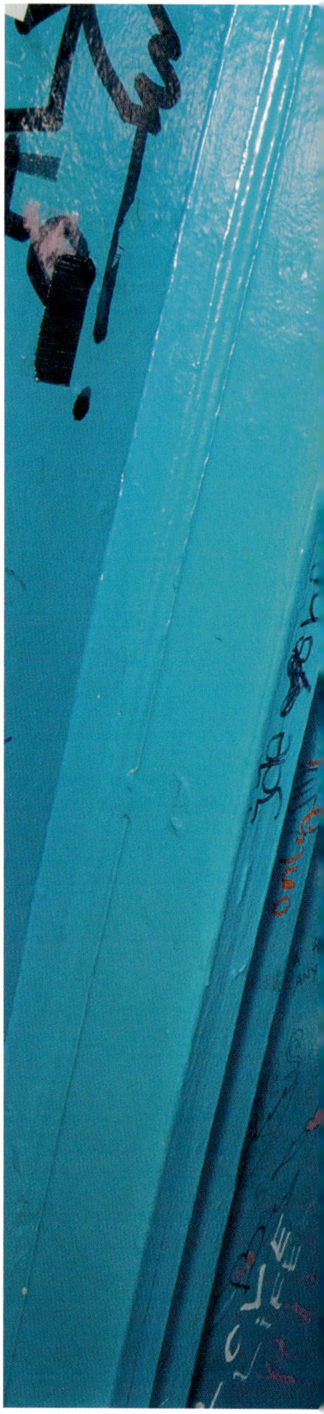

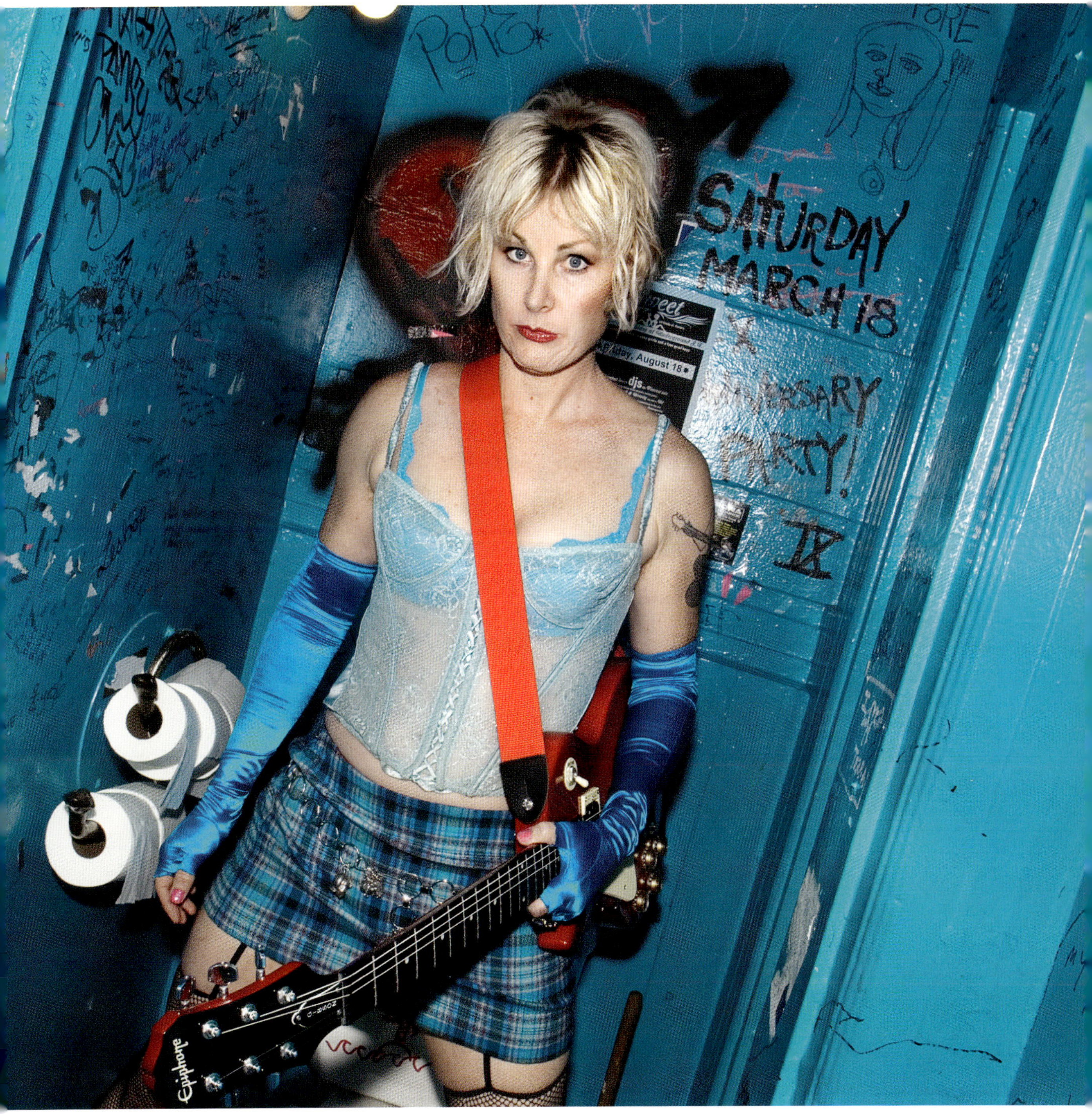
SATURDAY
MARCH 18
PARTY!
Friday, August 18
Epiphone

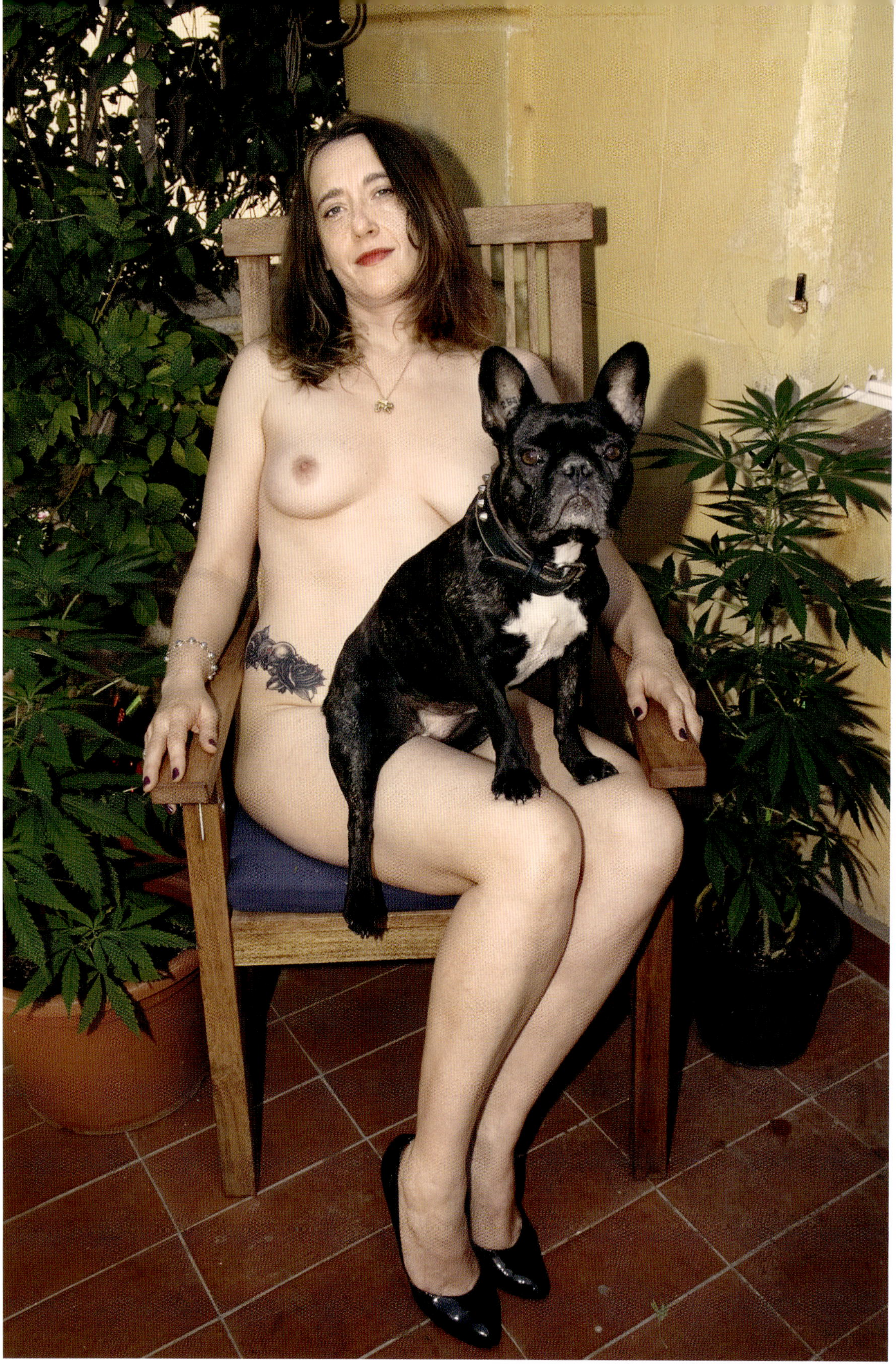

Femininity without a Country

In July 2007 Del and I visited the lovely home of his friends, the Spanish queer theorist Beatriz Preciado and the French writer and filmmaker Virginie Despentes, in a sleepy neighbourhood of Barcelona. While our hosts were away, we cared for Pepa, Beatriz's transgendered bulldog and Swan, a wild kitten rescued by Virginie. I marvelled in the author of *Baise-Moi*'s vast library of bad girl stories, comics and feminist fiction and enjoyed writing in the afternoon sun on the red tiled balcony. Upon their return, we were introduced to their good friend, American punk star and performance poet Lydia Lunch, who once upon a time provided a role model for a teenaged Virginie, along with the riot grrls of the early 90s. In the company of these bad ass girls, I felt a bit like a little sister in awe, taking copious notes, as always. Talking about film, violence and feminism, Virginie rejected the idea that we need a feminist justification for the violence or the sex in *Baise-Moi*. Rather, its themes reflect the contemporary obsession with violence as a necessary but gender-coded component of entertainment. In the cynical tone that began to seem so her, she said: 'I worked with porn stars, which to me was a feminist move. Give me the name of a famous male actor who you never saw with a gun and I'll give you the name of famous actresses whose breast you never saw. I am longing to see a film with dangerous psycho female characters and young men running half-naked in the wood, screaming and helpless. I'll find that a healthy re-balancing.'

Virginie Despentes & Pepa, Barcelona 2007

What are your thoughts on femininity, and especially queer femininity, in your self and in the world?

– I come from a heterosexual background, getting involved in a same-sex love story for the first time at thirty-five. It's like living in a country I was not born in: very intense, a strong relief and sometimes confusing, not that I have anything against confusion. I built myself out of straight femininity, so I wouldn't identify as a femme in a lesbian way. In the heterosexual community, aptitude for seduction is a woman's ultimate quality: it is best rewarded, best acknowledged. Any other feature, like expressing yourself, being funny, having ambition, aggression, strength, spirit must be underplayed, so it doesn't get in the way of your seduction. I still have a strong distrust of femininity because it's always primarily defining you in terms of what use others can make of you. Will they be excited, reassured, healed, understood, taken care of? It always distances you from your sincere emotions.

– That said, I enjoy femininity in other women, if it's what they are into, and I love the popular icons of femininity, especially porn stars, pop stars or comics icons. I prefer femininity melded with masculinity: I like it raw. My favourite female look is the porn star look, real porn or fake, like the MTV female singers in the 90s. I also love the slut business woman look of the 90s, for instance, Sharon Stone in *Basic Instinct* or the women in Abel Ferrara's *King of New York*. I'm OK with the pin-up from the 50s revival look – burlesque and whatever – it's sweet and sexy, but a little too strictly feminine for me, a little too harmless. And it's difficult for me to witness any 50s nostalgia without seeing it as nostalgia for a lost white supremacy. Every boy and every girl should experience a slut look at some point, it makes you view the world in a very interesting way. But you can get quickly lost in the game. To be feminine is a fake power. It is the same as drugs: a very immediate, very intense, very funny experience. But any power that is easily given and obtained should be watched over carefully. It might be a gross hallucination.

You are the only one who is naked in this book. Why did you choose this?

– I've been impressed and seduced by Del's work since I discovered it three years ago so this was not like just any photo session. It was an opportunity to work with Del LaGrace Volcano that I didn't want to miss. The only other time I have been naked for a photograph was for *Baise Moi*. I was naked and the two actresses wore black suits and white shirts. I love that photo. That was nine years ago. I still don't know precisely how Virginie Despentes should be dressed, whether she should be elegant, wear a wig, or some shades, a big red nose? Should she be dreadful, punk, dominatrix, classic or grotesque? Nakeness is a good costume for her. This is what I try to be when I write, when I get to be Virginie Despentes. Naked. Wearing nothing but my skin. Tattoos, high heels and a dog on my lap. This is my view of Virginie Despentes, and I wouldn't do it with any photographer, but I wanted to do it with Del.

One of the things that is clear among many of the subjects of our book is the overlaps and sisterhood between sluts, whores, femmes. Many of us long for sisterhood, perhaps a more twisted and perverted but ultimately fiercely loyal kind, especially among the marginalised. Do you see potential for sisterhood between bad girls?

– I don't pay particular attention to patriarchy, but I'm amazed at how difficult it is for men to criticise masculinity. As if they couldn't change anything about it, as if mummy's will was so strong they could never emerge from it. Men are so passive about what's imposed upon them in the name of virility... I respect some people's decisions to spread their wings inside the romantic or sexual seduction field, but I'd claim other fields for women as well, which wouldn't evolve around 'Did I seduce you good enough?' and 'How hard would you jerk off watching me move?' It's the compulsory nature of the game that makes me feel claustrophobic, not the game itself.

– Sisterhood is obviously not a feminine tradition. To build sisterhood, you need to get out of your kitchen, out of your family, out of your love story, you have to be allowed to get outdoors. That's why sisterhood is more a tradition for whores, alcoholics and outcasts. Good girls have husbands, good girls have children, good girls don't need a gang. It is pretty recent – since the 70s – that women can go out and think of a sisterhood without losing dignity. Sisterhood is under the same deep and cold influence as the unity amongst men: it's not a contemporary thing. Unless you're going to war in Iraq, where I suppose unity is still important... Everywhere else, and this concerns men as well as women, capitalism is not about unity, solidarity, collective struggles.

– One of the most important things that happened in the last ten years in entertainment is Reality TV and *Big Brother*. And the main message delivered to the audience is: be ready to betray your best friend. Be ready to vote against him or her. Be prepared to watch him or her get expelled and learn not to protest, because this is rule number one. You're gathered only to get rid of the weakest. 'You have no friend, you have no team and there will be only few survivors and disobedience is not an option.' Disobedience belongs to losers. So it's difficult to build sisterhood, or any solidarity, in the 2000s... the pride we had in the 80s in being 'punks', that is to say, losers, marginalised, underground, outsiders, is no longer an option. Sisterhood, like brotherhood, had to be built on a hatred of the dominant power, and a common willingness to fight. And I don't see much hatred of the dominant power, nowadays, only frustration about not belonging to the leading teams. That will come back. But we have to wait a couple of years. And then we can talk about sisterhood, again.

Lydia Lunch, Barcelona 2007

Creative Navigator of Heightism

Dear Trina,

Seeing you perform *The Bubble Show* at the Unisex Salon in NYC, I was spellbound. You danced and peeled off articles of clothing to reveal your glittered body inside a large balloon. At the end of the act, it exploded, releasing a million little white feathers into the crowd. It figuratively and literally took my breath away as I enhaled the plumage. Unisex Salon was inspired by John Cameron Mitchell's film *Shortbus*, which you and Bitch, another NYC subject of this book, were part of, and 'it provides a safe place to meet the most interesting, uninhibited people of the downtown queer art scene to party and celebrate variety' you later explained. 'My difference isn't stamped on my body, it envelops my whole body – it's in my skin, my shape, my voice, my body movement and in all of my bones. When I dance, I'm celebrating it and my excitement to be "of" it.'

We met to talk about activism and art in your Brooklyn home, where you showed your film *A Yellow Brick Road* and spoke of your closeness to your Italian-Polish family, and to your brother and mother. You later told me about the experience of making images with Del at the Yaffa Café in the East Village, 'Before working together, I sent Del a piece of poetic prose writing and herm's response made me feel connected, like we had a similar language and ethos. I'm glad I agreed to make the portraits. It was a warm, welcoming process.'

You outlined your theory of queer femininity, saying, 'I'm hyper-femme and I pass as femme in two ways. First, in the sense that we are all only "passing" as a gender. Secondly, I pass as "a real person" or as a subject among subjects through femme-ing. I enjoy using femme as a verb. I make sure that my lipstick is the reddest red so that while I'm femme-ing myself to navigate the world, I'm also calling out to the theatricality of gender. When you're different, you easily learn that you're walking on a stage, even if you're simply there to be an audience member. I'm always aware of the stereotypes attached to my body and so each step, performance, film, painting I make, I'm constantly looking at myself and the "thing" I'm creating with multiple eyes and from multiple directions.'

'The stereotype of "the midget" (throughout history) has been a creature of fantasy, luck, magic, evil, or representative of an immature adult. In a culture which doesn't welcome people with disabilities into the realm of sexuality, performing a femme gender enables me to participate in the world of the "Real". I'd love to live a world where the sexual binary system is considered a silly tradition of thought; but we're not there yet. I hope my work helps to paint myself and others as "Subjects", not "Objects".'

Trina Rose, NYC 2007

173

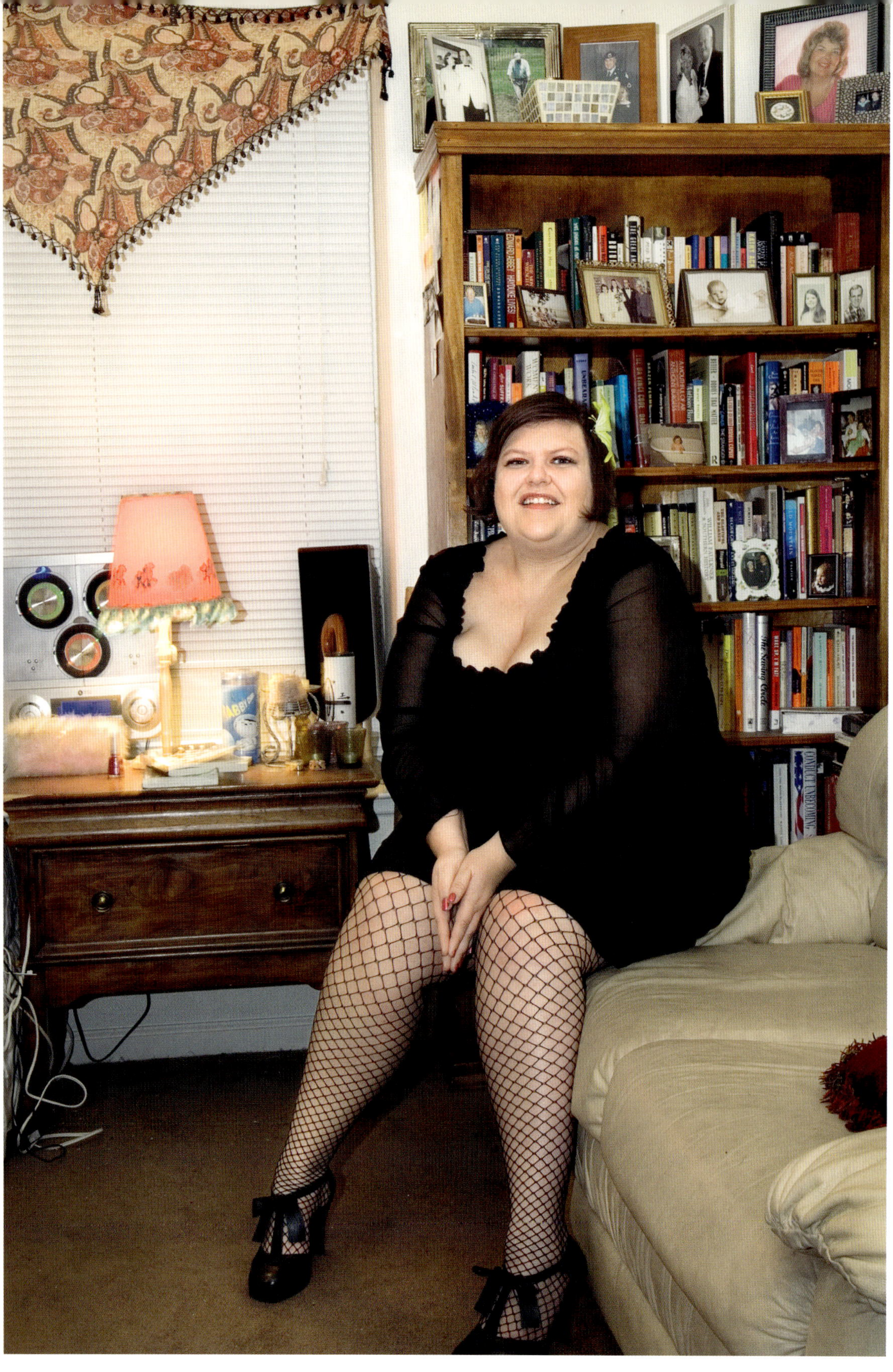

KRISTA SMITH | Fat... Femme... Fierce... Kentucky Fried

DESIRE IS THE VERY essence of queer identities. We define ourselves by who we desire. And while certainly, it is the sex and/or gender of the individuals that we desire that defines our queer identities, our desires play out in all kinds of beautiful and exciting ways. So, in a world where we bravely take our stance around our queer desires, why is it that so many of the representations of queer desires can easily be found in the pages of any heterosexual magazine? Where are the representations of the queers I desire? Where are the representations of queers of colour, working-class queers, gender-queers, fat queers, queers with disabilities, older queers? Sadly, these representations are lacking in most mainstream queer publications, art and performances. However, this fierce, fat femme is not having any of that. It's been my mission to bring visibility to those of us that have been made invisible, not only in mainstream heterosexual cultures, but also in mainstream and even underground queer cultures. Because it is through visibility that desires are named.

Krista performing 'GoodGirl'/'Bad Girl', Oakland 2006

I'm known in the San Francisco Bay Area queer community via my stage name/alter ego, Kentucky Fried Woman. Having spent my first twenty-four years in Kentucky and remaining 'southern' identified in all kinds of ways, it was important that the stage name I chose reflect that part of me. Whenever I tell folks I'm from Kentucky, their first response is usually about Kentucky Fried Chicken. And I love the image of something frying: the notion of something tasting good but being 'bad' for you, the saltiness, the fat, the kitchen imagery and how that connects me to my blood family. This one word, *Fried*, matches my personality in a myriad of complicated ways. As Kentucky Fried Woman I perform drag, burlesque, cabaret, ballet and tap in a variety of queer productions.

I started dancing when I was three years old and by the time I was in third grade, I was involved in competitive dancing. I was a chubby kid, causing my dance instructor to constantly urge me to lose weight. This culminated in being kicked out of my dance studio when I was twelve for being too fat. After that, I tried to participate in the arts through singing and theatre. But my weight often prevented me from being accepted. I was tired of fighting for the opportunity to perform, so I gave up my performance dreams and turned to academia. After graduating with my BA from the University of Kentucky, I moved to Santa Barbara for graduate school.

I'd always lived in the same town in Kentucky and was rocked to the core when I arrived in California. Though I'd been queer-identified for many years, this was the first time I was a part of a queer community. Of course this community was not perfect. I was surprised to learn that in many ways, the same issues of misogyny, racism, classism and body fascism were as present in the Santa Barbara queer community as in the straight culture in Kentucky. However, I was accepted and embraced by this community in a way that I had heretofore never experienced. This community challenged me in new ways and also gave me a safe space to explore leadership, social change, and my new performance identity. The drag king scene was starting to explode internationally and in Santa Barbara was represented by the group, the Disposable Boy Toys. While I was in love with every single drag king in the group and totally infatuated with their act, I wanted to perform femininity, not masculinity. The drag queen that had been living inside me was ready to bust out. I first performed as Kentucky Fried Woman in 2000 with fellow fat femme performance artist, Jessica Humphrey, aka Summer's Eve. We didn't know other women who were doing what we were doing, though we felt confident they existed. We were determined to illicit the same hot responses from our audience as our drag king counterparts. We were also determined to address the misogyny and body fascism of our queer community.

In the seven years since, I've been a part of several performance collectives, created a solo career and participated in a myriad of queer performance conferences. While I still focus on my fat and femme identities, I've also attempted to infuse my performances with politics of race, class, sexuality, ability, age, war, reproductive rights and other political issues. Examples include a recent performance with the Dangers to the Leonard Cohen song, 'Everybody Knows'. In this performance we visit 'Uncle Whitey's Carnival of Privilege'. Through clever use of the lyrics and a carnival theme, we were able to show our audience how white, male and heteronormative privilege is indoctrinated into society as well as the tools that can be used to resist it, or at least use this privilege to enact social change. While some of my performances critique aspects of the queer community others critique the US government or mainstream society. As an artist I have the opportunity to create and envision a new world when I am on stage. I can create a world that is free of the 'isms' and give my audience a new reality to hope and fight for. In my world, women of all shapes, sizes and colours are beautiful, respected and objects of love and passion. In my world, queer people are not oppressed and discriminated against. In my shows, George Bush is defeated and does lose to the power of the people. Audiences leave these shows reinvigorated in their own activism and lives. For folks who are not activists, it can be a provocative experience, introducing radical ideas to hopefully someday act upon. Finally, my audiences are given alternative representations of femininity – femmes of colour, working-class femmes, fat femmes, differently-abled femmes, older femmes, etc. and find themselves in the delightful position of desiring all types of queer femmes.

MY PERSONAL TRUTHS are found in the beautiful, challenging and fascinating ways that my fat, femme and queer identities connect. What further complicates these identities is how each one contains a mixture of essentialised and performative characteristics. For instance, my queer identity is in some ways an essentialised identity, while in other ways it is more of a performative one. I felt attracted to girls at the age of five, leading me to believe I was born this way. Yet, my queer identity encompasses much more than that lifelong attraction towards women. It also includes the attraction I sometimes feel towards men, the ways that I have incorporated queer community into my life, and my queer performance art.

While I cannot help but believe that I was born the girly girl I am today – my love of all things sparkly, pink, sweet and soft has been present for as long as I can remember – I'd be remiss if I didn't acknowledge the ways that I learned to perform femininity and the ways that I intentionally perform my queer femininity both on and off stage. One of my favourite drag queens, Rosie True, once said, 'I was not born in these false eyelashes'. Like her, I was not born with all of the hyper-feminine clothing, accoutrements, and movements that help identify me to the queer eye as a high-femme. I intentionally put these things on to perform femininity. This performance is closely tied to my body and part of the subversive nature of femme identity is to value bodies in all of their varied contexts. If femme identity is consciously engaging with femininity and one accepts that femme identity is not merely an essentialised identity, but also a performative one, then we must engage with what it means to perform this identity.

We live in a world that devalues the feminine. Labour that is tied to femininity is often not paid, very poorly paid, or illegal. Traditionally feminine qualities are constantly critiqued and we teach young women that if they want to be a leader they must take on more masculine traits. Even the second wave feminist and 70s lesbian movements sold out their feminine sisters as victims of the patriarchy. I refuse to devalue femininity and the daily performance of my femininity shows all who interact with me what it means to be strong as a femme, to find value in all things feminine and to celebrate femininity. Gender equality will *not* be achieved through erasing femininity and masculinity, but rather when we stop devaluing that which is feminine and define a masculinity that is non-misogynistic.

For femme to remain a subversive identity, we must question notions of desire and beauty. In the dominant straight culture a beautiful feminine body is one that is thin (though large breasts and asses are generally adored), hair-free, able-bodied, and white. This ideal femininity is further enhanced by the right hairstyle, make-up, clothing, shoes, money, etc. There is a feminine 'ideal' that is held up as the epitome of desire and beauty. While certainly some women fit into this 'ideal' not all do. Many women spend a lot of time and energy to fit this ideal through dieting, plastic surgery, laser hair removal, body hatred, internalised fat phobia, and internalised racism, etc. I believe that every woman should have the right to do what she wants with her body and if for her that means dieting, plastic surgery, and body modification, I do not blame her for doing what she can to become this idealised woman. Of course in dominant straight culture, it's difficult to define where the 'male' gaze fits into this equation. Plastic surgery is most common amongst heterosexual women and homosexual men, both groups of people seeking the male gaze. Though dominant queer culture often replicates dominant straight culture, queers have the option and I'd argue should choose the option to create their own standards of desire and beauty.

SEVEN YEARS AGO I took the stage for the first time as Kentucky Fried Woman, a skin-tight black velvet dress clinging to every curve of my body. I danced and pranced around the stage to a song by The Story called 'Fatso'. The lyrics sarcastically state, 'Someone will adore me when my ribs show clearly and I'm thin even when I sit down. Someone will admire my gorgeous arms and legs when I'm only 100 pounds'. The juxtaposition of these lyrics with my beautiful curvy body gracefully moving about the stage challenges the audience's desires. It's shocking that something as simple as a fat woman wearing tight clothing and happily dancing is a subversive act. What kind of world do we live in that such a thing is seen as subversive? A world that teaches all of us that we are never good enough, never beautiful enough, never desired enough. We are starved for women who will stand up and proclaim their desirability and sexuality, not for the male gaze, but on their own terms. Women react powerfully to my performances because my performances enable them to see themselves as objects of desire.

It's fascinating that queers are readily able to challenge socialised aspects of desire when it comes to sexuality, but not when it comes to bodies. They can see how heterosexuality is socialised and they are able to reject that socialisation, but they often do not draw the same conclusions with bodies and desire. I often hear queers say, 'I love fat people, I am just not personally attracted to them', as if what they desire exists in a vacuum and is not part of a socialisation process. If we can create and modify queer culture, then we have the possibility of creating a subversive femme-inism that refuses to create 'ideals' of beauty, but rather, finds beauty in all types of femininity: the skinny flat-chested femme, the deliciously round as an apple femme, the smooth-shaved femme, the bearded femme, the able-bodied femme, the differently-abled femme, the older femme, the youthful femme, and of course femme expressions in all of their diversely gendered possibilities.

Valuing and desiring all types of femme and femininities explodes and subverts strict ideals and allows folks who identify as femme room to express their femininity in a multitude of ways. If we don't acknowledge the role desire plays in our gender and body expressions, we don't engage with the politics of who we fuck. The politics of who we fuck are at the very root of our identity. Until we as a femme-inist community are able to value in each other and ourselves that which does not fit into the 'idealised' mode created by a straight, patriarchal culture, we'll still be tied to the chains that oppress our love for our own and each other's bodies.

In the world that I've dedicated my life to creating, we each value our own and each other's bodies and we continuously challenge ourselves around our desires. This is one of the most radical things that queers can do in battling some of the ugly 'isms' that haunt our communities. Every day I wake up feeling beautiful. Everything I encounter from the minute I get out of bed, to the minute I go to sleep tells me I'm not desirable. I will be invisible, ignored, pathologised, degraded, disrespected, made fun of and hated. I am a queer fat femme who refuses to be defined by this. I am a beautiful, healthy, happy femme who is fighting to create a world where every person knows that they matter. So tonight, before you go to bed, strip in front of a mirror. Trace the curves of your body and celebrate your beauty. You hold the keys to your own revolution.

The Bearded Lady & The Fat Lady, Elese & Krista, Oakland 2006

Femme futures

OVER THE YEARS there's been much tweeting about femme invisibility. In the time we have worked on this book however, femmes have studied our histories, risen in our heels, put on our combat boots, reapplied the lipstick and become even more articulate and proud. I'd say the femme movement is growing, and it transcends borders. Local and transnational community-making, like Femme 2006 and support groups like London's Bird Pride, the Paris Fem Menace and growing number of chapters of the Femme Mafia, not to mention the articulate voices of the transfeminist movement and of fat activists, are just a few examples of organised femme-inist resistance in the face of both patriarchal and feminist contempt for femininity. Their full significance is for other books and femme scientists like Maura Ryan, to address. The hope for these movements, it seems to me, lies in openness.

'Can I be straight and femme?' a student once asked me. 'It's up to you,' I responded, 'you have to work out what femme means to you.' Femme 2006 conference chair Jessica Humphrey insightfully said: 'There are two models for making community. One is the exclusionary model where you have to fit certain criteria. The other, the one we are using, is that anyone who identifies as femme, regardless of what that means to them, is welcome.' Open borders is a good start because the question of what queers femininity (a figuration in constant metamorphosis and refiguration) and how it intersects with other dimensions of identity can never fully be determined.

As this book closes, readers should remember that there are countless femmes out there, larger than life, in the world, who for a variety of reasons, cannot and do not want participate in the kind of visibility politics that a book inevitably comprises. In a world that privileges the visual and the spoken, however, queer femininities do continue to explode and femmes make our voices heard and our seductive power known on stages, in countless anthologies and magazines, and in films like *Female-to-Femme* set in San Francisco (Chisholm and Stark), *Fem* in London (Inge 'Campbell' Blackman), and forthcoming *This Femme Fucks Back* in Stockholm (Maria Niemi). All of this, one can hope, contributes both to countering hegemonic visions of femininity and to making femme-identified queers feel less alone and alien in queer and feminist subcultures. As Bird queen Kath puts it: 'Femme invisibility? So last year!'

We should always attend to the politics of location. While femme apparently continues to go in and out of fashion in predominantly white queer communities, this has not been the case in queer communities of colour and working-class

Stockholm Pride 2007

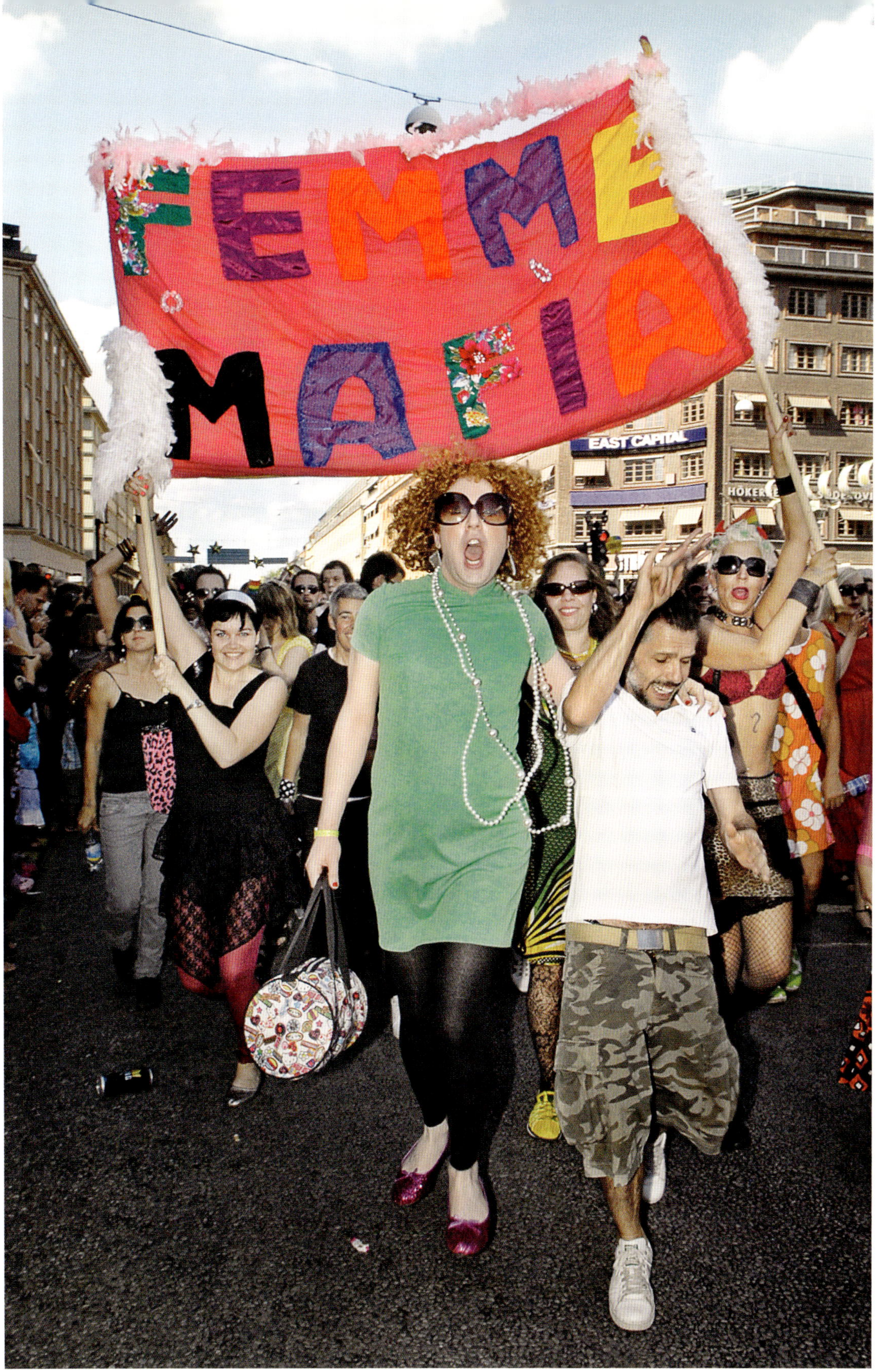
FEMME
MAFIA
EAST CAPITAL

communities, as Solange, Marla and Amber all point out. White privilege can obscure vision and, and as Leah observes, 'there's a tendency among some white femmes to argue that they face oppression solely on the basis of their queer femininity.' At best, the persistent and varied desires of femme can unify through posing challenges to hegemonic and heteronormative femininity, but only insofar as we humbly recognise that our experiences are rarely the same. As a figuration, not a unified identity, femme to me is routed and rooted in differential consciousness and awareness of the need for multiple struggles and strategies.

SO WITHIN THESE rising femme movements, is sisterhood always simple among the queerly feminine? Of course not. A figuration is not one as in same. As femme admirer Campbell once pointed out, misogyny and femme phobia is internalised by all of us and many express both ambivalence and hope. Caroline in London noted that 'femmes can be scary. There are negative stereotypes, of femmes being bitchy, stealing each other's boifriends, being competitive. But to me that's residue from straight culture.'

One US-based femme, who tellingly wanted to remain anonymous said: 'It's really difficult for me to loudly proclaim "femme" when all I see around me is this pretty but vapid, youth-culture obsessed, catty, manipulative, misogynistic and overtly emotional femme. I've never been some of those things and I try and quell those other qualities I see in myself.' Commenting on one femme organisation, another independent femme who also wanted to remain anonymous but still heard said 'while some may say that being femme is "not about clothes", it's always been an antifeminist environment for me. It's disappointing when something that has so much potential becomes a breeding ground for cattiness and femme on femme judgement.'

My queer sisters, let's remember that femme power doesn't reside in pretending that the potentially competitive qualities we've all internalised from growing up in a patriarchy don't exist. We must critique the patriarchal idea that femininity is the greatest and perhaps only asset and resource a girl really has and its demands that we measure ourselves against each other according to a scale that has never been fair. At it's best, as Krista notes, the femme movement values femme bodies of all sizes and hues – and, we might add, outfits and purses!

Lastly, while femmes don't care who you desire or how you fuck and while sisterhood between femmes and transwomen is a given for so many of us, and while we often meet in transsensuality and a partially shared sense of gender or body dysphoria, specificity remains important. This means honouring both lesbian pasts and presents and standing up for our queer and trans allies and for (being) both feminists and bad girls. We can only hope that in our femme futures we continue to address the thorny issues and that we remain willing to unpack privilege as well as prejudice and pain as well as pleasure. For the femme figuration to remain an emergent 'political fiction' [Braidotti 1994:5] with the power to explode feminine political agency, let's use our fierce bravery, our open closets, our desiring hearts and cunts and our generosity to both mirror and generate femme love and diffuse and enduring solidarity.

Debby, Andi, Marla, Turner, Carey, Rachel & Joelle, Atlanta, 2007

183

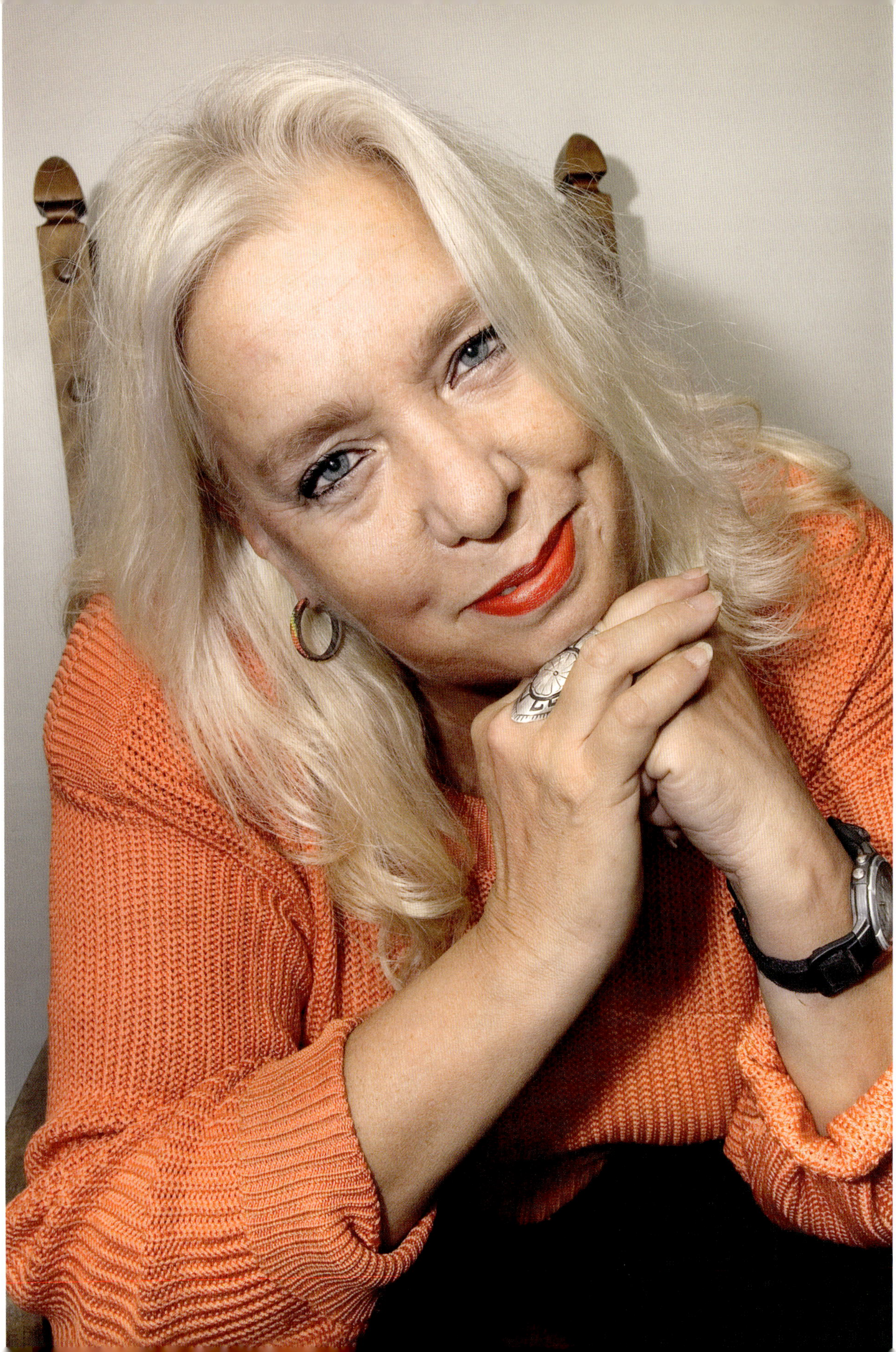

AMBER HOLLIBAUGH
Afterword: Femmes of Power

IN 2006 I STOOD on a stage in an auditorium in San Francisco as keynote speaker at the Femme 2006 Conference. It was one of the most powerful moments in my life. All I had dreamed of through the years of ridicule, enduring ugly humor at my own expense, long seasons of invisibility and loneliness in lesbian/queer femme identity – the dreams I had nurtured for kinship and connection, for finding voice and possibility, for discovering rooms filled with others who shared a passionate, difficult, impossible-to-nail-down kind of femaleness – seemed on the brink of realisation. Standing there, I remembered the countless times I had dreamed of a community of sisters who had somehow managed to figure out how to survive while keeping their defiance and extraordinary beauty alive. How terribly long I had wanted, finally, to enter a well-lit place and find others like myself. Standing there on that stage, I had arrived home.

When I told a queer co-worker I was speaking at a femme conference, he said: 'Oh, Amber, what are you wearing for the slumber party?' But when I looked out at the hundreds of people there, I saw the compelling results of our stubborn femme refusal to be a running joke embedded in queer geography.

I have always believed that the identity, the essence, the distinction that is Femme mattered – that an erotic, self-configured femme person was as intriguing, complex, gender-defying, and deliciously abnormal as all the other strangely configured, self-created, lived-inside-of-whether-you-like-it-or-not-mother-fucker identities occupying our queer universe. Because – like the rest of the clan – in order to survive we have imagined ourselves: we have made ourselves up.

Remember becoming conscious of your birth family one day and feeling as if you'd been unceremoniously dropped down there from another universe? Our fierce femme identities are partially determined by our defiance and resolution that we would salvage whatever we could from the tortured terrain of the biological female. And that is not an easy task. And, while I know the world of queerness has shifted and expanded in countless and powerful ways, the bottom line is still that femmes and femme identities don't really count for much, aren't valued or seen to be as truly queer as other homoerotic personas. It still seems that a femme identity is assumed to be a sort of default – not something forged in the fire of its own complex, unresolved human possibilities and hungers.

In fact, the real suspicion is that we are just faux straight people sleeping over at the LGBTIQ campground. And that tells you how despised women are, even by those of us born female. Femmes are read as imposters, betrayers of the authentic queer self. Yet, in working-class commu-

Amber Hollibaugh, New York, 2007

nities and communities of colour, we often flourish and shine – even though we are, at the same time, hated or treated with derision because of our queerness.

OVER THE YEARS I've struggled to determine whether I believe femme identity is a drag identity. Trans identities, butch identities, leather daddies and bear bait, drag kings and drag queens and all of the various variations of the drag persona have currently found homes in the land of queerness. I'm not speaking about the 'we're just like straight folks/we want our place at the table/we want our piece of the pie' kind of homosexuals; for them, all this difference flowering in the queer universe is an unfortunate side effect of coming out; and they want to change it so that they can be just like straight people – except gay; and, once that day arrives, they'll wish the rest of us would just stop marching in all of these unnecessary gay pride parades and embarrassing them. But that day isn't here yet – not even for them! The fights all continue, of course: Who matters most? Who speaks for whom? Who counts the most? And therefore: Who has a right to a voice?

The images in this book explore that question (among others), but don't resolve it. However, they do begin to make us visible – in all of our glory – yes, in all the complexities of our irreconcilable, besieged, magnificent queer personas. That is why these images and stories in *Femmes of Power*, generated by femmes from a world of femme-ness, matter now as profoundly as they would have mattered to me had I ever been lucky enough to encounter them when I was coming out. For me, at that time – a high femme, 'mixed race', white trash, sexually deviant, incest surviving, Romany/Irish lesbian (an identity that took me decades to decipher and understand) – these images and stories would have helped me save my life. Because, in confronting the irrefutable knowledge that I was a femme, I tried to kill myself. Nothing else in my life ever got me to that edge; nothing else seemed so impossible to understand, or to claim.

While many of us are defiant and elegant in our refusal to shut up, many more of us sink, and do not survive. These are the unseen femme configured corpses whose stories die with them. To me, *Femmes of Power* is a book of survivors' tales. It gives us a place to behold femme images, take risks, and contemplate setting off on dangerous journeys. There are small journeys here but also marathon treks, sly side trips, transgressive but resolute crossings – all sorts of voyages. And each one matters.

We matter.

Femmes matter... here.

Valerie Mason-John, London 2007 |
next spread: The New 3 Graces, San Francisco 2006

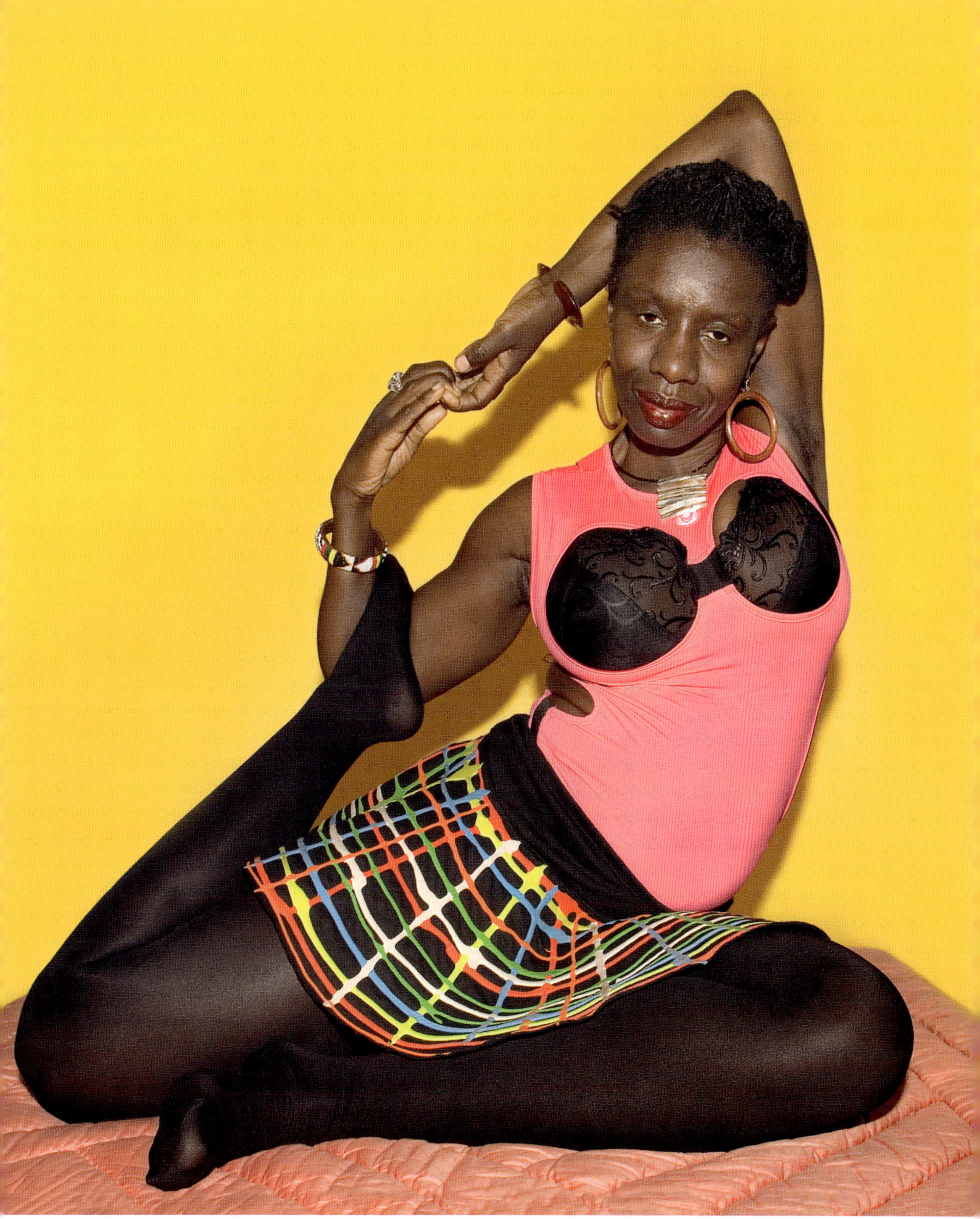

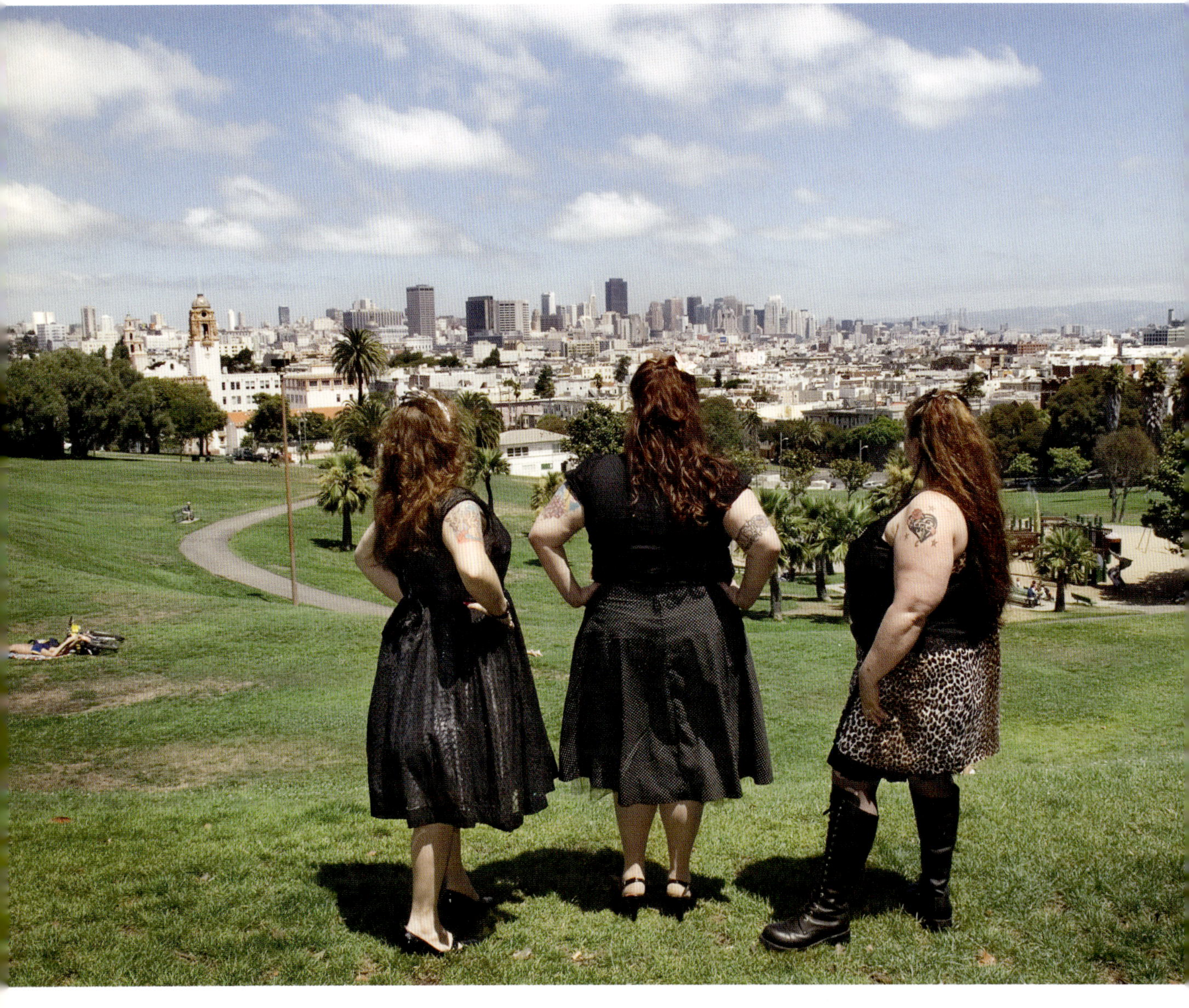

CONTRIBUTORS INDEX

Amber Hollibaugh | 13, 30, 97, 185–187
amberhollibaugh@aol.com

Amelia Mae Hess | 82–83, 148–149

Andy Candy | 78, 86–89
www.andycandy.se

Asynja Gray | 53–55

Barbara Carrellas | 34, 78, 115–117, 118
www.barbaracarrellas.com

Bird Club | 20, 68–71, 180
www.birdclub.org.uk

Bitch | 160–162, 172
www.bitchmusic.com

Campbell | 29, 182
www.blackmanvision.com

Caroline | 30, 35, 81, 84, 182
www.myspace.com/sexyrubbersoul

Celestina Pearl | 56–61, 115
www.myspace.com/celestinameowmeow

Charlotte Karlsdotter | 38–39

Clover X | 62–65
clovercutthroat@gmail.com

Debra Kate | 50–51 | www.debrakate.com

Del LaGrace Volcano | 8–15
www.dellagracevolcano.com

Deni Francis | 28, 31, 81

Diamond Daggers | 81, 148
www.diamonddaggers.com

Dossie Easton | 33–34, 112–113
www.dossieeaston.com

Elese Lebsack | 38, 147, 176–178

Femme Mafia | 20, 34, 81, 103–105, 132–137, 183 | www.femmemafia.com

Harlem Shake Burlesque | 62, 146–148

Indra Windh | 12–16, 50, 52–53, 78, 81
windran@hotmail.com

Itziar Ziga | 22, 72–77, 112
exdones.blogspot.com

Jaheda Choudury | 67, 98–101, 151

Jennifer Miller | 38, 148, 153
www.circusamok.org

Josefin Brink | 157–159
www.josefinbrink.riksdagsvanstern.org

Josephine (Allison) Wilson | 34, 40–44, 47, 148 | www.josephineallison.com

Jukie Sunshine | 56–57, 61, 115, 151, 188
www.jukiesunshine.com

Jun Wizelius | 34, 54, 78–79, 85, 164
www.missjuniversum.se

Kate Bornstein | 34, 78, 116–117, 118, 163
www.katebornstein.com

Kath Monan/Bird La Bird | 68–71, 81, 115
www.myspace.com/birdlabird

Krista Smith | 4, 11, 174–179, 147, 182
www.myspace.com/kentuckyfriedwoman

Lady Monster | 56–57, 61, 115, 151, 188
www.ladymonster.com

Laura Méritt | 115, 118–121
www.sexclusivitaeten.de

Leah Lakshmi Piepzna-Samarasinha
96–98, 151, 182 | www.brownstargirl.com

Leslie Mah | 53, 106, 160, 162–163
www.lesliemahtattoo.com

Lois Weaver | 140–145
www.splitbritches.com

Louis(e) de Ville | 10, 108, 110–111
www.myspace.com/louisedeville

Lydia Lunch | 169, 171
www.lydialunch.com

Maria Dixen | 34, 81
mariadixen@hotmail.com

Maria Lönn | 23, 138–139

Maria Rosa Mojo/Dyke Marilyn
46–49, 30, 70, 109, 148
www.myspace.com/rosamojo

Marla Stewart | 102–105, 133, 132–137
www.myspace.com/marlarenee

Maya Hald/D Muttant | 34, 154–156

Meliza Banales | 58–60
www.myspace.com/melizabanales

Michelle Tea | 58, 106, 160, 163–165

Morgana Maye | 19, 21, 34, 115, 128–131
www.morganamaye.com

Polly Mathies | 120–121

Pratibha Parmar | 90–95, 112
www.kalifilms.com

Rebecca 'Goldie' Goldfader | 66–67

Reina Lewis | 20, 25, 85, 130

Rosie Lugosi | 109, 124–127, 148
www.rosielugosi.com

Shanti Freed | 52, 71
www.myspace.com/shantifreed

Shawna Virago | 160, 163, 166–167
www.shawnavirago.com

Signe Flyvsk | 24, 34, 50, 122–123
frk.fup@gmail.com

Simone de la Getto | 115, 146–147, 150–151

Sofie Wahlström | 23, 34, 78, 80, 164

Solange Garjan | 33–34, 84–85, 105, 148
www.myspace.com/solangegarjan

Sossity Chiricuzio | 56–57, 61, 188
www.dieselfemme.com

Stav B | 53–54 | www.stav-b.co.uk

Tina d'Elia | 23, 36–37
grouchotd@aol.com

Trina Rose | 172–173
www.misstrinarose.com

Ulrika Dahl | 17, 21, 156

Vagina Jenkins | 53, 62–65, 115, 147
www.myspace.com/vagina_jenkins

Valerie Mason John | 30, 32–33, 187
www.valeriemason-john.co.uk

Virginie Despentes | 34, 115, 168–171

Wendy Delorme | 10, 34, 106–111, 115
www.myspace.com/wendydelorme

Ylva Maria Thompson | 114–115, 118
www.ylva-art.com

BIBLIOGRAPHY

Allison, Dorothy. 1995. *Skin: Talking about Sex, Class and Literature.* Ann Arbor: Firebrand Books.

Barry, Kathleen. 2007. *Femininity in Flight.* Durham: Duke University Press.

Bornstein, Kate. 1995. *Gender Outlaw: On Men, Women and the Rest of Us.* New York: Vintage.

–. 2006. *Hello Cruel World: 101 Alternatives to Suicide for Teens, Freaks and Other Outlaws.* New York: Seven Stories Press.

Braidotti, Rosi. 1994. *Nomadic Subjects: Embodiment and Sexual Difference in Contemporary Feminist Theory.* New York: Columbia University Press.

Buszek, Maria Elena. 2006. *Pin-up Grrrls: Feminism, Sexuality, Popular Culture.* Durham: Duke University Press.

Butler, Judith. 1991. 'Imitation and Gender Insubordination.' In Fuss, Diana, ed. *Inside/Out.* New York: Routledge. Pp. 13–32.

Carrellas, Barbara. 2007. *Urban Tantra: Sacred Sex for the Twenty-first Century.* New York: Celestial Arts.

Case, Sue-Ellen. 1993. 'Towards a Butch–Femme Aesthetic.' In Abelove et al. ed. *The Lesbian and Gay Studies Reader.* New York: Routledge, 1993. Pp. 294–306.

Cvetkovich, Ann. 2003. *An Archive of Feeling: Trauma, Sexuality and Lesbian Public Culture.* Durham: Duke University Press.

Dahl, Ulrika. 2003. 'Utkläd- ningslådan.' In Mobacker, Susanne, ed. *Såna Som Oss.* Stockholm: Tidens Förlag.

–. 2005. 'El Baúl de los disfraces – un manifiesto femme-inista.' In Romero Bachiller, Carmen et al eds. *El Eje Del Mal Es Heterosexual. Figuraciones, Movimientos, y Prácticas Feministas Queer.* Madrid: Traficante de Sueños. Pp. 151–162.

Delorme, Wendy. 2007. *Quatrième Géneration.* Paris: éditions Grasset.

Despentes, Virginie. 2006. *King Kong Théorie.* Paris: Éditions Grasset & Fasquelle.

Duggan, Lisa & Kathleen McHugh. 2002. 'A Fem(me)-inist manifesto.' In Rose and Camilleri, eds. *Brazen Femme: Queering Femininity.* Vancouver: Arsenal Pulp Press. Pp. 165–170.

Easton, Dossie & Catherine A. Liszt. 1997. *The Ethical Slut: A Guide to Infinite Sexual Possibilities.* CA: Greenery Press.

Glenn, Susan. 2000. *Female Spectacle: The Theatrical Roots of Modern Feminism.* Cambridge: Harvard University Press.

Gomez, Jewelle. 1988. 'Imagine a lesbian... a Black Lesbian'. In *Trivia* 12:45–60.

Gopinath, Gayatri. 2005. *Impossible Desires: Queer Diasporas and South Asian Public Cultures.* Durham: Duke University Press.

Grace, Della. 1993. 'The Dynamics of Desire'. In Harwood, Victoria, et al. *The Pleasure Principles.* London: Lawrence & Wishart.

Halberstam, Judith. 1997. *Female Masculinity.* Durham: Duke University Press.

Harris, Laura & Liz Crocker, eds. 1997. *Femme: Feminists Lesbians and Bad Girls.* New York: Routledge.

Haraway, Donna J. 2004. *The Haraway Reader.* New York: Routledge.

Hardy, Tara. 2006. *Dis-Coarse.* Chapbook.

–. 2000. 'Femme Dyke Slut.' In Damsky, Lee, ed. *Sex and Single Girls: Straight and Queer Women on Sexuality.* Seattle: Seal Press. Pp. 175–182.

Holland, Samantha. 2004. *Alternative Femininities. Body, Age, Identity.* London: Berg.

Hollibaugh, Amber. 2000. *My Dangerous Desires: A Queer Girl Dreaming her way home.* Durham: Duke University Press.

Jordan, June. 1980. 'Poem for South African Women.' In *Passion: New Poems, 1977–1980.* Boston: Beacon Press.

Kennedy, Elizabeth L. & Madeline Davis. 1994. *Boots of Leather, Slippers of Gold: The History of A Lesbian Community.* New York: Penguin.

Lemoine, Ingrid & Christine Renard, eds. 2001. *Attirances. Lesbiennes fems, lesbiennes butchs.* Paris: éditions gaies et lesbiennes.

Lewis, Reina 2006. 'Dress Acts: Performing Lesbian Identity 1980–2005', conference paper, Lesbian Lives XVIII: Historicising the Lesbian, University College, Dublin.

Loulan, JoAnn. 1990. *The Lesbian Erotic Dance: Butch, Femme, Androgyny and Other Rythms.* San Francisco: Spinster Books.

Lugosi, Rosie. 2000. *Creatures of the Night.* Manchester: Purple Prose Press.

Lönn, Maria. 2006. *Det blir bättre med tiden – femme-identifierades upplevelse av makt och agens ur ett intersektio-nellt perspektiv.* Undergraduate thesis, Department of Gender Studies, Södertörn University College.

Martin, Biddy. 1996. *Femininity Played Straight: The Significance of Being Lesbian.* New York: Routledge.

Mason-John, Valerie, ed. 1995. *Talking Black: Lesbians of Asian and African Descent Speak Out.* London: Cassells.

Morgan, Tracy 1993. 'Butch-Femme and the politics of identity.' In Stein, Arlene, ed. *Sisters, Sexperts and Queers: Beyond the Lesbian Nation.* New York: Penguin. Pp. 35-46.

Munoz, Jose Esteban. 1999. *Disidentification: Queers of Color and the performance of politics.* Minneapolis: University of Minnesota Press.

Munt, Sally, ed. 1998. *Butch/Femme: Inside Lesbian Gender.* London: Cassell Academic.

Nestle, Joan. 1987. *A Restricted Country.* New York: Firebrand.

Nestle, Joan, ed. 1992. *The Persistent Desire: A Femme-Butch Reader.* Boston: Alyson Books.

Newman, Leslea, ed. 1995. *The Femme Mystique.* San Francisco: Alyson Books.

Payne, Kathryn. 2002. 'Whores and Bitches Who Sleep With Women.' In Rose & Camilleri, eds. *Brazen Femme: Queering Femininity.* Vancouver: Arsenal Pulp Press. Pp. 47-56.

Parmar, Pratibha. 1990. 'Black Feminism: the Politics of Articulation' In Rutherford, Jonathan, ed. *Identity: Community, Culture, Difference.* London: Lawrence & Wishart.

–. 1988. 'Other Kinds of Dreams: An interview with June Jordan'. *Feminist Review.*

–. 1984. 'Challenging Imperial Feminism' with Valerie Amos. *Feminist Review.*

Pratt, Minnie Bruce. 1995. *S/he.* Boston: Firebrand Books.

Rednour, Shar. 2000. *The Femme's Guide to the Universe.* San Francisco: Alyson Books.

Robertson, Pamela. 1997. *Guilty Pleasures: Feminist Camp From Mae West to Madonna.* Durham: Duke University Press.

Rodriguez, Juana Maria. 2003. *Queer Latinidad: Identity Practices, Discursive Spaces.* New York: New York University Press.

Rose, Cloe Brushwood & Anna Camilleri, eds. 2002. *Brazen Femme: Queering Femininity.* Vancover: Arsenal Pulp Press.

Serrano, Julia. 2007. *Whipping Girl: A Transsexual Woman on Sexism and the Scapegoating of Femininity.* Emeryville: Seal Press.

Tea, Michelle. 2004. *Without a Net: The Female Experience of Growing Up Working Class.* Seattle: Seal Press.

Tyler, Carol-Anne. 2003. *Female Impersonation.* New York: Routledge.

Vance, Carol, ed. 1992. *Pleasure and Danger: Exploring Female Sexuality.* New York: Pandora. 2nd ed.

Volcano, Del LaGrace. 1991. *Love Bites.* London: Gay Men's Press.

–. 2000. *Sublime Mutations.* Berlin: Konkursbuchverlag.

–. 2005. *Sex Works 1978-2005.* Berlin: Konkursbuchverlag.

Volcano, Del LaGrace & Judith Halberstam. 1999. *The Drag King Book.* London: Serpent's Tail.

Volcano, Del LaGrace & Indra Windh. 2004. 'Gender Fusion'. In Morland, Iain and Annabelle Wilcox, eds. *Queer Theory.* London: Palgrave.

Walker, Lisa M. 2001. *Looking Like What You Are: Sexual Style, Race and Lesbian Identity.* New York: NYU Press.

Westerling, Kalle. 2006. *La Dolce Vita: Trettio år med drag.* Stockholm: Normal Förlag.

FILMS

Bauer, Gabriel. 2002. *Venusboyz.*

Blackman, Inge. 2007. *Fem.*

Chisholm, Kami & Elizabeth Stark. 2006. *Female-to-Femme.*

Despentes, Virginie. 2000. *Baise-Moi.*

Jouvet, Emilie. 2006. *One Night Stand.*

Parmar, Pratibha. 1991. *Khush.*

Rednour, Shar & Jackie Strano. 2000. *Hard Love/How to Fuck in High Heels.*

Sexpositive Productions. 2002. *Voluptous Vixens.*

Treut, Monika. 1999. *Gendernauts.*